Additional Praise for *The Great Reflation*

"Tony Boeckh is a first-rate investment intellect whose work I have read for years, and his thoughts on the crisis are well-worth reading and contemplating."

—Barton M. Biggs, managing partner, Traxis Partners;
Author, *Hedgehogging* and *Wealth, War, and Wisdom*

"*The Great Reflation* is part history, part theory, part textbook and part prophecy—lucid, persuasive and a good read. The title says it all. There was the 1930s Great Depression and the 1970-80s Great Inflation, but never before has a great recession been averted by an unprecedented great reflation. Nobody knows and history can't tell us what the upshot will be; there are no road maps. Instead, Tony Boeckh tells us what signposts to look for. It will have a place on my shelves and I expect many others."

—Brian Reading, founder of Lombard Street Research
World Service, former adviser to UK Treasury
and to the governor of the Bank of England

"Tony pioneered the concept of the debt Supercycle in the 1970s and his *The Great Reflation* has proven that he is the ultimate macro thinker. This book is a must read for all investors who strive for financial success in an extremely risky world."

—Chen Zhao, chief global strategist and managing editor,
Bank Credit Analyst Research Group

"Tony Boeckh, long time Editor and Publisher of the prestigious *Bank Credit Analyst*, has called on all of the experience of a brilliant analytical and forecasting career to write *The Great Reflation*. Weaving together today's unprecedented and complex economic, monetary, and investment conditions, Tony lays out the uncomfortable truths that investors must understand and deal with in order to protect capital and invest profitably in the years ahead. *The Great Reflation* is imperative reading for all serious investors and businesspeople."

—Eldon Mayer, former CEO and CIO of Lynch & Mayer, Inc.;
New York-based institutional asset manager

"Few people know as much as Tony Boeckh does about the relationships between the economies and the financial markets. In his book, he gives us a much-needed road map on how to invest given the tremendous convulsions we are going through. It is a must read for every investor."

—Charles Gave, chairman, GaveKal Research

THE GREAT REFLATION

How Investors Can Profit from the New World of Money

J. Anthony Boeckh

WILEY

John Wiley & Sons, Inc.

Published by John Wiley & Sons, Inc., Hoboken, New Jersey.
Published simultaneously in Canada.

For general information on our other products and services or for technical support, please contact our Customer Care Department within the United States at (800) 762-2974, outside the United States at (317) 572-3993 or fax (317) 572-4002.

Wiley also publishes its books in a variety of electronic formats. Some content that appears in print may not be available in electronic books. For more information about Wiley products, visit our web site at www.wiley.com.

Library of Congress Cataloging-in-Publication Data:
Boeckh, J. Anthony.
 The great reflation : how investors can profit from the new world of money / J. Anthony Boeckh.
  p. cm.
 Includes bibliographical references and index.
 ISBN 978-0-470-53877-7 (cloth)
  1. Investments—United States--History. 2. Finance--United States—History. 3. Business cycles—United States—History. 4. Financial crises—United States—History. I. Title.
 HG4910.B5985 2010
 332.60973—dc22

                                                                         2009054227

Printed in the United States of America
10 9 8 7 6 5 4 3

To Ray, my loving wife, muse, and best friend

Contents

Preface

The financial crisis, the speculative bubble leading up to it, and the aftermath have proven once again just how true the old saying is that if you want to know what's going on in the financial system, watch the banks. The banking system has always been the centerpiece of liquidity flows, and financial markets are driven principally by changes in liquidity. This is best assessed through indicators that monitor the flow of money and credit.

Richard Dana Skinner, writing in the 1930s, was one of the early pioneers in the study of money and credit, and the creation of indicators that monitor and forecast financial markets. Interested students of this approach will find plenty of value in his *Seven Kinds of Inflation*.[1] Skinner was instrumental in helping investors better understand financial markets. He, like many, was shocked, not only at the damage caused by the 1929 crash and the Great Depression, but by the fact that so few people saw it coming and that there was no acceptable theory or practice in dealing with it. A. Hamilton Bolton,[2] founder of the *Bank Credit Analyst* (BCA), picked up on Skinner's analysis and techniques and further refined them over the course of 20 years until his death in 1967. I came into the BCA as his replacement and was the principal owner and editor-in-chief for the next 35 years, during which time we continued to refine the money and credit approach to help in understanding and forecasting financial markets.

In its simplest form, this approach is based on the concept that when liquidity is expanding at a noninflationary rate, financial markets do well, and when liquidity is contracting, markets do badly. However, when money, credit, and liquidity expand too rapidly, inflation of general prices and various assets occurs, leading to speculative bubbles and ultimately to financial crises. The lesson learned from the experience over many decades and particularly in the past few years is that excessive debt and monetary inflation are the root causes of banking crises and stock market crashes. This is the principal theme that runs throughout this book. They are the two greatest dangers for investors, as the 2008–2009 episode so amply demonstrated.

Acknowledgments

A number of people have been extremely helpful in putting this book together and, from a longer-term perspective, shaping my views and educating me. In particular, I want to thank former colleagues at the *Bank Credit Analyst*. Warren Smith read the whole manuscript, and his insights, wisdom, and outside-the-box thinking made this a better book. Chen Zhao, Francis Scotland, Martin Barnes, Dave Abramson, and Mark McClellan, through various conversations and brainstorming over many years, have provided thoughtful insights and tremendous intellectual stimulation. I am extremely grateful to BCA Research Inc. for granting permission to access BCA's impressive database and software capabilities for charts and data, and to quote and use old BCA material.

I want to acknowledge the huge support I received from four other former colleagues at BCA. Cindy Jones, with whom I collaborated for many years, worked far beyond the call of duty in preparing charts and data of the highest standard—the only way she knows how to do things. Nicky Manoleas, with whom I also worked closely for many years as well, was totally supportive and helpful at all times. Ron Torrens, the fixed-income specialist at BCA, provided a lot of help on interest rate issues and data. Jane Patterson, BCA's tireless, good-natured, and knowledgeable librarian, was very supportive in tracking down material for me on short notice and made my life much easier.

I also want to thank and acknowledge my colleagues at Boeckh Investments and *The Boeckh Investment Letter* for strong support, ideas, and editorial feedback: sons Ian and Robert Boeckh, Bill Powell, Peter Norris, Inez Jabalpurwala, Natalie Kazandjian, and Cindy Lundell. Carol Boccinfuso was enormously helpful in preparing the manuscript and getting it to the publisher in a timely way. She cheerfully put in many hours at night and on weekends to meet deadlines that always arrived too quickly. I was extraordinarily fortunate to have a young genius, Kierstin Lundell-Smith, as a summer research assistant. She is creative, enterprising, and full of wisdom far beyond her years.

I am greatly indebted to dozens of other people who have played an important role in my 50 years in the financial business. Unfortunately, there is space to name only a few. The Bank of Canada is one of the great schools of higher learning for people starting off a career in practical economics, banking, and finance. I was extremely fortunate to have begun my first four years there, and to have been influenced by two giants, Louis Rasminsky and Gerald Bouey, great governors of the Bank and men of true wisdom. I learned much from other colleagues at the Bank of Canada, in particular Ross Wilson, still a close friend, who taught me a lot about discipline, focus, accuracy, and getting things right. I hope there hasn't been too much slippage since. The late Don McKinley was another bank colleague with whom I maintained a close and lifelong friendship and from whom I learned a lot, not just about economics but also about life.

At the Wharton School, there were Irwin Friend, Albert Ando, and Jim Walters, inspirational teachers and brilliant academics.

In the world of practical finance and investment, there are many to whom I am grateful for both friendship and support. Jake Greydanus and I were partners in a very successful money management business (thanks to him) for many years. Jake is a man of discipline, focus, strength of character, and integrity that is rare in this world. Eldon Mayer, an investment genius, a friend for over 30 years, and from whom I have learned a great deal over the course of hundreds of conversations;

Rudy Penner, BCA's fiscal policy consultant, an economist with wisdom and insight and a true Washington insider; Rimmer de Vries, former chief international economist at Morgan Guaranty; Charley Maxwell and Herman Franssen, two of the world's leading energy experts; Brian Reading, one of the world's most thoughtful economists for the past 50 years; Peter Fletcher, globetrotting investment guru and manager of one of the world's largest family offices; Gordon Pepper, for many years the most widely followed financial economist in London, author of several books on finance; John Mauldin, a best-selling author of investment books and editor of the famous financial e-letter, "Thoughts from the Frontline"; Joe Gyourko, real estate professor at the Wharton School, Philadelphia; Andy Smith, one of the world's top gold experts and editor of *Precious Thoughts;* Walter Eltis, professor at Oxford University and coauthor of *Britain's Economic Problem: Too Few Producers,* and Robert Mundell, Nobel laureate in economics—both were original leaders of the supply-side revolution in economics in the 1970s; William Rees-Mogg, former editor of the *Times,* London; A. Hamilton Bolton, founder of the *Bank Credit Analyst;* and many, many more.

Last and most important is my wife, Ray Dana Boeckh. She not only put up with my preoccupation with writing and the long hours over eight months, but also cheerfully read much of the manuscript and provided valuable feedback and insight.

Introduction

The U.S. government has thrown an avalanche of new money into the economy and the financial system. This is the Great Reflation, and its purpose is to pump new life into the economy after a near-death experience. The biggest financial crisis and recession since the 1930s created a black hole that was huge and frightening. It was caused by an implosion of the greatest credit and asset bubble in history, which nearly brought down the global banking system. The effort to reflate—pump air back into the balloon—has had to be on a scale at least as large as the bubble itself. It is an experiment never before attempted in the context of U.S. experience, and it will have consequences unlike anything seen before.

The purpose of this book is to help investors understand the new investment world we live in, what is likely to happen in the future, and how to profit from this new world of money. It is both a guide and a framework to help investors understand and navigate through all the complexities of an unstable, inflation-prone world.

No one knows exactly where the Great Reflation is going, what is going to happen, and what the end point will be like. However, there are some things we do know. When new money is created on a grand scale, it must go somewhere and have some major consequences. One of these will be greatly increased volatility and instability in the economy and financial system compared with the roller coaster ride of the past 15 years when the credit bubble was forming.

It is critical for investors to understand that there is a linked sequence of events that is leading to a potential disaster. Over the past 15 years, we experienced first the tech bubble, followed by a crash, then the recession and deflation of 2000–2002. Next came the Federal Reserve's first effort at massive reflation to avoid a debt collapse. This led to new bubbles—in housing, exotic new financial products, commodity prices, energy, and world food markets. They were financed by unprecedented amounts of credit that were unsustainable. Once again, the bubbles turned to bust, but with debt levels in place that were much more precarious. The ensuing crash in 2008–2009 pushed the financial authorities into the greatest of all reflations.

This sequence of events has an ominous undertone. The Great Reflation effort will doubtless give the economy a temporary boost, just as the preceding one did. However, it will do so only by creating much greater money and credit inflation and fiscal deficits than the last one.

Extrapolation of this out-of-control roller coaster suggests more bubbles in the short run. Hot markets already began forming by mid-2009 in such things as commodities, gold, and world stock markets. There are many assets that could be recipients of the new money created. However, another inflation of asset prices won't last as long as the previous one for several reasons. Private debt has been pushed to the limit; government debt will be pushed to the limit in a few more years; the U.S. dollar, as the world's main reserve currency, will not be able to withstand open-ended monetary and fiscal reflation; and finally, the world economy is too fragile to withstand another spike in energy and food prices.

The Great Reflation, if left unchecked, will run into a brick wall in the next few years, and another credit implosion and deep recession will occur. The result will be even bigger budget deficits and lower economic growth. Logic says that if the last crisis was caused by excessive money and credit inflation, even more of the same should cause an even bigger crisis. The ultimate end point to this trend is worrisome, to say the least.

The new investment world will be extremely challenging for investors. There will be opportunities in the Great Reflation to make a great deal of money and equal opportunities to lose a great deal of money on the downside of volatility.

Investors, unfortunately, do not have the luxury of riding out this turbulent period by sitting in short-term deposits and money market funds. After taxes and inflation, capital will erode. To earn decent returns, investors have to take some risk; but in the new world of money, these risks are above the comfort level of most people.

Investors must come to grips with this risky new world. To do so, it is essential to acquire a framework for understanding the dynamics of how the Great Reflation will play out, what indicators to watch, and how to shift assets within a portfolio to minimize high-risk, low-return assets and maximize exposure to lower-risk, high-return assets. In a world of stability, buy-and-hold investment strategies can be very successful. In the financial world of the future, they will be an even bigger disaster than the past 10 years. Stock prices suffered two 50 percent declines in the eight years from 2000 to 2008. The Standard & Poor's 500 index by late 2009 was still almost 25 percent below the level of 10 years before. Those who were content with 5 percent returns on money market funds in 2007 are now looking at returns of less than one half of 1 percent. In other words, people relying on short-term money market funds have seen their income cut by 90 percent.

From my 40 years in the business of trying to understand and predict markets, I cannot emphasize strongly enough the importance of having a mental framework of how markets work, and how to integrate into this framework indicators which reflect the various forces that drive markets. Without that, the investor is like a boat on the ocean without a rudder, with the direction determined by whichever way the wind is blowing. In the world of investments, Wall Street is basically a marketing machine, and it does not have the investor's well-being in mind, only profits and bonuses for employees and shareholders of the firms there.

Experience with markets over a long period teaches humility. The forces that are most evident, from the media and research reports, are only the tip of the iceberg. Investors are never going to be able to figure everything out. What is obvious is usually incorporated into market prices. However, as many astute observers, such as Benjamin Graham, Warren Buffett, and social psychologists like Gustave Le Bon, have noted, the market can be an idiot. The reason is that individuals on their own are usually intelligent and full of common sense, but collectively they can become hysterical and irrational, pushing prices to ridiculously overvalued levels. This has happened all too often in recent years because too much money and too easy access to credit fan the flames of blind greed.

A framework of analysis for understanding markets is not the same as building a model or set of indicators fitted to back data. I can assure you, from a lot of experience, that they always break down. An eclectic approach that is based on common sense, strong logic, and objective data, balanced by right-brain intuition and lots of curiosity, is what works best. The investment world will never be deterministic, never amenable to scientific models, at least for any period of time. Some approaches work well in some periods, other approaches in other periods. Successful investors not only know how to think outside the box but, from experience, know what to pay attention to in each market environment.

This book frequently takes a long look back at history because there are many lessons appropriate for today. Proper perspective is invaluable. Some things never change, whereas some change a lot. Investors can never hope to be successful without an understanding of what has happened before and why. This will be critical in understanding what will happen in the future.

The book uses the term *investor* in the broadest sense, to include everyone who owns a home, owns a business, or invests in stocks, bonds, or mutual funds. It includes people who have pension plans that invest in a variety of different asset classes. Moreover, taxpayers now have a stake in the investment world because the government has put huge amounts of money into financial institutions and corporations to prevent their collapse. These investments may cost the taxpayer heavily depending on how well or how poorly financial markets recover. So in this broad sense, almost all of us are investors now.

In Part I of the book, we discuss the bigger picture—the economic and financial environment—that is essential to forming an understanding of the markets and what drives the prices of different assets. We look at the global monetary system because it lies at the core of global and United States financial instability. Investors must understand not only its workings but also its failings to better anticipate how the future will play out. We examine the massive buildup in private debt over the past 25 years and the role it played in the sudden credit contraction of 2008–2009. The unprecedented attempts underway to reflate the economy open a new chapter in financial experimentation, one that creates great uncertainty and risk for everyone, but also opportunity.

Part I also includes a chapter on the long wave, an economic cycle of roughly 50 to 60 years. Its downward phase after the 1973 peak played an important role in the 25-year credit explosion, and it will also play a role in how the postcrash economy will evolve. One of the main conclusions from Part I is that volatility and instability will be much greater than in the past 10 years and wealth preservation will be more important than ever. Investors will have to be more agile in allocating their money across different asset classes. Buy-and-hold strategies did not work over the past 10 years. Those strategies will be even more damaging in the future.

Market crashes, almost by definition, seem like an act of God, a bolt of lightning, something no one could be expected to anticipate. That, of course, is a cop-out and a way for people to avoid responsibility. Investors were not the only ones caught by surprise in the recent crash. Central bankers, commercial bankers, regulators, and property developers were also blindsided. Almost no one saw this crash coming in a timely way, in spite of the fascination with the crash of 1929 and the Great Depression. Many important changes have been made to the financial system since then with the purpose of avoiding a repeat performance. Thousands of learned papers and books have been written since 1929 explaining the causes of that episode and informing policy makers so that this would never happen again. But it did!

Clearly, we have not learned much about the causes of financial crises and how to time them. However, the authorities, as demonstrated after the recent crash, have learned how to abort a self-feeding economic collapse in the short term. Their solution is to write checks, very big ones. However, they have not learned how to achieve stability and growth at the same time. They have clearly not convinced anyone that the Great Reflation underway won't cause an even bigger bubble and collapse than the ones we have just experienced.

Massive new financial regulations are being proposed, although it is not yet clear whether any will be implemented. Disastrously weak financial regulation surely had a major role in the debacle, but new regulation will not stop a repeat performance. The underlying causes of money and credit excesses remain because the system itself is flawed, a recurring theme throughout the book. There is no discipline in the system today to bring international payments deficits and surpluses back into balance and to keep money and credit growth in check.

In Part II, we look at different asset classes, such as stocks, bonds, currencies, gold, commodities, and real estate. We examine how they have performed historically and ways in which investors can assess how much exposure they should have to each. The Great Reflation will affect some asset classes more than others in terms of returns but also in terms of instability and risk. However, the time-tested principles of value, momentum, and market psychology remain valid. Investors need to be armed with the tools to use them. Part II also looks at some of the basic principles of diversification and allocation of money among different asset classes. In the world that lies ahead, investors will need to be concerned at all times with how much risk they are exposed to. Sound diversification is an essential tool to control risk.

One of the main themes of the book is the importance of money and credit for financial markets. Money and credit changes are the main drivers of bull and bear markets. When they are extreme, bull and bear markets become extreme. We use the terms *manias* and *crashes* to describe such markets, the topic of Chapter 6.

As people sift through the postcrash rubble in an effort to try to understand why we experienced yet another mania and then the crash of 2008–2009, they have naturally come back to the disease of credit excesses. This outbreak was no different from all the others in the postwar period and many before that, except for its magnitude and speed. It was perfectly predictable for anyone willing to look at the unprecedented growth in U.S. debt since 1982 and apply a little common sense; only the timing of the bursting was in doubt. By definition, in a mania people lose their rationality. This includes policy makers, regulators, central bankers, academics, and Treasury officials in addition to investors. An important question is: How could this have happened? Why were so many intelligent, well-informed professionals in every major and minor country asleep at the switch, ignoring obvious warning signs?

Alan Greenspan, chairman of the Federal Reserve, was on watch during the credit and asset bubble buildup in the United States. He famously argued that the central bank had no business trying to figure out what market prices should be, and if there was a bubble and it burst the Fed would pick up the pieces. Some pieces and some pickup!

One of the great challenges for investors is to make judgments on whether the authorities will be able to engineer a sustainable, noninflationary recovery. The danger is always that the policy reactions to a huge financial and economic crisis have the unintended consequence of creating the next one.

In Part III, we take a broader look at the question of whether the United States is in serious decline. There are a number of ominous, discouraging trends, not only in the economic and financial system, but in the realm of geopolitics, education, and social conditions, among others. Unstable money is both a cause of instability and a reflection of underlying decay. It is an integral part of the negative feedback loop. Historically, it is difficult to think of any empire in decline that didn't eventually succumb to monetary debauchery. That is never a direct policy objective. It happens because it seems like the least bad alternative facing the authorities when they have to make big decisions in difficult circumstances.

Serious U.S. policy issues are on the table. The direction in which the authorities move will be instrumental in determining whether the United States can reverse the long-term slide underway. Key questions will focus on whether the government takes a high-tax, interventionist, and tough regulatory approach as an overreaction to the disgraced Bush administration.

There are some positive alternatives. Policy could focus on reinstating some old-fashioned virtues that raise savings, investment, and growth; contain fiscal deficits; speed up new technologies and innovation; and educate the large underclass. Above all, the authorities must move to reform the international floating dollar system, impose meaningful monetary discipline, and eliminate the overhang of nearly $4 trillion held by nervous foreign central banks. Serious reform and revitalization of the United States is a very tall order, and the next five years will be critical as to whether the United States collectively is up to the challenge. It will, undoubtedly, be an extremely difficult time, but if the United States can skate through it without more disasters and counterproductive policies, there is every chance that the next long wave upswing, based on new technologies and innovation, will come into play. This would drive much faster growth in output and employment, and enable tax revenues to rise much faster and the fiscal deficit to contract rapidly without raising tax rates very much. The previous long wave upturn after World War II did precisely that: It brought the extraordinarily high ratio of government debt to gross domestic product (GDP) cf almost 120 down steadily and swiftly.

Continued major financial and economic instability in the United States will not be good for either Americans or foreigners. A declining superpower leaves a vacuum that is rapidly filled by new challengers trying to flex their economic and geopolitical muscles. Candidates like China, with its huge population and economy, rapid growth in incomes, massive capital investment and savings, large financial surpluses, and strong currency, are looming ever closer to fill the vacuum.

The Great Reflation will help investors navigate the tricky waters that lie ahead. It provides the knowledge, background, insights, and tools necessary for the complex task of wealth enhancement and wealth preservation.

Part I

FINANCIAL INSTABILITY

Chapter 1

The Age of Inflation

The inescapable conclusion of any factual study of the major kinds of inflation is that debt, in its many forms, moves restlessly and relentlessly beneath all of them.

—RICHARD DANA SKINNER[1]

The Great Reflation is the term we use to describe the government's massive monetary and fiscal stimulus program. Initially, its purpose was to stop the possible death spiral of the economy in 2008 and early 2009. Now its purpose is to prevent a relapse. The program has triggered an avalanche of new money. It will create a world that will be nothing like anything any of us have seen before. It represents a new and different chapter in inflation, a phenomenon that has prevailed off and on, but mostly on, since the outbreak of war in 1914. Then, almost every important country detached its currency from gold in order to finance the war with a free hand. That was the start of the Age of Inflation. Investors need to understand the historical context; it is important because the roots of inflation are long and deep, and it will not be easily ended.

The Age of Inflation has had a colorful history and consistently demonstrates the notion that money, not backed by something of value, does not look after itself. The discipline that comes with solid backing, traditionally gold or silver, makes it difficult to create too much money and prevents countries from running chronic deficits and surpluses vis-à-vis other countries. It also constrains banking systems from creating too much credit.

Some understanding of the modern history of inflation is important in gaining insight into the all-consuming problem of our day—where is the Great Reflation taking us and what can investors do to profit from the coming changes? In order to answer that question, we first need to focus on the origins of modern inflation, the nature and process of inflation, the different types of inflation, why it has occurred, and how it affects different assets. This understanding is critical for investors because it has the most profound effect on all investments—stocks, bonds, currencies, gold, commodities, real estate—literally everything that has a market price.

What Is Inflation?

Inflation is all about the creation of excess money and credit. Some would call it a disease, others a debauchery. Both would be correct and, unfortunately, the histories of all great empires are littered with monetary excesses and inflation. That is why we must all be so concerned when we see the U.S. empire heading down this path.

Many people think that inflation is just a rise in prices, but it's not that simple. Inflation does cause prices to rise, but it is important to be clear on *which* prices. Inflation is a process that begins with an increase in money and credit above what is needed for the production of goods and services. The second stage—rising prices—is actually a consequence of the first stage of inflation and that is what confuses a lot of people.

There is a clear distinction to be made between two types of rising prices. On the one hand, inflation can cause an increase in prices we pay for things we consume or use on a regular basis—food, haircuts, gasoline, washing machines. This is usually measured by the consumer price index (CPI), and it indicates whether there is a general rise in the cost of living. We will refer to this as CPI inflation.

On the other hand, inflation can raise the prices of assets we own or may want to own. For example, we can think of inflation raising the prices of homes, stocks, bonds, gold and silver, and foreign currencies. These types of assets don't necessarily move together or even in the same direction, nor does CPI or general inflation have to move in the same direction as asset prices. In the past 30 years, for example, the rate of general inflation has fallen while most asset prices have risen sharply (until mid-2008). Investors have to understand the different impacts that money and credit inflation can have on these two types of inflation.

Central banks, like the Federal Reserve or Bank of England, control the creation of money and, to a lesser extent, credit. When we are talking about inflation, we need to keep in mind the role played by central banks. Whenever there is inflation, whether it be in asset prices or the CPI, there is always a central bank to be found; and the central bankers are responsible for the integrity of the money, and that means responsibility for not creating too much of it.

Unfortunately, most central bankers have traditionally focused on the CPI type of inflation and have not applied the monetary brakes to asset inflation. The reason is that central bankers at the Federal Reserve and in most other countries were badly bruised by the raging general price inflation they created in the 1970s. The CPI rose to 15 percent or more in the United States and elsewhere, traumatizing the general public, the authorities, and foreign holders of dollars who saw its value collapse on the international exchanges. Afterward, central bankers focused on keeping increases in the cost of living low and stable and congratulated themselves when they succeeded. However, after the early 1980s, asset prices exploded upward in a series of waves, or cyclical bull markets. Figure 1.1 shows what happened to some key asset prices after 1982. Bonds and stocks began rising first, followed by house prices and much later by gold. However, by the late 1990s they all began rising sharply. Following the stock market decline from 2000 to 2002, all four asset markets exploded upward to the bubble peak in 2008. A rise in asset prices creates a feel-good atmosphere. There seem to be only winners, and the only losers are the ones who didn't play.

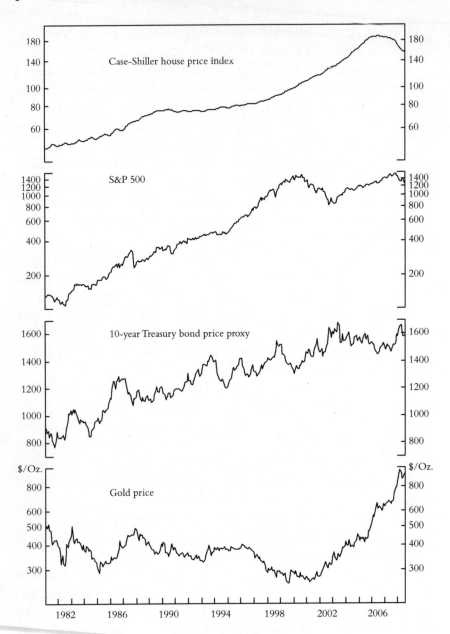

Figure 1.1 U.S. Asset Inflation 1981 to 2008
Source: Chart courtesy of BCA Research Inc.

Bull markets create a wonderful party, and it is not easy for the central bank to "take away the punch bowl."[2]

While central bankers were right to be very concerned when the CPI or some variant moved up rapidly, they paradoxically failed to understand that asset inflations are far more dangerous. They tend to be financed with too much credit. When the bubble bursts, as it always does, asset values drop sharply, as we saw in 2008 and 2009, but the debt remains. The assets can no longer support the debt, leaving balance sheets of people, banks, and businesses seriously compromised. Conversely, in a general CPI type of inflation, the real value of debt declines as prices rise. For example, if I borrow to buy a house and my income and the house value rises, I win on two counts. The mortgage is easier to service out of my higher income, and the debt I owe has fallen relative to the new higher price of the house.

When people use too much leverage in an asset inflation, it does not take much of a fall in prices to wipe out their equity. Creditors become suspicious that assets are no longer adequate collateral. Panic liquidation takes over, and a self-feeding spiral ensues. Prices fall to levels no one thought possible. This is what happened in 2008 and 2009, and is a familiar story to those who have read a little financial history.

The recent burst bubble and near-total banking collapse created a huge risk of another depression. However, it should be understood that the cause of the bubble in the first place was a massive inflation of money and credit that had its origin in the early 1980s, and was reinforced twice more, in the early 1990s and again in the early 2000s. The key to sustaining excessive monetary inflation over this period was falling CPI inflation and interest rates in the United States. The widespread view was that inflation was a nonissue. That is why so few, including the Federal Reserve, saw this crisis coming.

Major asset inflations, paradoxically, occur when the rate of generalized price inflation is falling and often very low. This is referred to as *disinflation*. *Deflation*, in contrast, is the term used to denote an actual decline in the price level. Severe deflation is a terrible disease because it is associated with recessions, depressions, mass bankruptcies, and high structural unemployment. Once started, it is very difficult to escape from, as the United States learned in the 1930s and Japan has learned since 1989.

Disinflation played a key role in the asset inflations of the 1920s and the nineteenth century. It was of critical importance after the 1970s for three main reasons. First, central banks had shifted temporarily to very restrictive monetary policies as a result of the dramatic rise in the CPI during that decade. Second, the cold war began to wind down after the late 1980s. Wartime spending is always inflationary; its ending is deflationary. Third, globalization opened up trade with rapidly developing low-wage, export-oriented countries like China.

During the almost 30-year period after 1982, interest rates fell steadily to low levels in a series of waves, triggering a borrowing binge. The U.S. government under Ronald Reagan started to run huge budget deficits which, at the time, caused mistaken fears of a new rise in CPI inflation. However, instead of pushing domestic prices up, the deficits resulted in a flood of cheap imports, leading the United States into a huge negative trading balance with foreign countries.

We can visualize this by thinking of Wal-Mart sourcing vast and growing amounts of goods from China at lower and lower prices, which it then passed on to its customers. The result was falling CPI inflation, as excess U.S. spending was deflected overseas, and China became the workshop for the United States and much of the rest of the world. Price inflation in the United States went down, and China created tens of millions of new low-wage jobs. It seemed like a win-win development.

Globalization, rapid growth, and a high savings rate in developing countries had another major effect: Their total savings rose rapidly and the savers were happy to lend virtually unlimited amounts to the United States so it could pay for the flood of new imports. The large inflow of foreign savings allowed the United States to save much less and borrow more, all the time pushing U.S. interest rates down. This, in turn, further stimulated the frenzy of U.S. borrowing and spending.

Central banks have no real mandate to restrict money and credit creation to stop asset inflations. Their focus, as we said before, has traditionally been on keeping money stable in terms of the cost of living.

Disinflation brings great benefits and almost always marks a time of prosperity and well-being. Interest rates are falling, asset prices are rising, and business activity and employment are strong. Everybody seems to be a winner. However, under the surface, big trouble is brewing because excess credit creation and asset bubbles are unsustainable. The longer they last, the longer people and the country as a whole, have to get in over their heads with debt. By 2008, the vulnerability was so great that it took only a modest tightening of monetary policy and a rise in short-term interest rates to just 5.5 percent to topple the debt structure.

The asset inflations in the United States in the 1920s, Japan in the 1980s, and the United States from the 1980s to 2008 fit this pattern perfectly. Before the 1920s, there were repeated bubbles and manias and, for the most part, they also followed the script closely.

To understand asset inflation, think of money and credit inflation as water coming out of a giant hose that has been stuck in the ground. The water must come out somewhere, but you can't be sure where. When the hose pumps out money, eventually some prices will have to rise. If CPI inflation is weak and falling, the pressure must flow to assets and push their prices up.

The aim of the Great Reflation was to abort a potential depression, repair balance sheets, and generate economic recovery. It is an unprecedented experiment. Subsequent chapters will focus on where the new money might go.

Origins of Modern Inflation

The Great Reflation now underway should be seen as another chapter extending the long-running saga of inflation—excess money and credit expansion—that began in 1914. A hundred years of financial background may seem a little esoteric to some, but it is important to understand that we have been living for a very long time in a monetary world that is without an anchor. When there is no anchor, the monetary system has no discipline. And it is this lack of discipline that is fundamental to where we are now and where we may be going. The Age of Inflation is deep-rooted and enduring but it is not sustainable forever. Anything that is not sustainable has an end point. When that time comes, it will not be pretty.

Money without an anchor to something of solid value is called fiat money. It is money that is in the form of paper, or a book entry in a financial institution. The traditional anchor to prevent excesses was gold, and to a lesser extent, silver. The anchor provides a constraint on central banks. They can print paper but they cannot print gold or silver. With the discipline that comes with gold or silver backing, monetary expansion can exist only to the extent that central banks have additional metallic reserves. It is normal for countries to go on a fiat paper money system temporarily during major wars to finance huge military expenditures. The United States did it during the Civil War and the United Kingdom did it during the Napoleonic Wars. After such wars, what inflation that had occurred was brought back down by the return to a disciplined monetary standard. However, after World War I, the authorities badly bungled the attempt to go back to an externally disciplined system. The gold standard was reestablished at a price for gold that did not take into account the wartime inflation of money and credit, the rise in commodity prices, and the general cost of living. Hence, the value of gold reserves was inadequate to support stable growth, and central banks felt they had to supplement their gold reserves with foreign currencies.[3]

This proved to be a disaster for a system that was already fragile because of war reparations, hyperinflations in the early 1920s in belligerent countries, and widespread political instability. The inclusion of foreign currencies in reserves in the late 1920s aided and abetted the credit inflation and asset bubbles that led to the 1929 stock market blow-off. When the crash came, followed by bank failures, central banks yanked their currency holdings out of other central banks by asking for conversion into gold.

Effectively, central banks ran to gold because they didn't trust each other, a lesson that may become relevant today. As budget deficits ballooned, trust fell even further and no central bank risked losing gold. Countries were then pushed into contractionary policies, such as tax increases, government expenditure cuts, tighter monetary policy, and trade protection, even as economies sank. As a result, the gold standard was blamed for causing the Depression. That was, in good part, an unfair rap, but certainly strict adherence to it while the economy and debt structure of the world were collapsing was catastrophic. Later, we will come back to the danger created by currencies, particularly the U.S. dollar, when used as central bank reserves.

After the Second World War, the authorities avoided some of the mistakes of the post–World War I period. As a result, we got 15 years of relative stability under the Bretton Woods system,[4] which was a mutation of the gold exchange standard of the 1920s. By agreement, the United States pegged the dollar to gold at $35 per ounce, and other countries pegged their currencies to the dollar. It provided stability as long as the U.S. dollar was scarce and had the appearance of enduring value.

However, in the 1960s the first of the postwar asset bubbles formed and the U.S. dollar came under pressure as foreign central banks became concerned with U.S. deficits, too much monetary expansion, and the Keynesian policies of President John F. Kennedy's economic advisers. Their view was that governments should stimulate the economy to get full employment and that a little inflation was acceptable if you could create a few more jobs. Significantly, the free market price for gold rose above the $35 per ounce peg for the first time. The future value of the dollar had now become suspect, and hence the Bretton Woods system was no longer viable.

To delay the inevitable, the U.S. policy response to growing pressure on the dollar was controls, a clear indication that the policy makers had no intention to rein in money growth. They imposed restrictions on who could convert dollars to gold (the gold pool), a tax on U.S. portfolio investments abroad (the interest equalization tax), and manipulation of the government bond market (Operation Twist), and various other interventions were tried. None of them worked, because U.S. policies remained inflationary with the money taps left wide open.

For most of the 1960s, the United States wrestled with the impossible problem of how to keep the dollar/gold-based Bretton Woods system intact while at the same time ignoring market pressure for monetary discipline in the United States. The market won, as it always does in the end: Controls to hold back the consequences of monetary inflation ultimately break down. They are like a dam to hold back running water; eventually the water will find a way around. The markets finally forced the United States to break the link to gold and float the dollar in August 1971, a watershed event in world monetary history. The dollar fell sharply, triggering the greatest peacetime rise in the cost of living in U.S. history. The CPI rose at a 15 percent rate at its peak. The experience was pretty traumatic. Articles on hyperinflation regularly appeared in the press. Cynical money managers extolled the virtues of moving to a log cabin in the woods and loading up on canned food, gold coins, and machine guns for protection against the anticipated mobs!

Paul Volcker, the chairman of the Federal Reserve, came to the rescue and will probably always remain the most revered central banker in the Fed's history. He courageously gave inflation and the economy a cold bath with very tight money. This created a serious recession and high unemployment, but brought interest rates and the CPI down sharply.

Once the back of that inflation was broken, the Federal Reserve was once again able to become expansionary. The Fed grew the money supply rapidly but the CPI kept falling, confounding the monetarists (people who believe there is a tight link between changes in money, the economy, and the CPI). Monetarists were very influential at the time, and they kept forecasting (wrongly) a major rise in general prices. The explanation was that confidence in U.S. money had returned and people were prepared to hold a lot more of it.

This seeming paradox was what led to the start of the great credit expansion after 1982. Because the CPI and interest rates were falling, no one paid much attention to the surge in credit. It continued to accelerate in a series of waves, with market crashes occurring along the way—1987, 1990, 1997–1998, 2000–2002. After each bubble burst, the Fed stepped up its expansion of money and credit inflation. After the panic of 2008–2009, the Fed moved to once again reflate; but this time its efforts, combined with fiscal stimulus and bailout money, have dwarfed anything ever seen before in peacetime. This is why we call it the Great Reflation.

As evidenced by the short history just discussed, monetary instability clearly has been a regular feature of the investment landscape since the Age of Inflation began almost a hundred years ago. It has produced a roller-coaster economy and financial system because there was no brake on the monetary engine, and we cannot count on politicians and central bankers to provide one in the future. As investors, we need to think about what the limits are to this process. Just as a car needs brakes, so does the monetary system.

The Great Reflation experiment now underway, while critical in avoiding a 1930s debt deflation spiral, ensures that we are a long way from writing the last chapter on the post-1914 Age of Inflation. The managed paper money system has been a huge failure, and lies at the root of the persistent tendency to inflation, instability, and debt upheavals. There are obvious political advantages to inflation in the short run, and a paper system with no brakes is a great temptation to politicians with one eye always on the next election. For that reason, it is important to explore what lies behind this temptation to inflate.

Why Do We Have Inflation?

Money, as we explained before, is at the root of all inflations. When there are no effective brakes on the monetary system, the creation of too much money and credit inevitably follows. And in the modern world, there is a central bank to be found whenever there is inflation. However, the political authorities are the ones that ultimately pull the trigger. They have the power to create or stop inflation. If the government wants monetary stability, no central bank will try to subvert that policy.

The reason we have inflation is because there are political advantages in the short term. It is all too common for politicians to try to exploit them, particularly when economic conditions are dismal and the public is looking for easy solutions. The central bank is merely the tool of governments when push comes to shove. Almost always governments would like interest rates a little lower, credit a little easier, and the economic environment more supportive to financing their deficits so they can spend more money.

We have centuries upon centuries of experience with inflation, from the Greeks and Romans onward. Politicians inflate to save their own necks, either when economic conditions turn the people against them or to finance wars, lavish public works, or other expenditures that cannot be financed with higher taxes. Whenever there is inflation, there are always political promises that it will be temporary and the people are told that they should not be concerned because they will be the beneficiaries of better times.

Goethe, one of the Western world's greatest writers, captured, in his *Faust,* the spirit of the inflation process and how it unfolds—from money creation, false promises, short-term full employment, and the early signs of currency depreciation to disillusionment, collapse, and popular disgust.

> Here and behold this leaflet rich in fate
> That turns our woes to prosperous estate
> "To whom it may concern, this note of hand
> Is worth a thousand ducats on demand,
> The pledge whereof and guarantee is found
> In treasure buried in the Emperor's ground."
> None has the power to stay the flying chits,
> They run as quick as lightning on their way,
> And money-booths kept open night and day,
> Where every single note is honoured duly
> With gold and silver—though with discount truly.
> From there it flows to wine-shops, butchers, bakers,
> With half the world as glutton merry-makers, ...
> "His Majesty!"—toasts flow and cellar clatters. ...
> Now see the charming mob all grabbing rush,
> They almost maul the donor in the crush.
> The gems he flicks around as in a dream,
> And snatchers fill the hall in greedy stream.
> But lo, a trick quite new to me:
> The thing each seizes eagerly
> Rewards him with a scurvy pay,
> The gift dissolves and floats away. ...
> Some grab, and catch frail butterflies.
> The rascal offers wealth untold,
> But gives the glitter, not the gold.[5]

Investors should never forget that politicians, unless they are elected on a hard money platform following disillusionment with inflation, will always be tempted to buy short-term popularity when economic and financial conditions are difficult, even though experience demonstrates that all inflations end in disaster. Ultimately, the public discovers it got only "the glitter, not the gold." Nor should people forget that, if there are no effective brakes built into the monetary system, as we discussed earlier, the creation of excess money is all too easy a temptation for politicians.

The Inflation Process

Lenin, in referring to the consequences of inflation, may have said it better than anyone: "The best way to destroy the capitalist system is to debauch the currency." Inordinate increases in money and credit—those beyond the needs of production—have a profound effect on prices, but the way such increases enter the economic system and have their impact is complex and not well understood by the average person.

Extreme forms of general inflation are called hyperinflation when money becomes worthless. Fortunately, these are rare in developed countries and always occur during major wars or in their aftermath when the government has no tax revenue because the productive system has been destroyed. In that case, the government must print money to finance itself. The central European powers all experienced hyperinflation after World War I. More recently, the only countries that have experienced hyperinflation are economic basket cases like Zimbabwe. In these situations, the only limit on the government's ability to inflate is how many zeros it can get on a banknote. Figure 1.2 shows a reproduction of the recently issued 100 trillion Zimbabwe dollar note, which became worthless in a matter of days. It is now a collector's item.

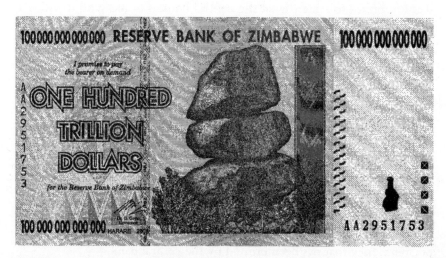

Figure 1.2 Zimbabwe $100 Trillion Note

Even though hyperinflation is rare in advanced economies, that doesn't mean that CPI inflation cannot rise to dangerous levels. As we pointed out earlier, it did reach 15 percent in the United States at the end of the 1970s and an even higher rate in some other countries at that time, and that was enough to create havoc in financial markets and near panic among a large part of the population.

Asset inflation has also hit extraordinary extremes in virtually every advanced economy in the past 30 years, sometimes repeatedly. It is therefore important to understand the mechanics of the inflation process—how inflation is actually created.

Central banks—formerly called banks of issue—are at the center of the money and credit creating process through their monopoly of the issuance of paper currency and, more importantly, through the requirement that commercial banks must hold reserves in the form of deposits at the central banks. These reserves are assets of commercial banks and liabilities of the central bank. They are normally set as a certain proportion of bank assets. The ratio limits the growth in commercial bank assets and liabilities. The latter are mainly deposits, which together with Federal Reserve notes make up the money supply. Banks also have to hold a certain amount of capital relative to their assets, another rule that helps to control them.

The main liabilities of the central bank are composed of currency held by the public and reserves held by commercial banks. Therefore, it is important to watch what the central bank is doing with its balance sheet. When it is adding to its assets, its liabilities must be rising, and hence the money and credit generating engine is expansionary. When the engine runs too fast it causes inflation.

Fast-forward to the Great Reflation. Figure 1.3 shows the extent to which the Federal Reserve expanded its balance sheet after the crisis. The unprecedented explosion in Federal Reserve credit reflects the Fed's response to the liquidity crisis by buying securities with all kinds of risk attached in order to bail out the financial system. Figure 1.4 shows the monetary base, which reflects the reserves of commercial banks when the Federal Reserve creates credit. It is also called high-powered money because it lies at the heart of the money and credit-generating process for the economy as a whole. It shows clearly the vast magnitude of high-octane money that has been created by the central bank.

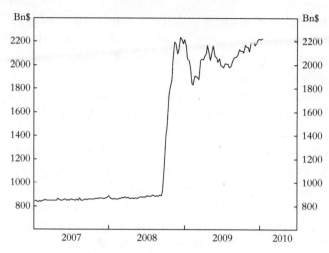

Figure 1.3   U.S. Federal Reserve Bank Credit
Source: Chart courtesy of BCA Research Inc.

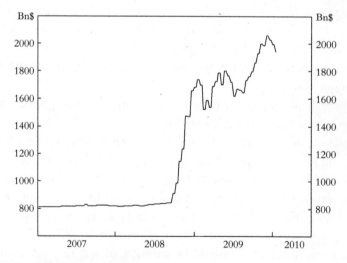

Figure 1.4   U.S. Monetary Base
Source: Chart courtesy of BCA Research Inc.

The Fed's emergency response to the crisis, which is so clearly portrayed in Figures 1.3 and 1.4, was an absolute necessity to avoid a complete meltdown of the financial system. However, the Fed must reverse the massive liquidity injections as soon as borrowing and lending start to normalize if it hopes to achieve long-term stability. The Fed is in the extremely uncomfortable position of having little or no room to maneuver, because very strong forces of deflation will linger while fears of inflation increase.

The Fed does have the distant precedent of 1937 to keep in mind, as well. Fearing a return of inflation then, the Federal Reserve embarked on a premature tightening of monetary policy when the economy looked like it was recovering. However, the reality was that the recovery was fragile, and the tightening policy sent the economy and stock market into a tailspin and ratcheted up the fiscal deficit even further. This could easily happen again because the economy and financial system will require years in the convalescent ward. But inflation scaremongers are already sounding the alarms. Failure to address the risks of future inflation potential could easily affect expectations and send asset prices out of control, eventually forcing the Fed to act in an even more dangerous situation. The Fed has received plenty of well-deserved criticism for ignoring the last bubble. It will almost certainly move faster on the next one—but how and when is an open question. Such action would increase short-term volatility but would not stop the inflationary engine over the longer run.

There is a systemic reason for this concern. The global financial system is and will remain flawed as long as it is based on fiat paper money. Lots of proposals to fix this have been floating around for years, but trying to do it immediately after a banking collapse and near depression would be a high-wire act. It would be better left to a time when conditions are more stable, if that is possible. In the near term, the lesser risk is letting reflation push asset prices higher, which improves balance sheets—a key objective of reflation efforts. In 2009, the rise in asset prices, while substantial, should be thought of as a recovery from very depressed levels, not yet a new bubble. However, market action in 2010 and beyond will have to be watched carefully for signs that the so-called recovery has become something more dramatic. In the meantime, we must rely on the discretion and judgment of the central bankers themselves and, unfortunately, that has not worked very well for many years. As a result, we will all have to live with the great uncertainty of whether a return to stability is even possible.

The Advantage of Stable Money

Earlier, we emphasized the inherent conflict between the short term and the long term in a managed paper money system. The short term is driven by political/populist demands for low interest rates, full employment, and perpetual prosperity. The long-term focus should be on achieving stability and equilibrium. Only with the latter conditions will key economic decisions relating to savings and investment be made with some degree of certainty as to what the more distant future will be like. However, very few politicians are concerned with anything beyond the next election. Their short-term focus creates instability and severe fluctuations in prices and economic activity, which, in turn, forces economic decisions to become even more short-term oriented.

Prior to 1914, most countries of the Western world adhered to a monetary regime that *legally* restricted the amount of money a central bank could create based on its gold holdings.[6] It was an external, rules-based system that avoided the inherent conflict between politicians and central banks that occurs in a paper money system. Countries adhered to the discipline except in time of major wars. This system has had many critics[7] and certainly did not prevent fluctuations in the economy. Nor did it prevent asset inflations and market panics. However, it did produce stability of prices in the long run, something with which people today are not familiar. Figure 1.5 demonstrates what long-term price stability can look like. The purchasing power of the dollar was little changed in 1914 compared with 1820. Figure 1.6 shows that over the 95-year period from 1914 to 2009, the purchasing power of the dollar fell by 95 percent.

Interest rates over the 100-year period up to 1914 fell on average. By the early years of the twentieth century, companies and governments could sell bonds with a maturity of 100 years, such was the confidence people had in the purchasing power of long-term contracts. People developed strong habits of saving and planning for the future, and these were deeply ingrained in decision making.

The experience since 1914 has demonstrated that instability and inflation cause needless hardship for people and enormous resentment. Windfall gains go to the lucky or successful speculators, and hard work is less well rewarded. It should be noted, however, that countries do not

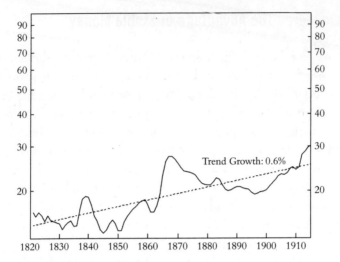

Figure 1.5 U.S. Consumer Prices and Time Trend, 1820 to 1914
Note: U.S. producer prices from 1820 to 1830.
Source: Chart courtesy of BCA Research Inc.

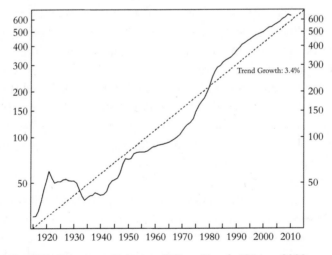

Figure 1.6 U.S. Consumer Prices and Time Trend, 1914 to 2009
Source: Chart courtesy of BCA Research Inc.

need a lot of monetary inflation to grow. Germany and Japan achieved seemingly miraculous growth out of the ashes of World War II with very stable prices. China did so as well after 1978 when market reforms were introduced, although price stability did not occur until more recently.

The United Kingdom and United States grew steadily more prosperous in the nineteenth century with long-term stability of money. Japan got into trouble only after it had created a credit inflation and asset bubble in the 1970s and 1980s.

In spite of signs of economic recovery in 2009, those who downplay the advantages of stability in the purchasing power of the currency and the dangers of asset inflations should not forget that the final bill for the credit bubble of the previous 25 years has not yet been presented.

A monetary system based on an external discipline provides a set of rules for money, just as a constitution works for its citizens. A rules-based monetary system prevents politicians, apart from emergencies, from messing with a country's money for short-term electoral advantage. Long-term stability creates the expectation that it will endure. Short-term instability also tends to be self-perpetuating because it destroys a sense of predictability.

Some people, fed up with our chronic inflation and instability, advocate a return to the gold standard in a search for sound money. It did work to bring about stability and prosperity for 200 years before 1914 for the countries that followed the so-called rules of the game.[8] There were a number of reasons why it worked so well, but probably two were most important. First, governments were small and fiscally conservative. They did not run budget deficits in peacetime and were not expected to take responsibility for full employment and business prosperity. They would never sacrifice external stability for domestic political considerations. Second, wages, which are by far the largest cost component in any economy, were relatively flexible prior to 1914. As a result, deflationary adjustments that were needed could be accomplished without political upheavals, even though they were not without pain. Hence, politicians in stable countries like the United States and United Kingdom were not tempted to inflate except in wartime, when they had no choice but to do so.

After 1914, conditions changed dramatically. The rise of trade unions made wages relatively rigid and, therefore, downward adjustments became impossible without severe political disturbances and steep declines in output. Since the Great Depression, governments have taken on unquestioned responsibility for domestic employment and would never sacrifice jobs for external reasons unless they had absolutely no choice. Therefore, the preconditions required to make a return to the gold standard possible are not present. If it were tried now, it would be a deflationary catastrophe, particularly given the fragility of the world economy and tremendous fiscal imbalances in all developed countries as a result of stimulus packages.

Unfortunately, no one has come up with a practical, acceptable alternative to the gold standard that would have the basic virtues of discipline and the elimination of currencies held as central bank reserves. We will, therefore, remain on an undisciplined paper money system with a huge and precarious overhang of dollars in the hands of foreign central banks. The authorities continue to believe or hope that they can fine-tune the paper system and avoid the mistakes that caused previous disasters. That is wishful thinking. After each bout of inflation and instability, the authorities go on to either make new mistakes or repeat the old ones.

The key point is that, in the absence of a system that has real discipline, we will remain on a purely paper, anchorless fiat money system with its inherent tendency toward inflation and instability. Periods of stability will occur, but they will be temporary and result in increased risk taking and accelerating credit expansion because the system has no brakes.

The Globalization of Inflation

Before 1914, inflation was a domestic matter with the one exception of new gold and silver discoveries. The reason was that the gold standard rules of the game not only allowed, but automatically caused, countries to increase money and credit when they had an inflow of precious metals. Without an increase in the world stock of gold and silver, one country's increase was matched by another country's loss. There are two good examples of inflation caused by an increase in precious metals. When gold and silver poured into Spain from the New World discoveries in the sixteenth and seventeenth centuries, a general inflation occurred. The same was true after the South African discoveries in the late nineteenth century.

In the 1920s, with the introduction of the gold exchange system whereby countries could hold dollars and pounds sterling (mainly) and other currencies as reserves, inflation could and did occur much more easily.[9]

The globalization of the inflation process works like this. The world monetary system is based on the U.S. dollar, which is a floating currency, not redeemable into anything except other currencies at whatever exchange rate is prevailing at the time. It is at the center of the international monetary system because most central banks' reserves, which are held for a rainy day, are kept in dollars. When the United States runs large, persistent balance of payments deficits, it means that more dollars are spilling out of the United States than are coming back in. The overall international deficit can arise either from trade or from net capital outflows. The latter occurs when Americans buy foreign financial assets such as stocks and bonds, or invest in plant and equipment in foreign countries. Capital outflows can also occur when foreigners pull their money out of U.S. assets.

When a foreign country is faced with a net inflow of dollars, its central bank can either buy those dollars to prevent its own currency from rising or it can let the dollar fall. If it buys the dollars, it must do so by creating more of its own currency, which expands the central bank's balance sheet and domestic bank reserves in that country. We discussed earlier how such an action creates high-powered domestic money. The result is that buying dollars tends to flood a country's own economy with too much liquidity, causing domestic inflation, asset bubbles, and frequently excessive capital spending. If the country doesn't buy dollars, its currency will rise, which creates deflationary pressure. In a world with high unemployment, every country is trying to avoid deflation and hence does not want its currency to rise. So, to put it simplistically, U.S. balance of payments deficits get monetized by foreign central banks. Foreign countries that peg to the dollar effectively adopt the monetary and interest rate policy of the Federal Reserve.

The current international monetary system is called Bretton Woods II. It allows surplus countries like China to keep their own currencies artificially cheap by buying dollars on the foreign exchange markets. China has bought almost $2 trillion in recent years to keep its currency from appreciating, and it is still doing so. This has tended to inflate credit and asset prices in China, as can be seen in its property and stock market booms, prior to the crash and once again in 2009. However, that is not the end of the story. When China reinvests those dollars back in the United States, the credit base of the United States is further increased in spite of the U.S. balance of payments deficit that initially moved dollars from the United States into the hands of the Chinese.

Under a system with external discipline, the U.S. deficit would have led to a contraction in credit in the United States and reduced the expansion of credit in other countries. That would have tended to restore equilibrium in the U.S. balance of payments, restrained U.S. spending and credit creation, and significantly reduced the tendency for asset bubbles. However, the current undisciplined system is like a perpetual motion machine. Jacques Rueff called it "deficits without tears." The debtor keeps spending and borrowing, and the creditor keeps building industrial capacity, lending, and experiencing asset inflation. This goes on until a crisis puts an end to it. At that point, the debtor has too much debt and the creditor has inflated asset prices and excess productive capacity. Both create deflation, a view well articulated by Richard Duncan.[10]

We have always agreed with this concept that inflation and deflation are two sides of the same coin with the difference being in the timing. Too much inflation always ends in deflation, and deflation paves the way for the next inflation so long as the central bank is able to reflate. The great flaw in the world monetary system is that the United States— the main reserve currency country of the world—runs unlimited deficits that inflate foreign economies while at the same time progressively undermining confidence in the dollar's future value. It is a system that is unsustainable and dangerous. If not reformed, it will ultimately end in a very big crisis that the United States and the rest of the world may not be able to reflate their way out of.

As mentioned earlier, a financial and credit system without brakes does not have a natural tendency toward stable equilibrium. All persistent debtors—those living beyond their means through the good graces of foreign lenders—come to enjoy the seeming benefits of such behavior and assume that their creditors will allow it to go on indefinitely. The United States is no exception and, like all chronic debtors, has become arrogant and blind to the long-term consequences of its behavior. Experience shows that debtors really come to think that they have an entitlement. As long as the United States is allowed to live beyond its means, the global money and credit system will remain inflation prone and the dollar vulnerable to crises. That is, until the music stops.

Conclusion

Investors face an obvious conundrum: Do they bet on inflation or deflation and over what time period? The dilemma is natural. Inflation and deflation are two sides of the same coin. The more advanced an inflation, the greater the threat of deflation and debt defaults.

In this chapter we discussed how each bust triggers a political response and the authorities revert back to reflationary stimulus—easy money and fiscal deficits. Over time, it is evident that crises have been getting more severe. Experience shows that it has taken increasing amounts of money, credit, and fiscal deficits to generate each recovery. And then inflation, with a lag, accelerates once again. The unsettling question is: When and how will it end?

It feels like we are traveling down a narrowing road with inflation on one side and deflation on the other. We keep bouncing from one side to the other with increasing force. The implication is that eventually we will get to an end point and experience both inflation and deflation together. The monetary and fiscal levers won't be able to pull us out. At that point, some prices may be going up, but living standards and wealth will be falling.

After the crash of 2008–2009, most people ceased to be concerned about inflation. They started saving again, paying down debt, doing whatever they could to get liquid and restore their balance sheets. However, astute market observers have not forgotten that inflation follows deflation.

(continued)

In the latter part of 2009, the early signs of another potential asset inflation were already visible. Real estate prices were rising sharply once again in China, peripheral Asian countries, Canada, Australia, London, and elsewhere. Stock prices had risen from their lows by between 70 percent and 120 percent in many developing countries such as China, India, Russia, and Brazil. Commodity prices had also risen sharply, and gold broke well above the magic barrier of $1,000 per ounce, the top in 1980 and in 2008–2009. Oil prices doubled from their lows by late 2009.

Asset inflations occur, as we pointed out earlier, when economies tend to be weak and CPI inflation is low, stable, or falling. They are frequently driven by investor expectations of higher prices in the future, otherwise known as speculation. As a result, market conditions can become extremely volatile.

It is likely that the Age of Inflation will remain intact for at least one more cycle. An avalanche of new money appears to have already started the next round of asset inflation. How fast and how far it goes can only be conjecture, but it is not likely to last long, because the economic underpinnings are not solid.

Investors will be playing a cat and mouse game with the Fed. As investor expectations of inflation heat up, pushing asset prices higher, the Fed will be tempted to stop it. The Fed could easily tighten too much too soon, or it could do too little too late out of fear of triggering another bust in housing, stock prices, and the economy. The reality is that the Fed has little or no room to maneuver because the underlying structure of the economy and financial system is still rotten. The problem is too much debt, the subject of the next chapter. Debt got us into the crisis, and it has not come close to being sufficiently liquidated to avoid another one.

Chapter 2

The Debt Supercycle, Illiquidity, and the Crash of 2008–2009

Debts are nowadays like children begot with pleasure, but brought forth in pain.

—MOLIÈRE

As the crash and banking collapse start to fade into the past, there will be a growing tendency for people to forget the cause—too much private debt. This would be a huge mistake. The debt must be dramatically reduced if we are to gain a solid footing to support the currency and financial system. However, private-sector debt reduction is not easy and has consequences.

The effort to reduce debt, called deleveraging, will happen one way or another and will profoundly shape the future of financial markets in a complex way. On the one hand, it is deflationary; people save more, spend less, sell assets, and do what is necessary to pay down debt.

This reinforces the weakness in the economy and lowers price inflation even to the point of outright deflation. On the other hand, the government is trying to offset those depressing forces by printing money, running up big deficits of its own and subverting the need for borrowers to reduce their debt. These actions are initially anti-inflationary but ultimately become inflationary. In the next few years there will be a tug-of-war between these two forces. The outcome is not at all clear and unfortunately leaves investors in a quandary as to where to place their bets. Investors need to follow this saga closely on account of its critical importance, a theme on which this chapter, and the book in general, focuses.

With the government trying so hard to pump air back into the balloon, investors are right to be skeptical as to whether the post-1982 trend in debt growth will be reversed. They must pay attention to see whether it actually happens. That will determine whether risk in the financial markets is really declining. Investors can assume that if the rising trend of private debt resumes, there will be an even bigger debt scare than the one in 2008 and 2009. As we said earlier, one way or another, private debt must be significantly reduced. The question is: Does it happen gently in the next year or two or do we need another crisis to make it happen?

Background to the Debt Supercycle

A supercycle involves a series of short-term fluctuations that build over many years into a very large and powerful long-term cycle. We use the term *debt supercycle* to denote a persistent long-term increase in private-sector debt significantly greater than the nation's potential growth of output or gross domestic product (GDP). Historically, in a noninflationary economy, increases in debt beyond the growth of GDP tended to be temporary and self-liquidating. For example, from a seasonal perspective, farmers borrow in the spring when they plant and repay debt in the fall when they sell their crops. From a business cycle perspective, companies borrow money to buy inventory, plant, and equipment and then pay off the debt as new sales bring in extra cash. Individuals borrow to buy a car or a house and pay it off according to the amortization contract.

To understand the debt supercycle, we have to look at the usual recessions that typically occur every three to five years. These recessions cause people and businesses to get caught unexpectedly with too much debt. It is prudent to reduce the debt before it becomes a serious problem. Bloated inventories are cut, capital spending is curtailed, and consumers retreat. Savings are increased and the surplus liquidity is used to pay down debt. Recessions should be a time for correcting excess debt so that over the course of the full business cycle, a balance, or equilibrium, is achieved.

In a debt supercycle, however, equilibrium is achieved only temporarily. Each correction of the previous rise in debt is only partial, and in the next expansion debt is taken to new highs relative to incomes, a measure that indicates ability to service that debt. In a supercycle, private-sector debt just keeps rising to new highs, and disequilibrium continues to grow. Over the course of a few business cycles, debt reaches levels that are ultimately unsustainable and therefore very dangerous when they start to unwind. Figure 2.1 shows the rise in U.S. private debt relative to GDP since the early 1960s.

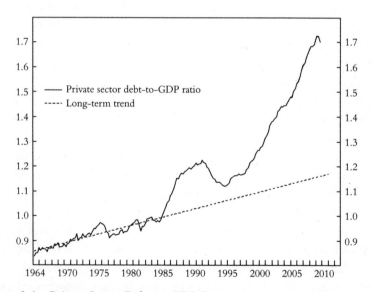

Figure 2.1   Private Sector Debt-to-GDP Ratio
Note: Excludes state and local instruments. Trend based on average ratio for 1964 to 1984.
Source: Chart courtesy of BCA Research Inc.

Until the early 1980s, debt rose moderately and pretty much in line with GDP After that, it began to rise much faster. Corrections were only partial or nonexistent. Each new business upswing took the ratio to a new high. Disturbingly, during the 2000−2002 recession after the tech bubble burst, debt never corrected. That was a very signi-ficant tip-off that serious trouble was already brewing in the early 2000s. The debt was so big then that the Federal Reserve and U.S. government became terrified of actual deflation, fearing a repeat of the Japanese experience since 1989. That country has been waging a deadly bat-tle with deflation for 20 years. There was also a lot of talk in the early 2000s of a possible replay of the 1930s experience, and the Federal Reserve was not shy about joining the discussion, so great were its con-cerns. Ben Bernanke, the current Federal Reserve chairman, acquired the nickname "Helicopter Ben" because in the early 2000s he said the United States would never have deflation because the Fed could always drop dollar bills from a helicopter!

A point to keep in mind is that deflation—an actual fall in price levels—is a serious problem only if there is excessive debt. Falling prices in that case increase the burden of debt. People stop spending because they anticipate that prices will be lower in the future. A self-feeding spiral occurs that is extremely hard to reverse. Irving Fisher[1] described this process as debt deflation. Each fall in prices raises the burden of debt, forcing more selling, which raises the debt burden even more, and so on.

Earlier, we pointed out how inflation begets deflation, which in turn begets the next inflation. The U.S. fear of deflation after the tech crash caused policy makers to keep interest rates artificially low far too long in order to encourage faster credit creation and spending. The result was that they extended the debt supercycle trend in the first years of the 2000s and a major new high in the private debt-to-GDP ratio was reached by 2007−2008.

There were other factors at play that certainly aided and abetted the American love affair with debt—and we include both borrowers and lenders. The avalanche of foreign savings that entered the U.S. financial system gave U.S. long-term rates an extra downward push, with the 10-year Treasury bond reaching almost 3 percent by early 2003. This gave rise to Fed Chairman Alan Greenspan's reference to the bond market "conundrum." What he was saying was that he didn't understand that the financial system was awash in money that needed to find a home.

In the world of finance, supply will always rise to meet demand. Financial entrepreneurs are skilled at creating products to get their hands on loose money. As time went by in the 2000s, the quantity of new products rose sharply while the quality fell precipitously. Lending standards declined, particularly in the new subprime mortgage arena, including the creative repackaging to sell them to unsuspecting investors. Excess money created a widespread culture of spending and borrowing. The Federal Reserve and others in positions of authority and responsibility failed to pay attention, not only to the quantity of debt building up but also to the sharply deteriorating quality. Large numbers of people were borrowing with no hope of servicing the debt under normal conditions, much less the stressful ones of 2008-2009.

Liquidity

The reality of the debt supercycle is that it expands seductively over time and, in doing so, creates artificial prosperity. The initial extra spending from the proceeds of new debt creates jobs, profits, and asset appreciation. However, as debt rises to new heights in each cycle relative to incomes and assets, there is a secular, or long-term, decline in liquidity that takes place in the private sector. Liquidity is a slippery concept and in this chapter we discuss it in some detail. The basic idea is that when you don't have liquidity—cash or near cash—you will have trouble meeting unforeseen demands for quick payments.

Common sense tells us that debt cannot rise faster than GDP forever. At some point, debt cannot be supported, because the under-pinnings—incomes, profits, and asset prices—cannot keep up. During the expansionary phase of any particular cycle, a given level of debt appears to be much more sustainable than it actually turns out to be. However, it is fully exposed only after the economy starts contracting, incomes fall, and unemployment rises. As Warren Buffett is fond of saying, you only find out who is swimming naked when the tide goes out! No one worries much about liquidity on the upswing because the mood is optimistic. Lenders and markets are lowering standards and throwing money at would-be borrowers, who are enjoying their newfound ability to spend more.

In a debt supercycle expansion, the gap between expectations and reality becomes enormously exaggerated. Not surprisingly, the end comes as a sudden shock. It is as though termites are eating away at the support beams of your house. You don't notice anything until the structure gives way.

The unwinding process is always one of extreme violence and panic. Markets collapse because buyers disappear, leaving only forced sellers, who dump assets at any price. Liquidity evaporates because everyone wants it. People hoard cash out of fear because they don't know what will happen next.

As liquidity declines over time, the greater the threat of a debt crisis and debt deflation each time the economy turns down. The authorities, fearing such an outcome, are tempted to reflate excessively and prematurely after each crisis to ease the burden of debt. They failed to do so in the 1930s, which was a disaster, both economically and politically. That experience was so painful that the central bank and government became determined never to repeat it.

The evidence in recent years shows that to generate recovery after each recession the authorities have had to increase the amount of stimulation. They get less bang for the buck as debt burdens rise and liquidity falls. As households and businesses become less and less liquid, they need increasing amounts of money after each recession to repair balance sheets, and it takes longer and longer. The pattern of ever-rising credit in each cycle relative to GDP is clear from the data in Figure 2.1. In the expansion of 2002–2008, it took $10 trillion of credit to generate just $4 trillion of GDP. The economy has become like a heroin addict, needing increasing dosages to get the same high.

The postwar trend of increasing amounts of debt to generate each new recovery raises the question of where and when this process will end, because it is obviously unsustainable. Will the experience of 2008–2009 qualify as the end, or can the authorities successfully pump it up again? This is the essence of the tug-of-war we discussed earlier and is a key question on the minds of all investors. We can all make guesses, of course, but the reality is that no one knows the answer. Only time will tell.

The most likely outcome from this tug-of-war, at least for a few years, is a compromise. There will be some deleveraging, but probably not enough to regain full equilibrium and a solid footing for the economy. There will be some economic recovery, but not enough to generate full employment, because the recovery is artificial. It is dependent, for the most part, on government programs and nearly free money. It will be an unstable situation, not only in the United States but in many other countries as well.

We have used the word *liquidity* frequently. It's a highly complex subject and brings to mind the famous statement on obscenity by Supreme Court Justice Potter Stewart:[2] "I shall not today attempt further to define [obscenity]; and perhaps I never could succeed in intelligibly doing so. But I know it when I see it."

Liquidity means different things to different people. It is difficult to describe in the financial world, and is a slippery concept and confusing to many. To begin with, liquidity is relative. You can say that one asset is more liquid than another if you can sell it more easily and realize close to full value. The same asset may be more liquid today than it will be tomorrow.

The term *liquidity* can also refer to balance sheets. For example, we can say that one company is more liquid than another if it has half of its assets in Treasury bills and no debt compared with a company with no liquid assets and a lot of debt.

We can extend the description to countries. For example, let's take the United States and China. China is far more liquid because it has very little foreign debt and about $2.5 trillion in foreign exchange reserves. The United States, in contrast, has roughly $4 trillion of net foreign debt.

These are pretty straightforward concepts. But in practice they are anything but simple, and one of the key reasons has to do with what economists call the "fallacy of composition." For example, the governor of a small central bank may want to sell $1 billion U.S. dollars of its reserves and buy euros because he thinks the dollar will fall. The foreign exchange market is so big that this transaction would not even be noticed. If China wanted to sell a significant amount of its trillions of dollars for euros, the dollar would collapse just on the rumor and China would find that its dollars really weren't very liquid.

John Maynard Keynes[3] has made this point when he said that financial assets, which people think are relatively liquid, are essentially a creation of financial intermediaries and are based on confidence. Ultimately, what lies behind those claims are real assets like houses, office buildings, factories, boats, railroads, and airplanes. These assets are not at all liquid. Individuals and companies acquire financial assets because they want a liquid repository for their savings. They can cash them in at a later point if they need the money for expenses, to buy an asset, or for an emergency. Countries need reserves to tide them over an adverse swing in their balance of international payments. However, if numerous individuals, businesses, or countries cash in their chips at the same time, liquidity evaporates and no one has any.

The essence of a debt crisis and crash is a collapse in confidence and a panic scramble to get money *at any price*. The scramble itself causes the liquidity crisis and can be relieved only by the central bank coming to the rescue and providing the money needed by pumping cash into the banking system and financial markets. An economy may appear relatively liquid and tranquil at one point in time and a shock can create panic the next. Psychology is critical. When we think that we don't need liquidity, there is always enough; when we desperately need liquidity, there is never enough.

Liquidity, or lack of it, is intimately connected to the private-sector debt supercycle we described before. The longer the supercycle lasts and the greater the debt relative to GDP, the less liquid the economy is, although it usually takes a shock for people to realize it. A good way to visualize the process of liquidity deterioration is to picture an elastic band that represents liquidity in the economy. If you increasingly stretch the elastic band, it becomes less and less resilient and increasingly vulnerable to a shock that would cause it to break. Debt is the same. As it expands, the financial system becomes more vulnerable to shocks, and these are an inevitable fact of life. By definition, shocks are surprises. Examples would include an unexpected drop in a country's currency, triggering a sharp rise in interest rates; revelation of a major fraud; a sudden bankruptcy; speculation gone wrong; or military conflict. There are many candidates. A liquid economy can absorb shocks, whereas an illiquid one cannot. Moreover, there is an asymmetry that should be noted. A decline in liquidity can go on for a seductively long time. When it snaps, using the elastic band analogy, collapse is immediate.

Central Banks and Liquidity

One of the most important roles of central banks is to act as a lender of last resort in a financial crisis by providing ample liquidity to the financial system to prevent a freeze-up. This role evolved during the nineteenth century in England as a result of frequent financial panics. When they occurred, otherwise solvent financial institutions were faced with massive deposit withdrawals as a result of a collapse in confidence. Because commercial banks borrow short term from their depositors and make longer-term loans, they are always at risk. The successful banks understand that long-term loans must be made with prudence. A comfortable cushion of cash must be held for normal withdrawals, and a cushion of equity must exist to absorb loan losses. The problem arises when a shock triggers panic withdrawals. This is called a bank run, because depositors fear that the bank can't return their money. To stop the fear and panic from spreading, the central bank must step in with emergency loans.

Over the course of the nineteenth century, the Bank of England refined its lender of last resort role through experience in dealing with a series of financial crises. The objective was to prevent a panic bank run from toppling sound institutions. Walter Bagehot, the famous nineteenth-century British financial writer, laid out the basic principle in his classic *Lombard Street*.[4] In a financial panic, he advised that the central bank should lend freely but expensively.

Bagehot did not foresee that 130 years later there would be a private debt supercycle causing systemic banking failures around the world on the scale of 2008–2009. The Fed and other central banks became the lenders of *first* resort and not at the high rates Bagehot prescribed. Rather, they lent freely and massively at virtually zero rates, and they bought many hundreds of billions of dollars of illiquid assets of dubious quality that the markets had rejected. Thus a new chapter opened in central bank experimentation.

Given the circumstances, central banks, including the Federal Reserve, did a good job of saving the system from what would certainly have been a total collapse. They did provide liquidity on an unprecedented scale to banks, brokers, other financial institutions, and the markets. However, by breaking from Bagehot's dictum that the lending should be targeted and expensive, the U.S. authorities have created unprecedented risks of unintended consequences later for the dollar, as well as inflation, whether it be reflected in the cost of living or asset prices or both. This raises the question of whether there is a limit to the liquidity a central bank can provide, a question that could be critical as the Great Reflation works its way through the U.S. and world economies.

Clearly, the answer is yes, there is a limit to central bank liquidity injections. During the recent crises, there were a number of countries, such as Iceland, Ireland, and Eastern European nations, where external confidence in banking systems evaporated, causing extreme pressure on the currencies. The same thing occurred in a number of Asian countries and Russia during the financial crisis of 1997–1998. Central banks were stymied; if they lent too much, flight from their currency mushroomed and liquidity shrank faster than the central bank could provide it. These countries had too many liabilities in foreign currencies, so if their currency dropped, the value of their foreign debt went up. In addition, their banks had become far too big a percentage of GDP to be bailed out. In Iceland, bank liabilities amounted to 10 times GDP! Large multinational banks of most countries have operations in many other places where local central banks are loath to bail out the branches of banks headquartered in deadbeat countries.

At a time of crisis, when local residents who have some liquidity fear a currency collapse, they exchange their money for another currency as fast as they can. This process, if unchecked, can quickly lead to uncontrolled inflation and soaring interest rates, as we discussed in Chapter 1. No country wants to put itself in this situation unless it has no choice, because it would probably lead to a worse outcome than draconian domestic restraint. Countries in situations where central banks cannot act as lender of last resort experience precipitous declines in GDP and asset prices. This is discussed in Chapter 6.

The Federal Reserve could face the same sort of constraint in providing liquidity in a future crisis if the dollar came under severe selling pressure. As we pointed out, the U.S. external balance sheet is precarious and vulnerable to a loss of confidence. Many large holders of dollars, such as China, Russia, and some South American and Middle Eastern countries, are already taking action to diversify away from the dollar.

The dollar has fallen about 25 percent since 2001, and many dollar holders fear that the trend will continue. China and India, for example, have increased their gold reserves and holdings of other key currencies. There are other techniques they have also used to minimize dollar exposure. For example, Chinese companies and the China Investment Corporation (CIC) have been making commercial deals to get their hands on oil and other commodities, and have been buying stakes in foreign resource companies. Declining confidence in U.S. policy and the dollar, if continued, could create a run out of the dollar and the Fed might have to actually remove liquidity from the market instead of adding it in the next crisis.

Such a situation is unlikely in the short term but will be a growing reality in the longer run. There has to be an end point to the increasingly boom–and–bust character of the U.S. economy and repeated flooding of the world with excess dollars. If the Fed loses its ability to pump money into the system, should there be another financial crisis, it would be a disaster similar to what happened in the early 1930s. Then, the Fed and other central banks either couldn't or wouldn't add sufficient liquidity to the financial system when it was imploding because they were worried about external confidence in their currencies. They were frightened that central banks and others would convert their foreign currency holdings into gold, which was held as legal backing for the domestic currency. The gold standard rules of the game then meant that if a central bank lost gold reserves, it had to contract its money supply. When confidence was shattered, central banks reduced their money supplies and raised interest rates during the Depression just to preempt possible gold losses.

The experience of the 1930s is relevant for today, even though we are no longer on the gold standard and subject to its rigidities. The critical issue was, and still is, the confidence people have in a currency. If a country loses that, it loses the ability to throw liquidity into the banking system in a crisis.

Unfortunately, trust in the United States has fallen sharply in recent years. If a major dollar crisis occurred, the Fed would have limited, difficult, and painful choices. It might be able to borrow foreign currencies or special drawing rights (SDRs).[5] These are international reserve assets and units of account of the International Monetary Fund (IMF) and are backed by the four main currencies in proportion to their importance in world trade and finance. SDRs, therefore, have stability that no single national currency has. But with such borrowings, the United States would have a liability in foreign currencies that would greatly restrict its ability to depreciate the dollar. The reason is that the new liabilities go up as the dollar goes down.

Another alternative for the United States would be to guarantee the exchange value of dollars held by foreign central banks. While this could stave off a panic liquidation of dollar balances, it would further mortgage the U.S. national balance sheet and make devaluation of the dollar next to impossible. Another possibility would be for the United States to start selling its gold stock; but this would be like selling the family jewels and would appear as an act of desperation. In the extreme, it is possible to envision the United States coming up short with not enough acceptable collateral to borrow abroad. That scenario is too scary to think about and is reason enough for the United States to get its financial house in order quickly.

Liquidity: How Much Is Enough?

The financial system will remain fragile until private debt is reduced substantially and banks have restored their capital bases. Until then, how will we know whether there is enough liquidity? The short answer is that we will never know for certain.

As pointed out earlier, liquidity is a relative concept and what may appear as adequate liquidity for an individual, corporation, or country today may be entirely inadequate tomorrow if confidence is suddenly shaken. Over long periods of stability, rules of thumb are created. Some of these are based on ratios like debt to equity, liquid assets to total assets, and debt service to income. The rules were built from long experience and generally provide enough protection under most circumstances. However, conditions change. The way it works is like this: After a big crisis, say like the 1930s, everyone gets extremely conservative, fearing a rerun of the last crisis. When everyone becomes liquid, there will be no crisis. However, over time, people start to lose their fear of risk, and corporations and institutions find that holding too much liquidity reduces profit margins. As the crisis recedes in time and memory, people worry more about missed opportunities than about risk. They invest longer term and in riskier projects, they start to take on some debt, and they spend a little more to live better. In general, they start to move out on the risk spectrum, and the debt supercycle begins.

In the early stages, these actions create a positive feedback loop: Profits rise, incomes rise, riskier investments pay off, and debt servicing is easily handled. Copycats follow. The process is self-reinforcing and stability is not greatly affected in the early stages, although business cycles start to get accentuated. Different measures of liquidity show deterioration, but from a starting base that was too conservative. The problem is that there are no accurate measures to indicate when the rundown in liquidity has gone too far and the next crisis is about to arrive. There are plenty of coincident indicators that show when a country has moved into the risky danger zone. Unfortunately, the self-feeding nature of the process of running down liquidity almost always means that the aura of prosperity goes on far longer than anyone imagined and hence the development of a "new era" mind-set. Liquidity falls far below a stable, long-run equilibrium level. However, there are no reliable leading indicators of when the elastic band, to repeat our earlier analogy, is about to snap. That is why almost everyone is completely caught off guard when it happens.

What astute investors and businesses must do is act contracyclically and begin to reduce risky exposure when the coincident indicators start to flash yellow. This is a lot easier said than done. When to start is always subjective and depends on people's risk aversion. Going against the crowd is difficult; people can look very foolish for a while. Unsustainable trends have a habit of going on much longer than seems possible. However, those who are wise will start to build up liquidity and cut debt when they think the supercycle has moved into dangerous territory. Those who start early have lots of time to get their balance sheets in good order. However, most people are complacent and greedy, and they procrastinate until it is too late.

Picture a farmer cultivating rich, loamy soil on the edge of a smoking volcano. Life is prosperous and the temptation is always to stay a little longer. After all, the volcano has been smoking for a long time and it is hard to leave. The same goes for financial markets. Often the biggest returns are at or near the end of the cycle. Ultimately, experience and intuition are critical. Left-brain analytics and data study—Wall Street's forte—didn't work in calling this crisis, nor has it ever. Public data can be very distorted. For example, how many people knew the massive size of off-balance-sheet liabilities of banks before this crisis broke? Most people, including the Fed and other regulators, thought the banks were liquid enough and well capitalized. They weren't. Investors must rely on their own intuitive skills and common sense. When the acts of borrowing and speculating push market values far beyond what is historically normal, it is time to look for the exits. Even though you may be a year or two early, the money made at the end by taking large balance sheet risk is never kept, except by luck.

New Regulation

Governments in the United States and elsewhere are hoping to impose tough regulations on lending institutions to avoid a repeat credit bubble. How successful governments will be is another question. Lax regulatory standards and oversight played a huge role in the credit excesses of the past 25 years. Effective, sound, and conservative new standards make a lot of sense from a stability point of view. However, that alone will not prevent another wild frenzy of overlending and speculative market behavior, some signs of which are already apparent. In the short term, even without new regulations, lending standards always tighten dramatically after a credit crisis, and borrowers are much more attuned to risk and their ability to service and pay back debt. However, as we pointed out earlier, risk aversion erodes as the most recent crisis fades away and prosperity returns. The paper money, floating dollar system provides no effective brake on money and credit inflation, and there will be nothing to stand in the way of a repetition of recent bubbles once people become financially brave again. And we must remember that the same people who created the previous credit binge are still in charge.

The Great Reflation following the crash may, in the short run, look so successful that people will once again lose their respect for risk. After a while, conditions will likely stabilize, memories of the crisis will fade, support for regulation will decline and aggressive credit institutions will reappear, innovate, and take advantage of new profit opportunities. This will push the older, traditional, more conservative institutions into doing the same thing. For example, we can look back a few years and see how major investment banks decided to enhance their risk profile to play competitive catch-up with their more aggressive rivals. They did so after conditions stabilized following the bursting of the tech bubble. As a result, they and their rivals played a huge role in the most recent bubble and collapse. Lehman Brothers is gone now and most of the others had to be absorbed by banks to survive. Ironically, six months later, some financial institutions were making record profits.

Hyman Minsky,[6] the famous economist and authority on the instability of credit, made the point frequently that stability begets instability because regulatory systems always break down. The reason is that the crises that the new regulations were designed to avoid don't occur until after regulations are loosened or eliminated and stability creates complacency. The history of the Glass-Steagall Act is a case in point. It was introduced in the 1930s to separate investment banks from commercial banks to eliminate one of the villains in the 1929 crash. The Act was progressively watered down in the 1990s and repealed in 1999, just in time for the new gunslingers to play their part in the crash of 2008–2009.

In general, the history of the past 25 years is marked by a progressive dismantling of many of the controls put in place in the 1930s to avoid a repeat of the 1929 banking collapse!

Paradoxically, the more that governments try to protect us against financial disasters, the more likely they are to occur. Take, for example, deposit insurance, seemingly a wonderful idea that arose from bank runs in the 1930s. As a result, bank depositors stopped checking to see if their money was safe. Banks lost their fear of bank runs and became much more reckless with their lending and capital ratios. There are other examples. The high regard in which Keynesian countercyclical policies were held after World War II led to the price inflation of the 1970s because governments became overconfident that they could fine-tune the economy. The result was that they stopped recessions prematurely before the corrective forces had a chance to run their course, and so the perception of risk changed. Prudence became old-fashioned and got in the way of making money, and people began eagerly to expand their debts.

Federal Reserve lender of last resort bailouts in the past 40 years have been successful and led to an assumption that there was no systemic risk in the system. People came to believe that financial crises were a thing of the past. As a result, virtually the whole nation became reckless with its money.

It would be a great tragedy if the lessons from the crisis of 2008–2009 were forgotten. Already, there is fierce opposition to tighter regulations. Proposals are being either watered down or dropped, and the Federal Reserve is intent on ramping up the monetary machine. If successful, it may be difficult to curb another round of excessive credit creation.

Conclusion

This chapter explained the debt supercycle of the past 25 years, and how it caused a collapse in liquidity in the financial system and brought about the greatest market and banking collapse since the 1930s. The lessons have been extremely painful for borrowers and lenders alike. The economy and financial system have been left fragile. The Great Reflation is an attempt to pump it up again but it is far from clear whether it will work. There is a tug-of-war between debtors trying to deleverage and the authorities trying to get them to stop deleveraging and start borrowing and spending again. Investors must pay particularly close attention to see who will win the tug-of-war. Continued deleveraging could lead to sustained deflation and stagnation like that experienced by Japan. Successful reflation could lead to another round of major asset inflation and potentially another mania and out-of-control credit growth.

The next chapter looks at the long wave economic decline in the United States that began in the early 1970s. It was interrupted for 15 years by an artificial boost from the asset and credit bubble of the 1980s and 1990s; the down wave has resumed, and this will add additional deflationary pressure in the United States in the next few years that will offset, in part, the effectiveness of the reflation program.

Chapter 3

The Long Wave in the Economy

Man must accept motion.

—Lao-tzu[1]

Investors and economists have long been fascinated by research purporting to show that there are cycles in industrial economies that evolve over a period of roughly 50 to 60 years. Our particular interest in the long wave is twofold. First, it provides an additional, useful perspective on the private-sector credit inflation of 1982 to 2007. Second, it will continue to provide important insights as to how effective the Great Reflation will be in the evolution of the postcrash economy and financial markets.

It appears that the United States entered a long wave downturn after 1972–1973, but the wave was interrupted from its natural course by the credit and asset bubble that formed after 1982. The bubble artificially inflated certain industries, resulting in an unsustainable boom in income and investment. Now that the bubble has burst, the long wave downturn has resumed and income and capital investment are falling again. The decline, unfortunately, may have several years to run. The Great Reflation is needed not only to mitigate the damaging effects of the crash and credit deleveraging, but also to dampen the deflationary effects coming from the long wave. Much of this chapter looks at the connection between the debt supercycle discussed in the preceding chapter and the long wave.

Economies and financial markets have a lot of moving parts, and they are all connected to each other. This is basic to Taoist philosophy. Everything revolves around some central axis in an interrelated way. Men, governments, and the actions of both play a crucial role in this interconnectedness. Long-term fluctuations in economic and financial activity result from these actions. In this chapter we show how this comes about, the role it played in the crash, and what follows on from that.

The Long Wave

The long wave is not a competing or alternative theory to the debt supercycle but rather an important adjunct. The way in which the two interact should help to broaden investors' understanding of how financial markets operate and provide important insights into their behavior. Taoist philosophy and markets are all about change, and the key to successful investing is the accurate anticipation of change. Conventional thinking, particularly around important turning points, is usually not very helpful because it tends to focus on the extrapolation of past trends into the future.

In this section we look at the background to the long wave and the role it played leading up to the financial crisis of 2008–2009. This is particularly relevant now because the long wave forces are down and will provide a strong headwind against the government's efforts to reflate. Long wave forces are very powerful and operate slowly over time, making them hard to recognize by most people. The long wave is like the tide in the ocean, powerful and operating below the surface.

A Russian economist of note, Nikolai Kondratieff,[2] was the best known of the first researchers interested in the long wave. His research in the early 1920s purported to show the existence of a long cycle of 50 to 60 years from peak to peak in industrial economies. One of Kondratieff's principal conclusions was that capitalism was self-correcting and not headed for destruction, a view that should dispel some of the gloom coming from the arch-pessimists of today. His view obviously did not go over well with his Marxist bosses. His relative intellectual freedom ended after Stalin consolidated power in 1927. In 1930, he found himself with a one-way ticket to Siberia for his trouble and he was executed in the 1938 purges.

Kondratieff's work was based mainly on prices and interest rates and received considerable favor in the West for apparently forecasting the asset bubble of the 1920s and the depression of the 1930s. One of his greatest adherents was Joseph Schumpeter, arguably one of the most influential economists of the twentieth century. In his monumental *Business Cycles*,[3] Schumpeter outlined his general theory of business cycles and capitalist evolution. His contribution was highly original and focused on recurring innovation and new technologies that are fundamental drivers of the economy in the long run. He painted a vivid picture of continuous, large, and often abrupt changes in the economy that verge on chaos, something that most of us can relate to after the turbulence of the past two years. Looking through the chaos, there emerges a long-term fluctuation, driven by entrepreneurs who are the key innovators. They respond with creativity to economic pressures and incentives, whereas most people and institutions only adapt to change. In our focus on investors, we can see that the same model is true. Most are adapters and followers; very few are innovative, creative, and intuitive.

Schumpeter brought important sociological insights to his historical analysis of capitalism and business cycles, making his work unique because of its focus on human behavior in the cycles of innovation. He also pointed out how powerful elements in society resist major innovative changes because of the damage they do to existing business arrangements. This insight is particularly true today as we observe tremendous resistance to changing, fixing, and removing two of the primary causes of the crash and deep recession—lack of financial regulation and a flawed international monetary system.

A second wave of followers, building on the early work of Kondratieff and Schumpeter, surfaced in the 1970s and early 1980s as the economy then began to falter badly and comparisons with the 1920s and 1930s emerged. These disciples were attracted to the idea of long cycles in economic life, particularly as the pessimistic down-phase of the cycle seemed to fit the gloomy atmosphere of the early 1970s. That was triggered by the 1973 and 1974 stock market decline, the worst since 1929. Stagflation, a new phenomenon of high inflation and low growth, had taken hold. People were looking for explanations in the face of the obvious failure of conventional theory to explain the predicament in which the U.S. and other Western economies found themselves. The long wave seemed to do the job.

The experience of the 1970s stimulated a number of researchers to undertake serious studies of the long wave. This group would include people such as Walter Rostow, Jay Forrester, John Sterman, and others at the MIT System Dynamics Group.[4] Using more sophisticated statistical techniques and drawing on new historical research, these people showed that a cycle of about 60 years in duration can be observed using data back to the early 1700s, when the industrial revolution got into full swing. They show a cycle that is composed of a lengthy upswing and a lengthy downswing. There are transitions in between lasting for some years, when positive and negative crosscurrents affect different industries and different countries at different times. The effect of these crosscurrents is to stretch out the transition periods over several years and make it difficult to date precisely the beginning of the major up- and down-phases of the overall cycle.

The major phases of the cycle are, as we said, driven by innovative new industries or techniques of business arrangements. In earlier periods, we can think of cotton and the steam engine in the late 1700s; canals in the early 1800s; railroads and ocean-going steamships in the mid to late 1800s; and steel, automobiles, electricity, and the telegraph in the late 1800s and first half of the 1900s.

More recently, the Internet, globalization of supply chains, wireless communication, and financial innovation have created vast new industries. Historically, the great new innovations were associated with huge infrastructure spending as the process of diffusion was extended. For example, the automobile required vast new steel mills, oil refineries, roads, and gas stations. The spread to the suburbs meant construction booms requiring lumber, cement, drywall, new sewer systems, and so on. The adoption of electricity meant building electricity grids and requiring copper and transformers. As Schumpeter said many times, the capitalist process and long wave fluctuations are an explosive phenomenon, upsetting conditions of location and calculations of cost of the products affected.

It is also important to keep in mind that innovation and newer techniques unleash powerful forces of growth that create a positive feedback loop leading to overinvestment and overemployment. The down-phase of the cycle is characterized by the previously new industries reverting to average or below-average growth. This creates excess capacity and structural unemployment, which must be eliminated eventually. Later we discuss why the current long wave decline has further to run and how that will greatly complicate the efforts to reflate the economy.

The time factor is naturally of critical importance for those looking for turning points in the long wave cycle, and there has been no shortage of people and investment services that have attempted to use long wave analysis to make forecasts of the economy and financial markets. Many that fit into this group could be described as "fortune sellers."[5] They create deterministic models for investment forecasts that purport to show a regularity that doesn't exist. This long wave forecasting approach was popularized in the mid- to late-1970s but fell into considerable disrepute among investors in the 1980s because the forecasts went spectacularly wrong.

At that time, most were warning of a repeat of the 1930s, a multiyear stock market collapse and depression that failed to materialize. The reason these forecasts went wrong is because the long wave is not, and never will be, a deterministic phenomenon. It should be seen as an integral part of the process of capitalism and markets and is influenced by many things that affect our daily lives. We believe that the evidence is supportive of a long wave, and understanding its dynamics can be extremely useful to investors but only if used properly as a framework for analysis and to understand important dynamics in the markets. It is not useful as a precise forecasting tool based on a pre-ordained, fatalistic cyclical path.

Dating Long Wave Cycles

There is little dispute over the basic concept that there have been bursts of technological change and innovation in capitalist economies over the past 250 years, which have created long periods of dynamic, above-average growth rates, followed by periods of prolonged decline. The controversy surrounding long wave analysis arises from attempts to date the different phases of the cycles. For descriptive purposes, some have broken the overall cycle into four phases—spring, summer, fall, and winter.

1. Spring is the beginning of the long upswing, driven by the growth of new industries and an ending to the adjustment of surplus capacity and the excesses of the previous boom.
2. Summer is characterized by accelerating growth as the new industries blossom.
3. Fall is the transition to the declining phase of the economy. Real wages slow to well below trend, excess capacity builds, and the excesses from the summer period have become apparent. This stage is sometimes referred to as the plateau period and characterized by asset inflations spawned by both falling interest rates and falling general price inflation.
4. Winter is the trough phase when conditions are bleak, asset bubbles collapse, and the economy is weak relative to trend. The economy is moving closer to the next upswing, but is not yet there.

Great controversy had been generated, as we pointed out before, by efforts in the late 1970s and early 1980s to use the model for forecasting purposes. The assumption was that 1972–1973 was the beginning of the current long wave decline. That seemed to be a reasonable proposition based on data shown later in Figures 3.1 to 3.3. However, forecasters went on to predict a market collapse and depression rivaling the 1930s that would occur sometime in the late 1980s. Stocks were indeed poor performers from 1972 to 1982, but that was due to very high rates of price inflation, not the deflation that long wave adherents predicted. After 1982, stocks had the best bull market in history, lasting for 25 years. The fortune sellers had some good instincts but the analysis and timing were horrible, missing the boom of the 1980s to the early 2000s. The reason for the great error is that forecasters made the assumption that the long wave is like a great wheel that takes some 60 years to go around. The implication is that we are all strapped to this wheel, and on each revolution we get rolled through the mud for quite some years.

The problem, as we pointed out earlier, is that economics and financial market behavior cannot be made to fit into a deterministic model. To paraphrase Lao-tzu, you can't understand running water by trying to catch it in a bucket. Schumpeter, supported by the work of the MIT System Dynamics Group, made clear in his work that the economy does not work that way. The economy never has been a mechanical phenomenon, nor will it ever be. It is not like a pendulum or the orbiting of bodies in the solar system. Changes in technology, innovation, economic structure, regulations, financial institutions, and social and political attitudes are ongoing and an essential part of the flow. The economy is subject to all these and many more interconnected influences. There are both exogenous and endogenous forces and they interact in a continuous process of feedback loops. This is an important insight for investors and is consistent with the reflexivity thesis of George Soros,[6] probably the most successful hedge fund speculator in history.

The important point for investors is that change in the economy and financial system is continuous. There are many moving parts in the overall dynamic and many cycles of different duration. Probably the most important one, and the least visible, is the long wave. But even that cycle keeps changing. Over the past three centuries, U.S. and other Western economies have shifted from an agrarian to an industrial and currently to a postindustrial economy. Each time the long cycle spins around, it goes off in new directions. Some things are the same; some are intrinsically different. This observation will be extremely important to investors as they try to cope with the investment implications of the Great Reflation against the backdrop of a continuation of the current long wave decline.

When Will the Current Long Wave Decline End?

As stated earlier, most experts date the start of the current long wave downturn around 1972–1973. This is based on, among other things, a decline in the rate of real wage growth far below trend. This is shown in Figure 3.1.

Additional data support the hypothesis that the postwar long wave upswing peaked in the early 1970s. Real GDP and nonfarm business productivity, shown in Figure 3.2, follow the same pattern, rising to a peak in the early 1970s and then declining.

Figure 3.3 shows real (inflation-adjusted) manufacturing shipments and real nonresident producers' durable equipment detrended. The data also support the same conclusion of a peak in the long wave in the early 1970s.

The period following the apparent peak of 1972–1973 seemed to confirm that the long wave was in a clear downtrend. By the early to mid-1980s, many were postulating a trough around 1998. However, something went wrong with the forecast. Real wages

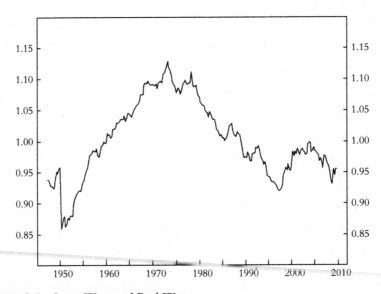

Figure 3.1   Long Wave and Real Wages
Note: Nonfarm business compensation per hour, shown as a deviation from long-term trend.
Source: Chart courtesy of BCA Research Inc.

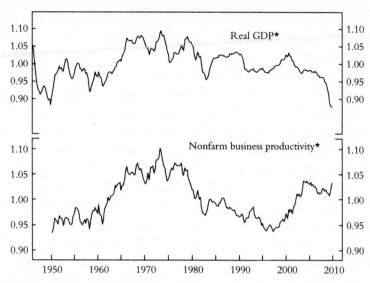

Figure 3.2   Long Wave and Productivity
*Shown as a deviation from long-term trend.
Source: Chart courtesy of BCA Research Inc.

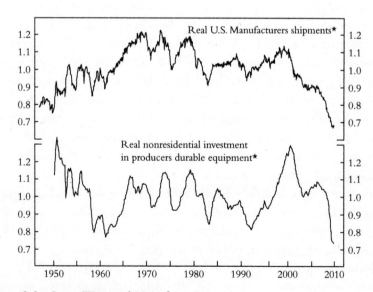

Figure 3.3   Long Wave and Manufacturing
*Shown as a deviation from long-term trend.
Source: Chart courtesy of BCA Research Inc.

began to accelerate around 1995, the stock market and profits boomed all throughout the 1990s, and the economy seemed to be doing pretty well until 2008.

Our interpretation is very different from that of most long wave adherents and seems to fit the evidence much more closely. The long wave downturn, in our view, did remain intact, but was masked by a significant but unsustainable countertrend movement for the reasons outlined in the following paragraphs. This countertrend movement can be seen in each of Figures 3.1, 3.2, and 3.3. It is more pronounced in some series than in others, and the timing varies. But the overall picture is one of a renewed upward movement in the late 1980s and the 1990s, followed by a resumption of the downtrend. In overall length, the decline has extended far beyond the usual 25 to 30 years.

There were two main factors behind the countertrend move. First, the weakness in real wages from 1973 into the 1980s and beyond impacted the social and political process and resulted in massive government stimulus. The initial focus was on money creation and devaluation in the 1970s, discussed in Chapter 1. The resulting inflation, in turn, caused a huge political backlash, not against the stimulus in general, but against its consequences—the sharp rise in the cost of living. As a result, the stimulus agenda shifted to other techniques. For the most part, these were taken from the playbook of the so-called supply-side economists[7] and implemented under President Ronald Reagan after 1980. They included huge tax cuts, fiscal deficits, and credit creation, all made possible because of falling general price inflation and interest rates. The unintended consequence of these policies was the asset bubbles in the late 1980s, in the 1990s, and for a good part of the 2000s. One result was a boom in the incomes and wealth of people working and investing in the industries that benefited from the bubbles. The most obvious were in residential and commercial real estate, retailing, finance, and technology. The household borrowing and spending binge, built on massive capital gains and reinforced by large budget deficits, raised the incomes of a significant minority of workers and investors, both directly and indirectly.

The second major factor temporarily reversing the long wave decline was the surge in growth in China, India, and other developing economies where globalization and deregulation unleashed long wave upswings. This was a textbook Schumpeterian effect and not the first time that globalization created long wave upswings in developing countries. In the late nineteenth century and up to World War I, globalization opened up the Americas, which were then the developing countries of the day. The result was enormous economic growth both there and, via feedback, in Europe as well. While competition from newly created agricultural supply depressed conditions for European farmers, it greatly increased demand for European manufactured products.

As Schumpeter had pointed out, long wave upswings and the rise of new industries and techniques are disruptive for old industries and forms of organization, but they create vast new opportunities for the innovators and the population as a whole. The dramatic rise of some developing countries is once again having a similar effect. It is creating disruptive competition for the mature industries of the West. At the same time, developing country growth is adding significantly to world demand, particularly demand for commodities, something that many investors have taken note of and that we will touch on in Chapter 12. Moreover, the surge in exports from low-wage countries lowered U.S. and world inflation and interest rates. This, in turn, helped to lift real incomes and wealth temporarily in the United States. For a while, the beneficiaries of the bubble era outweighed the losers, who were hurt by the stiffening competition in mature industries.

Four ominous signs in recent years have pointed to the disruptive nature of these developments. First, income and wealth disparity in the United States widened dramatically, much like the 1920s. Second, the current account deficit of the United States rose alarmingly to 6 percent of GDP, a direct indication that the nation was living far beyond its means. The low and stable consumer price index numbers, the relatively stable U.S. dollar, and the effects of massive purchases of dollars by foreign central banks to keep it stable disguised the unpleasant reality that U.S. living standards were heading for a big fall. Unsustainable income disparities and chronic balance of payment deficits always lead to painful adjustments, proportionate to the previous excesses. Third, U.S. savings and capital investment as a percentage of GDP declined sharply during this period, as can be seen in Figure 3.4. They are the source of future prosperity. Fourth, the huge trade

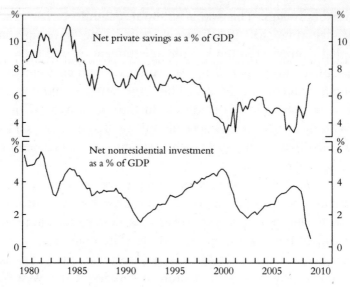

Figure 3.4   U.S. Savings and Investment
Source: Chart courtesy of BCA Research Inc.

surpluses of many developing countries led to massive financial inflows to their economies, creating credit and asset bubbles that matched or exceeded those in the United States, while at the same time creating huge capital investment in building capacity in those countries.

With the end of the asset and credit bubbles of the 1982–2007 period, severe weakness is again showing up in many industries, particularly the beneficiaries of the post-1990 excesses. Structural unemployment in these and other mature industries such as autos and steel has sky-rocketed and will likely stay high for years. Real income growth has decelerated again. This is a typical phenomenon during the long wave winter. The good news is that innovation is creating new industries at a rapid pace. Most are still far from hitting their full stride, and there will be a long lag before workers in the old industries are retrained and absorbed, or new ones with the needed skills become available. But the key point is that forces of rejuvenation, as Schumpeter described, are emerging and will eventually drive the next long wave upswing.

China, it should be noted, has not been immune to the long wave forces, particularly its capacity overbuilding to service indulgent

American consumers. The painful readjustment in the United States to the excesses of the past 20 years has meant a collapse in demand for billions of dollars' worth of Chinese exports. Chinese GDP had received a huge lift from the demand for plant and equipment to build the capacity to supply U.S. consumers. The U.S. retrenchment has cost something approaching 30 million Chinese jobs, both in export industries and in industries that produced the capital goods to create the export-oriented factories. This is textbook creative destruction outlined by Schumpeter in which overcapacity leads to a sharp decline in capital goods industries.

Fortunately, China's financial strength has enabled it to create massive new infrastructure spending without risking a U.S.-style government debt-to-GDP explosion. China has been able to create new jobs, stimulate growth, and weather the great recession very well—at least in the short run. Further out, China's long wave upswing appears to have many years to run, an important dynamic for Western economies and financial markets in the future, and investors will need to look to China and other well-placed emerging markets for growth in their portfolios.

Conclusion

The long wave decline and the timing of its bottoming process have been greatly complicated in the past 20 years by the asset boom, temporary inflation of incomes, and the bust of 2008–2009. It is also clear that there are significant differences from previous long wave declines. One is extended government intervention, which prevented a self-feeding debt deflation catastrophe in 2009. Another difference is that excess capacity in the United States is not so much in heavy capital goods industries as in the 1930s and 1880s. It is much more evident in finance, housing, and retailing.

In the past, the U.S. government has never attempted to transform so much private debt into public debt. One result is

(continued)

that private sector deleveraging has begun, as evidenced by the sharp increases in the household savings rate and substantial corporate bond and equity issuance in the much improved financial markets. However, serious questions about long-term stability and fragility remain and, in particular, whether households will continue to deleverage or will go back to their love affair with debt and overconsumption.

Deleveraging of the private sector, if continued, bodes well for speeding up the transition process to the next long wave upswing. Our sense is that the U.S. long wave decline is very long in the tooth. Its duration far exceeds declines in previous cycles for the reasons mentioned in this chapter. Our guess, and it is only a guess, is that the bottoming should be complete within four to five years at the most.

While it is always difficult to anticipate the diffusion of technology and innovation into new industries, it is not difficult to see that the next upswing will be based on microchips, information, and other technologies. Peter Drucker has theorized that knowledge will be the cornerstone of the new society, becoming the key means of production. This innovative revolution is advanced but far from over, and the United States has a strong comparative advantage. It is in an excellent position to apply its technology in a variety of other areas, such as the resolution of supply shortages that have created high relative prices. This would certainly include energy. There will be other areas of shortage in the coming years, such as water and food, and the United States is well positioned to lead in those areas as well.

The United States will recover economically and financially. What goes down does come up. How well the United States recovers, how quickly, and with what degree of stability will essentially depend on how the difficult transition to the next long wave upswing is managed and the sort of policies that will be put in place in the next year or two. Just as the economy is in disequilibrium, so too is the financial system.

The continuing concern is how the Great Reflation will play out in this context and whether it will turn into another Great Inflation like the 1970s.

Part III looks at some of the policy options. The trickiest and potentially most dangerous issue is the explosion in the fiscal deficit and the projected steep rise in the government debt-to-GDP ratio to levels that, in the past, have been seen only in wartime. This is the subject of the next chapter.

Chapter 4

Government Deficits and the Great Reflation

When national debts have once been accumulated to a certain degree, there is scarce, I believe, a single instance of their having being fairly and completely paid. The liberation of the public revenue, if it has ever been brought about at all, has always been brought about by bankruptcy; sometimes by an avowed one, but always by a real one, though frequently by a pretended payment.

—ADAM SMITH[1]

The crash, panic, and Great Reflation have unleashed an explosion in public debt that will last for years. This will have a profound effect on investors' portfolios and their ability to protect, and it is hoped, expand their wealth in the future. Like all experiments, the Great Reflation will have an uncertain outcome and investors owe it to themselves to understand how the financial world will be transformed by unprecedented peacetime fiscal deficits.

Chapters 2 and 3 discussed the debt supercycle and its role in the asset inflations of the past 25 years. Burst bubbles created by too much debt destroy balance sheets by causing asset prices to fall sharply. Liabilities, which are on the other side of the balance sheet, are fixed at any point in time. The difference between the two is net worth, or equity. The bigger the actual or expected fall in asset prices, the greater the risk that lenders won't get their money back. Their fear sets in motion a process called *balance sheet recession,* a term coined by Richard Koo,[2] a recognized authority on the Japanese deflation. As creditors try to get their money back or stop lending, debtors panic as well and the scramble for liquidity is set in motion. However, the true balance sheet recession does not end with the abatement of the crisis. Debtors continue their efforts to improve their balance sheets, one aspect of which is to repay debt when they get their hands on liquidity. Creditors also continue their efforts to get liquid by cutting back on lending and using cash to acquire liquid, safe assets regardless of the low level of returns. Balance sheet recessions can last for years, as Japan can attest, and don't end until balance sheets are thoroughly repaired. Normal recessions are fundamentally different because the damage to balance sheets is temporary.

The typical recession is brief and, after a short adjustment period, demand can be stimulated by easy money, lower interest rates, and government stimulus. In a balance sheet recession, monetary policy by itself is impotent. Low and even zero interest rates don't stimulate borrowing and spending. Because of this, government deficits must play a different role than in normal recessions. They fill the hole created by debt liquidation, collapsed asset values, and excess savings. They allow the private sector to accomplish the needed debt repayment to bring assets and liabilities back into equilibrium. Fiscal deficits in a normal recession are generally caused by automatic stabilizers, such as employment insurance and a drop in tax revenues; they support final demand in the economy during the brief downturn.

In a balance sheet recession, if the government fails to support private debt reduction by increasing its own borrowing and spending, private efforts to get liquid simply cause a self-feeding downward spiral in the economy, turning a balance sheet recession into what Irving Fisher[3] called a debt deflation. This is what occurred in the 1930s.

In the modern world with today's political realities, governments cannot simply stand aside and let mountains of private debt just collapse. Debt that cannot be repaid is obviously a mistake that someone has to pay for. It is true that both lenders and borrowers were equally responsible for the current crisis and ought to be the ones to pay. However, the government has no choice but to socialize these costs and stick it to the taxpayers, unfair as it may seem. The alternative would be an economic catastrophe for everyone.

In the past, overextended private debtors would default and then would work out an agreement with lenders according to bankruptcy laws and their relative power. Today, the government absorbs most of those losses by replacing private debt with public debt. This transformation from one to the other means an eventual transfer of hugely increased government liabilities to future generations through higher taxes, fewer government services, inflation, or a combination of all three.

The Great Reflation is an experiment, as we said before, in transforming U.S. private debt into public debt on a vast scale. With the exception of Japan, it has never been done before in a major developed country in peacetime. It is incumbent on all investors to understand what balance sheet recessions are all about, what is at stake, and how the process of sharply rising government debt could affect the value of assets in the future.

The Private-Sector Debt Overhang

A balance sheet recession implies that private debt has somehow become excessive. To get a handle on how big this excess had become by 2009, we must look at how private debt has grown relative to gross domestic product (GDP), which is the source of income to service the debt. Figure 4.1 shows that private-sector debt rose to successive new highs in the postwar period, particularly after 1984 (also presented as Figure 2.1 in Chapter 2). Then, it was about 100 percent of GDP but it rose to a peak of over 170 percent in 2008. The crash and financial panic in 2008 and the unprecedented difficulty households and businesses have had in coping with their debt have demonstrated dramatically

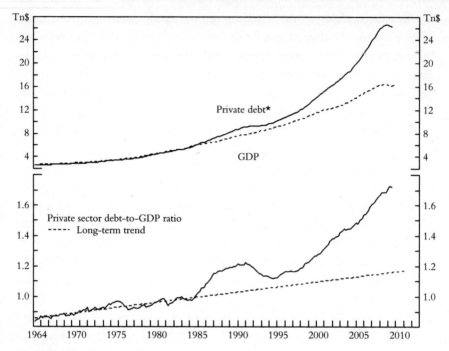

Figure 4.1   Credit Inflation: U.S. Private Sector
*Excludes state and local instruments.
Source: Chart courtesy of BCA Research Inc.

the extent to which borrowing in the United States had expanded far beyond the point where it could be supported by incomes and underlying asset values.

Figure 4.1 also shows that there was a close and stable relationship between private debt and GDP until about 1984. There was an uptrend in the ratio, but it was very modest. That changed after 1984 when debt began to accelerate much faster than GDP. We then began to experience a series of financial crises, each more severe than the previous one. There were stock market crashes in 1987, 1997–1998, 2000–2002, and 2008–2009. However, none of the economic downturns that followed each of these market peaks took on the characteristics of a full-blown balance sheet recession until the most recent one.

Recessions should be a time for healing, a time to eliminate real and financial excesses and, in particular, to restore balance sheet strength. As Figure 4.1 shows, that did not happen, and by 2008, when the peak was reached, private debt had come to exceed GDP by about $10 trillion. This is a measure of the amount of excess debt, or debt overhang, that had been created over the course of the debt supercycle. It was an indication of the magnitude of the danger and vulnerability of the financial structure just prior to the shock that was delivered by the sudden Lehman Brothers collapse in September 2008.

There are only four ways for individuals to cleanse balance sheets of too much debt. The first is to cut spending, increase savings, and repay it; the second is to sell assets and use the proceeds for debt reduction; the third is to default on the debt. Each is deflationary in one way or another; they drive the economy, employment, and prices down and, in extreme cases, cause a self-feeding spiral. The fourth way to reduce excess debt is to inflate it away. That works sometimes because debt is fixed in nominal dollars and, to the extent that prices and incomes rise, the real value of the debt is reduced. This assumes, of course, that incomes of debtors rise, and it works only in the short term because lenders catch on quickly and push up interest rates to get compensated for the loss of purchasing power. A variation of the inflationary route to fix balance sheets is to inflate asset prices. When they rise relative to liabilities, improvement in equity (net worth) and solvency result. At the time of writing, the Great Reflation was moving along this track, a theme we will return to in Chapters 5 and 6.

It should be noted that corporations have additional options to improve balance sheets, such as issuing new equity to investors or converting debt to equity. This improves liquidity for the issuer by sucking liquidity away from others.

From a practical point of view, the deflationary options are the only ones that promise to repair the financial system permanently. However, when balance sheets have become extraordinarily overextended, as they became by 2008, history has demonstrated that it can be dangerous and costly to let the financial system go into a liquidating free-fall in which the debt gets wiped out, through either bankruptcy, draconian retrenchment of spending or asset liquidation. More colorfully, this is described as letting the fire burn itself out. This is what happened in the 1930s and for most of the crises before that. However, debt levels and illiquidity were far greater in 2008 than in any of the earlier crises.

Coming to the rescue at a time of severe crisis involves creating another set of risks that must be managed with intelligence and great care. The only effective way to do this is for the government to transform excess private debt into public debt, exactly what the authorities have been doing. This is one component of the Great Reflation. It unquestionably entails the risk of turning the Great Reflation into the Great Inflation, as discussed in Chapter 5. In short, the dilemma facing the authorities is not unlike the dangers faced by ancient Greek sailors attempting to sail between Scylla and Charybdis.[4] There were monsters on both sides, and sailing between the two left little or no margin for error.

The government has several ways to transform private debt into public debt, including government debt guarantees; direct loans to, and investments in, corporations and banks; and the purchase of private-sector debts by U.S. government entities (for example, the Federal Reserve, Fannie Mae, and Freddie Mac). Governments can also accomplish this transformation through an increase in budget deficits, which puts money into the economy and into the hands of individuals and companies. This facilitates private-sector savings and debt reduction.

Bankruptcy and other forms of forced debt liquidation are immediately painful and can be catastrophic in a debt deflation like the 1930s. Since the crash, the government has been using an intelligent, creative process of managed bankruptcies (e.g., auto manufacturers) and quasi-bankruptcies together with bailout money to get concessions from unions and management while avoiding much of the fallout from uncontrolled debt liquidation.

Increasing budget deficits and transformation of private to public debt appear to have little downside risk for the authorities when the economy and markets are crashing. As recovery unfolds, opponents of the government begin to appeal to people's fear of inflation and increased taxation. The risk then is that the government gets pushed into fiscal retrenchment before deleveraging is complete. Richard Koo has described how this happened in Japan in 1997 and 2001. Both times the economy sank, pushing the deficit even higher. The same happened in the United States in 1937. Fiscal and monetary retrenchment pushed the economy back into depression, and unemployment remained at 25 percent until World War II started. These are stark lessons that should not be forgotten in today's fragile economic environment.

The total government borrowing requirement, which adds to outstanding government debt, always increases sharply after a major financial crisis. Reinhart and Rogoff[5] have pointed out that on average, the real value of government debt has risen a whopping 86 percent in the major post–World War II episodes, which includes 13 examples. The main cause of the debt increase is ballooning deficits due to collapsing tax revenue and, to a lesser extent, government bailouts. The United States is on track to repeat the experience of these other countries that have had major financial crises.

Government Deficits and Public Debt: A Look at the Numbers

The U.S. federal budget deficit amounted to $1.4 trillion or 10 percent of GDP in 2009. This compares with a deficit of 6.5 percent of GDP in 1975, the previous postwar record. Using the government's own figures and its assumptions, deficits are projected to remain in the range of $700 billion to $1 trillion. The important but fairly optimistic assumption is that growth in the economy will average about 3 to 3.5 percent per annum, a ridiculously optimistic forecast and includes no recession for almost a decade. If that forecast turns out to be too high, the debt ratio will deteriorate much more. Each year's deficit plus interest adds to the stock of outstanding government debt. Government projections show that publicly-held debt will rise from a level of around 44 percent of GDP at the end of 2008 to over 80 percent by 2018–2020 and 180 percent by 2035. This projection is shown in Figure 4.2. It is an extraordinarily high ratio, far exceeding anything ever recorded in the past 100 years.

As a reality check on the government's projection of the government debt-to-GDP ratio moving toward the 100 percent plus area and beyond, we can also look at the amount of debt overhang or excess private debt that must be eliminated to achieve some basis for future stability. Referring back to Figure 4.1, it would require a little over $7.5 trillion of private debt reduction, or ¾ of the $10 trillion

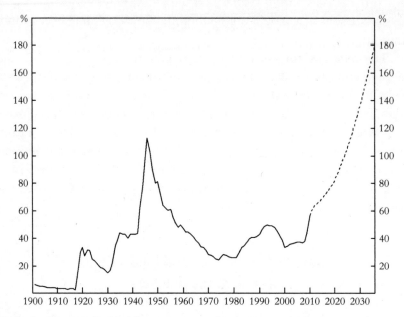

Figure 4.2 U.S. Federal Government Debt as a Percent of GDP
Source for data: Congressional Budget Office, "Debt Held by the Public."
Note: Dashed line represents Congressional Budget Office projections from 2009 to 2035.
Source: Chart courtesy of BCA Research Inc.

overhang, just to get back to the early 1990 level. The $7.5 trillion reduction will have to be transformed into public debt if we wish to avoid the risk of another sharp downturn in the economy. If that happened, the deficit would increase well beyond the projections in Figure 4.2.

In addition to the private and public debt transformation, there are ongoing fiscal deficits we mentioned before, probably averaging $700 billion to $1 trillion for years. Then we have to add something for state and local governments. Currently, they have debts equal to 16 percent of GDP, and most are running large ongoing deficits. Some, like California, are already broke and issuing IOUs. Reliable estimates of state deficits of up to $350 billion annually are floating around by groups such as the nonprofit Center on Budget & Policy Priorities,[6] and Washington is the ultimate backstop for state and local governments.

Another huge component of the government debt picture is the contingent liabilities of the federal government. Currently, the net present value of these liabilities, principally for Medicare and Social Security for federal employees, veterans, and the general public totals about $43 trillion (yes, trillion) or about equal to three times GDP according to the Government Accountability Office (GAO). There are, of course, other contingent liabilities that arise from, for example, the Federal Deposit Insurance Corporation (FDIC)'s guarantee of $4 trillion of deposits and other liabilities of banks. However, the FDIC holds only $52 billion of assets. There are also potential liabilities that arise from the guarantees of Fannie Mae and Freddie Mac, the government-backed mortgage lending institutions. There are also claims that inevitably arise from the government's intervention in the auto and other industrial sectors. Moreover, there is immense pressure on the government to make up a good part of the huge shortfall in private pension assets. They are woefully inadequate to pay the benefits that retirees are counting on. And then there is the unknown but massive cost arising from new health insurance coverage that might be legislated.

It is very difficult to assess how much of the government's colossal contingent liabilities will actually become real liabilities. For example, the government could cut benefits, extend the working age for retirees, or cut off financing of insolvent states. None of these are politically attractive. They lower living standards and risk depressing the economy further. The reality, though, is that as the baby boomers age, claims on the government will skyrocket under any scenario. The government debt-to-GDP ratio will almost certainly pierce the 100 percent level within a few years, approaching the 115-120 percent level reached at the end of World War II, and keep rising if substantial action is not taken.

In short, the U.S. government's financial position is almost certainly going to become increasingly precarious just as the private sector's position is now. The government is really only an intermediary, and its balance sheet is ultimately the balance sheet of the nation and its people. The government has used its monopoly power of taxation to make promises that artificially inflate expected living standards. These promises will not be kept. If a credible plan to achieve fiscal stability is not soon developed, confidence in the government's financial viability could erode rapidly. People will increasingly assume that it cannot maintain its ability to finance ongoing cash requirements in a noninflationary way, and this would have a profound effect on investors and their assets.

Too Much Government Debt?

How much government debt is too much? That is always an intriguing question. There is no hard-and-fast rule, only experience from other countries. There are many factors that are critical in assessing the sustainability of government debt ratios. For example, much depends on credibility and confidence in the government, the size of the existing deficit, and whether it is growing or shrinking. The size and direction of the domestic tax base, the level and direction of interest rates, the domestic savings rate, the strength or weakness in the currency, and inflationary expectations are also important factors and must be taken into account in assessing whether a country is on the road to financial ruin.

The experience of other countries is useful in establishing some guidelines on appropriate levels of government debt. It is generally agreed that countries with government debt that is stable and under 40 percent of GDP are fiscally sound. However, the European Union, for example, has set a maximum permissible debt ratio higher than that level for its members at 60 percent. Yet, Italy has continuously breached even that level by a wide margin and has not yet gone into bankruptcy in spite of many predictions that it would.

Countries that push the ratio up to 70 to 80 percent and beyond clearly move into the arena of instability and are, of course, seriously at risk if the economy implodes or some other shock suddenly hits. They have left little or no room to maneuver in times of distress when it may be necessary to reflate and to bail out banks and others. Currently, we can think of Italy, Greece, Ireland, Iceland, and much of Eastern Europe in this camp. The United States with a debt ratio of 55 percent is currently in the gray area between 40 and 60 percent, but it is rapidly moving to much higher levels and will soon have to contemplate the politically unthinkable—much higher levels of taxation.[7]

Japan's experience of the past 20 years with enormous budget deficits and extraordinarily high government debt ratios is worth examining in the context of where the United States might be going. Japan's bubble economy imploded after 1989 and it entered a full-blown balance sheet recession, which does not yet appear to be over. The government responded with huge fiscal stimulus and sustained large deficits, pushing the gross government debt-to-GDP ratio over 200 percent. However, Japan has managed to maintain confidence in its currency, finance cash requirements at very low interest rates, and avoid fears of inflation. The fact is that Japan, following its 1990 post-bubble crash, avoided a depression even though the loss in wealth as a result of the stock market and real estate decline was equal to about three years of GDP. To put this in perspective, the U.S. loss of wealth in the 1930s was only about one year's worth of GDP, yet it suffered a decline of almost 50 percent of GDP and the unemployment rate rose to 25 percent. Thus, if Japan had not run such large deficits, it is likely that it would have gone into a very deep depression.

Richard Koo has outlined the lessons he believes the United States should learn from Japan's experience.[8] He claims that in a balance sheet recession monetary policy is useless and the government must run deficits equal to the increased savings of the private sector until deleveraging has ended and the private sector is ready to borrow again, no matter how large the government debt gets in the meantime.

In the short term, his prescription is undoubtedly correct. However, there are critically important differences between the two countries. The United States has had a much lower savings rate than Japan and therefore it is harder to finance large deficits internally. The dollar is the reserve currency of the world. Central banks hold about $4 trillion in highly liquid form. The United States typically runs a large balance of payments deficit, whereas Japan is a surplus country. Therefore, the United States would be putting itself in a very danger-ous position if it didn't soon address its precarious fiscal position. The United States has not allowed itself much room to maneuver should depressed economic conditions and high unemployment extend for a long time.

On the positive side, the United States has great advantages over Japan. It has a far more flexible, adaptable economy; the loss in wealth relative to GDP from the crash was about one-third of the Japanese loss. Last, it has a growing population whereas Japan's is shrinking. Therefore, while the United States should take to heart Koo's major point, it cannot be complacent about the deficit and the debt increase. The United States has far more potential for disaster, even taking into account its advantages, if confidence in the currency crumbles and foreigners and residents alike scramble to dump the dollar for other currencies or gold.

Some argue that the U.S. government escaped rather easily from its very high wartime debt ratio in 1946. It fell to 30 percent by 1970, with little or no pain. The data are shown in Figure 4.3. The question is: Why couldn't the government do it again once the appropriate time for fiscal consolidation arrives? Unfortunately, there are a number of reasons why the conditions in the United States now and in the fore-seeable future will not resemble those in the early postwar period, and any escape from spiraling debt will be neither easy nor painless.

In 1946 there were virtually no contingent liabilities of the U.S. government; private sector debt had been reduced to about 60 percent of

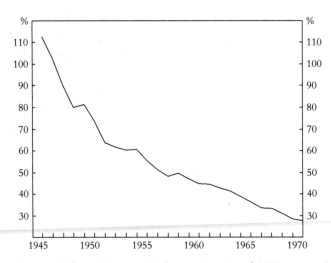

Figure 4.3 U.S. Federal Government Debt as a Percent of GDP
Source for data: Congressional Budget Office, "Debt Held by the Public."
Source: Chart courtesy of BCA Research Inc.

GDP compared with the 170 percent today, and the domestic savings rate was high. Demand for U.S. products was enormous because of wartime destruction in Europe and Asia, combined with the huge surge in domestic population from the birth of baby boomers and immigration. The United States had a young, hardworking labor force, whereas now it has a rapidly aging labor force that frequently shuns hard work, particularly relative to the developing countries. The United States ran a large balance of payments surplus after World War II, adding to its already hugely positive net foreign asset position. This made the U.S. dollar powerful and highly sought after. Moreover, the banking system was sound and highly liquid, as were households and corporations from years of forced savings during the war and the depression before. The U.S. government ran budget surpluses most of the time until 1970 without impeding growth, because underlying demand in the economy was very strong.

The United Kingdom also managed to escape from very high government debt ratios in the nineteenth century and again after World War I and World War II. But, like the United States, in 1946 it had the preconditions to do it. At present, the United Kingdom and most other developed countries are in the same boat as the United States today in facing a very difficult environment in which to reduce government debt.

The lesson is that strong economic growth, a high savings rate, and low interest rates are essential to the restoration of manageable government debt levels. Japan never followed a pro-growth strategy but rather a bailout–save jobs–public works strategy, all of which avoided the need for restructuring. The result was stagnation with government debt becoming progressively more burdensome and damaging to the confidence of the Japanese people themselves.

The necessary conditions for escaping from what is generally known as the debt trap—a continuing upward spiral in the government debt-to-GDP ratio—is quite straightforward. The economy must grow faster than the rate of interest the government pays on its debt, and the government must run a deficit no larger than the interest payments on its outstanding debt. At present, interest rates are very low and the U.S. government's interest payments are relatively small. However, the underlying growth in the economy—net of the artificial stimulus for support programs—is probably significantly lower. The government budget deficit is around $1.4 trillion and may, under optimistic conditions, shrink to the $700 billion to $1 trillion range in the next few years. But even these numbers are far higher than the interest payments on outstanding debt (the difference is called the primary balance and it is in big deficit). Therefore, the United States is, and will remain for the foreseeable future, in the so-called debt trap—an upward spiral in the debt-to-GDP ratio.

The great problem in the United States now is that underlying demand is weak from private-sector deleveraging, excess capacity in many industries, and enormous pressure from hypercompetitive countries like China and India, which have high savings and investment relative to GDP. It is precisely because of this weakness in the economy, deleveraging, and a failed financial system that the United States has to run such large deficits in the near term. Failure to do so would cause the economy to slide again, resulting in even larger deficits. The United States must get growth back on track because that is the only way that the greatly enlarged debt can be brought under control in the long run, allowing the United States to escape from the debt trap. Otherwise, the country risks drifting into multiyear stagnation like the Japanese, where government debt has risen so dramatically.

Conclusion

Investors can rejoice in the short run because the U.S. government has made sure to avoid a 1930s debt deflation and depression by running massive fiscal deficits. These have been used to allow the private sector to start deleveraging, to bail out banks and companies, and to sustain demand in the economy and get some growth. The deficits and stimulus programs will give the economy a lift for a while and have been supportive of higher asset prices after the March 2009 lows.

Whether investors can rejoice in the longer run remains to be seen. That will depend on whether the government can rein in its deficits and sharply rising debt-to-GDP ratio which, in turn, will require, among other things, strong economic growth. However, in past cycles, growth has depended on ever-rising private debt and the ability of the United States to run increasingly large current account deficits. That will not be possible after the crisis of 2008–2009. If the United States cannot reduce its debt-to-GDP ratio in a timely manner, investors will be faced with a public-sector debt supercycle that will be an even bigger monster than the post-1982 private-sector debt supercycle. Monetization—money printing—is one of the implications, a subject we take up in the next chapter.

Chapter 5

Money and the Great Reflation

Inflation is always and everywhere a monetary phenomenon.
—MILTON FRIEDMAN AND ANNA SCHWARTZ[1]

Investors are understandably concerned that the Great Reflation will turn into the Great Inflation. In this chapter, we look at some of the issues relating to those fears. In previous chapters we pointed out why inflation is the single most important factor affecting investments. We also emphasized that inflation should be understood as an increase in money and credit beyond the growth requirements of the economy. In the previous chapter, we explained how the implosion of the 25-year private debt binge is creating a government debt supercycle of its own. The explosion of government debt is one component of the Great Reflation. The other is money printing and near-zero interest rates. The Federal Reserve is the institution behind the monetary component, and it will play the starring role in whether we have another inflationary drama.

The Great Reflation experiment is pushing an avalanche of new money into the economy and financial system. This new money must find a home somewhere. By the end of 2009, the government had succeeded in its initial purpose of stabilizing the financial system, reflating asset prices, and generating economic recovery, albeit a hesitant and artificial one. However, being an experiment, the ultimate outcome of the total reflation package is far from certain. That is a reality that all investors must continuously keep in mind as they struggle to understand how the future will unfold. The Great Reflation has ensured that the 100-year-old Age of Inflation remains intact. Possible outcomes are further declines in the purchasing power of the dollar, another mania in asset prices, or some combination of both. But eventually, all inflations result in deflations.

Central Banks and Inflation

The central bank is at the core of the modern inflationary process through its creation of excess money and credit. Historically, before World War II, central banks were independent and frequently privately owned; and, before the eighteenth century, very few countries had them. Paper money that circulated was substantially backed by specie—gold and/or silver. Therefore, inflation was not easily created by governments, even though they frequently had a desperate need for money.

There were two main causes of inflation before central banks. The more frequent was the clipping (shaving the edges) of coins by monarchs to pay their bills when they could not squeeze more taxes out of their people. An inflow of new gold and silver was the other main cause of inflation, as we discussed in Chapter 1.

There have been some paper money inflations in countries without central banks, but they have been rare. Probably the most famous was the assignat inflation in France associated with the French Revolution.[2]

The assignats were originally bonds, later currency, issued by the National Assembly after the French Revolution, and were backed by confiscated church properties. There were no brakes on the issuance of notes (a theme running through this book), which were increased to the point where they had no value (i.e., hyperinflation). The Bank of

France was created in 1800 to bring monetary stability and to introduce the new French franc in 1803.

Inflations in the nineteenth century up to 1914 were temporary and episodic, almost always related to war. Since then, inflation has become chronic; periods of stability have been temporary. There is one overriding reason why we have had this experience since 1914. The monetary system is based on fiat paper money, which we described in Chapter 1. It is money that has no backing other than promises made by the issuer, usually a central bank. Therefore, we must look to central banks for an understanding of the modern inflationary process. They are the heart of the financial system with the monopoly power to print money if they so desire.

The Challenges of Central Banks

It is not easy being a central bank. They face many challenges that are as old as central banking itself. Two hundred years of history suggest clearly that central banks have had mixed success, at best, in meeting these challenges. The primary ones are maintaining the stability of the purchasing power of the money they issue and maintaining the financial system on an even keel. Horrendous mistakes have been all too frequent; money has not retained its value and the financial system has experienced frequent crises of great magnitude. What periods of stability there have been may have had more to do with luck than skill.

Because of this sorry track record and the fascination with financial crises, there have been thousands of books and learned papers written on money, central banks, and the challenges they face. One of the earliest and most important of these was the Bullion Committee Report[3] of 1810 that resulted from an inquiry into why the pound sterling had fallen on the exchanges, and why the gold price and inflation had gone up during the earlier part of the Napoleonic Wars. The report was one of the early attempts to understand the issues surrounding inflation, the definition of money, and the role of the central bank. That and the great volume of other literature on the subject is testimony to the great challenges that central bankers have faced over the centuries. The following summarizes seven of these because they relate particularly to the challenges the Federal Reserve faces in the aftermath of the Great Reflation and the implications if the Fed fails to meet these challenges.

1. Money does not look after itself. It has a long and varied history of running to excess or deficiency.
2. Money defies accurate definition. Financial innovation and technology continually create new instruments with money-like properties, and the central bank always has trouble knowing what to control, and how much is too much or too little.
3. The time lag between a central bank's action and its impact is long and variable.
4. Central banks are frequently conflicted in objectives. For example, the necessary action of supplying lender of last resort liquidity in a crisis may exacerbate inflation and moral hazard (the increasing tolerance for risk) later.
5. Central bankers often disagree among themselves on what they should be targeting. The choices are: money supply, interest rates, price inflation, asset inflation, credit, or the foreign exchange value of their currency.
6. One of the greatest challenges for central banks is knowing to whom they are ultimately responsible and knowing clearly what their ultimate objectives are. These are muddy issues even in the best of times. Most would argue that the central bank is, in the final analysis, responsible to the government; but that is a tricky one, particularly in the United States where the executive branch of government is separate from the Congress. Both the president and Congress derive their power from being elected by the people. The Federal Reserve chairman is not elected. He is appointed by the president but must report to Congress, a murky situation. Short-term political objectives can frequently trump long-term stability objectives, and the Federal Reserve is caught in the middle. It is clearly responsible for the long-term purchasing power of the currency, but, in the short term, it does not have a mandate to defy elected politicians. They are responsible to the people who all too frequently clamor for easy money and low interest rates. Regulation of financial institutions and markets is only partly in the hands of the Federal Reserve. Many other regulatory authorities are also involved.

Frequently they have views different from the Federal Reserve, and conflict results.

7. The responsibility for the dollar's international role belongs to the U.S. Treasury, which is always going to be more politically oriented than the Fed. The key currency role of the dollar in foreign central bank reserves is critical for international monetary stability and U.S. inflation. The potential for conflict is obvious. The Fed will always have at least one eye on the stability of the dollar and general prices, while the Treasury will always have at least one eye on politics, unemployment, and the next election.

The history of central banking shows clearly, as we have just summarized, the great difficulty that those in charge have in fulfilling their mandate of fostering a stable economy, currency, and price level. Central bankers, with full access to the reams of literature and research over the past two centuries, have still managed to make a mess of things on a pretty regular basis. Take the Federal Reserve, for example.

It is managed by highly intelligent, academically solid, experienced, dedicated, well-meaning people. However, they are nonetheless just humans, and humans can make huge mistakes. Unfortunately, there have been many since the Federal Reserve was set up in 1913. As pointed out in Chapter 1, the purchasing power of the dollar has fallen by 95 percent since then, indicating that the Federal Reserve, on balance, has preferred to listen all too often to its political masters rather than risk the consequences of a single-minded focus on stable money.

There have been great economic booms and busts over the Fed's century-long history. The experience includes repeated asset inflations and deflations and enormous volatility in the foreign exchange value of the dollar. Any way you cut it, it's not a great scorecard for generating the sort of confidence investors need to see as the Federal Reserve enters into perhaps its biggest challenge of all—managing the Great Reflation—in the aftermath of the biggest credit bust and banking collapse since the 1930s.

The Fed, in contrast to its performance from 1929 to 1932, did achieve a timely rescue of a collapsing financial system. It showed great financial leadership in fulfilling its classic role of lender of last resort at a time when there was a political vacuum in Washington. However, the reflation story is far from over. The Federal Reserve in the years ahead will be faced with an activist, interventionist, populist government that will stand or fall on getting the United States out of its economically depressed, high-unemployment quagmire. The age-old conflict between short-term political objectives and long-term stable money objectives will be a constant feature of life until full recovery is secured, balance sheets are rebuilt, and the government fiscal house is put in credible order. And that is not going to happen anytime soon.

Mechanics and Operations of Central Banks

The mechanics and operations of central banks are for technicians, and we needn't spend much time on them. The interesting things are what happens in the real world of decision making and the consequences of those decisions.

Central banks, formerly called banks of issue, have two main technical functions: the issuance of paper money, for which they have a monopoly, and the depository for commercial banks to hold their reserves.

The overwhelming majority of the central banks' assets are held in government bonds and Treasury bills. The Fed can hold foreign exchange, but, in practice, amounts are small. The liabilities of the Fed are notes in circulation and deposits, the latter being an asset of commercial banks that make up the bulk of their reserves. Various securities and loans make up most of the rest of commercial bank assets. Their liabilities are mainly deposits, made up of different types—demand, savings, and certificates of deposit (CDs). Capital is the difference between the assets and liabilities of the commercial banks. One hopes that it is positive and by a large enough margin so that depositors are confident, not just that the bank is solvent, but that it has sufficient liquidity to honor, beyond question, demands for deposit withdrawal. Hard bank capital is composed of issued common and preferred stock, and retained earnings.

The control mechanism, in very simplified form, works as follows. Let's assume that the Federal Reserve wants to increase the money supply by 5 percent. In the short run, currency in circulation is fixed, so the Federal Reserve focuses on increasing its liabilities (reserves) to commercial banks. It can do this only by increasing its assets. Typically, it would buy Treasury bills in sufficient quantity to increase commercial bank reserves by 5 percent. After the first-round effect, commercial banks would find that they have excess reserves earning nothing, so they would put this money to work either buying securities or making loans. They would write checks on themselves to buy securities or, when they make a loan, credit the depositor's bank account.

Money starts to move around the banking system as each bank adjusts its assets and liabilities to the increased reserves it holds. When all the activity is completed, the great mystery of paper money creation has done its magic. Excess reserves no longer exist because commercial banks, in their profit-maximizing mode, have done their job. Bank deposits, alias money supply, have increased by 5 percent, and the reserve ratio is once again equal to what it was before. Bank reserves and other bank assets have risen together by 5 percent, just managing to equal the increase in commercial bank liabilities (money supply). As banks' earning assets have increased, they would acquire the additional profits to add to their capital base to meet the increased need as a result of their increased liabilities. This example applies to a healthy financial system. In a balance sheet recession, the money-creation process breaks down because either the banks don't want to lend new reserves or borrowers want to repay loans, not borrow more. This is financial constipation, and the government must short circuit the breakdown by doing the borrowing through increased deficits to keep money circulating and growing.

Financial constipation occurred after the crash in 2009. The Federal Reserve, remembering the lessons of 1929, flooded the banking system with reserves by doubling the size of its assets. As we pointed out, when the Fed adds to its assets, it also must add to its liabilities and these become additional reserves of the commercial banks. These reserves are the base for monetary expansion. It increases the base on which the banks can make more loans and expand the money supply.

Figure 5.1 shows how the Fed's extreme efforts at monetary ease through asset purchases caused the monetary base to double in a matter of months. This has given rise to fears of accelerating inflation. However, the commercial banks simply held the excess reserves at the Fed rather than putting them to work. The result was that the money

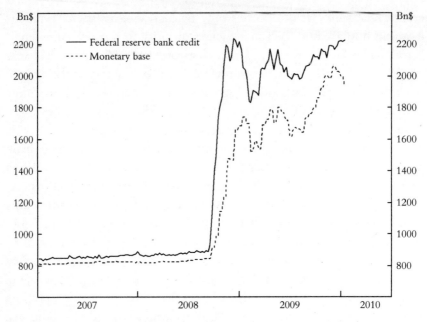

Figure 5.1   Federal Reserve Bank Credit and Monetary Base
Source: Chart courtesy of BCA Research Inc.

multiplier—the ratio between bank reserves and the broad measure of
U.S. money supply (M2)—collapsed, almost completely neutralizing
the potential inflationary impact of the Fed's action, at least for the
time being. This is shown in Figure 5.2. The collapse in the multiplier
is also true of other measures of money.

When the financial system moves out of the convalescent ward and
people want to borrow money again, the banks will want to put their
excess reserves to work. The money multiplier would then reverse, and
the money supply would start to grow again. Then fears of accelerating
inflation would become more realistic. When this might happen is difficult to gauge, and investors will have to pay close attention to these
relationships. The reason is that the Fed's long-discussed exit plan from
the massive monetary ease will have to be executed at some point. The
Fed will have to tighten policy, shrink its balance sheet, reduce bank
reserves, and raise interest rates at a time when the economy may still
be vulnerable and fragile. Such are the difficult decisions central bankers will soon be forced to make, and they spill over to investors and the
decisions they, in turn, have to make.

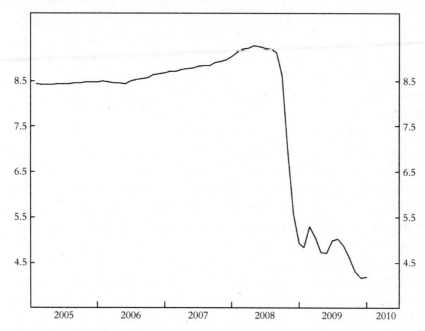

Figure 5.2 Money Multiplier
Note: M2 divided monetary base.
Source: Chart courtesy of BCA Research Inc.

Another control mechanism over commercial banks is the requirement that capital be maintained at a certain percentage of bank assets.
The purpose is mainly to provide a cushion against inevitable losses on
loans or securities. If a bank wants to grow its assets (as in the preceding
example), or if it faces losses greater than predicted that would eat into
its cushion, it must acquire more capital, either out of profits or by the
sale of eligible securities.

Central Banks and Monetary Control

The mechanics of monetary control are deceptively easy in theory. In
practice, central banks never know with any certainty how to manage the
financial system. This is critically important as the Great Reflation unfolds.

First, central banks cannot control both the amount of money in
the system and the rate of interest at the same time. They must focus

on one or the other and that can make life very difficult. For example, in the 1970s the Fed made a huge error by focusing on interest rates. As it raised rates, it thought it was tightening monetary policy. However, price inflation was rising faster and hence policy was actually becoming more expansionary, which in turn fed the inflation in a classic self-reinforcing feedback loop.

At other times, the Fed has tried to control the growth of the money supply, but the perennial question always pops up—which definition of money? Should the Fed control narrow measures such as the monetary base and M1 or should it control a broad measure such as M2? Frequently, the different measures of money move in opposite directions, undermining this so-called monetarist approach.

In more recent times, the Federal Reserve has focused on price inflation, adjusting interest rates as an intermediate-term objective. However, the rate of price inflation has been falling on average for 27 years for reasons mainly external to the United States. The result was that the policy of the Fed became too easy, which encouraged excess credit growth, which in turn fed the previous asset bubbles.

A second age-old issue for central banks is one of rules versus discretion. Should there be a fixed rule, such as a certain percentage of gold backing their liabilities (gold standard) or a Milton Friedman[4] rule, which advocates a fixed percentage growth of the money supply depending on structural factors and the desired rate of inflation. With a rules-based system, the central bank sticks with it come hell or high water.

Pre-1914, the Fed and most central banks operated on a rules-based system derived from the gold standard and a fixed ratio of gold to central bank liabilities. It brought long-term stability but periodic short-term pain. However, the experience in the 1930s under the restored but flawed gold standard was entirely different. The Fed stuck with the rules until it got *both* hell *and* high water as the country drowned in the ensuing debt collapse. That killed the idea of a rules-based system, and the Fed has operated on a discretionary basis ever since.

Central banks took the rap for the experience of the 1930s, which was so painful that the Fed and most other central banks lost their independence. Those that were private became nationalized or at least totally controlled by the government. Rules were out, discretion was in, and inflation accelerated. Proposals to reestablish rules reappear from time to time, but no one has come close to providing a credible system that has gained significant support. We remain on a discretionary-based policy framework, relying on central bankers' judgment to target whatever they think is appropriate for the environment of the day. That environment, in the near term, will continue to be deflation, deleveraging, anemic growth, and chronic unemployment. The prescription is full-throttle monetary expansion, with the target being consumer price index (CPI) inflation. If it undershoots Fed objectives or threatens to turn into deflation, monetary policy will remain super easy. If in the unlikely event that CPI inflation, actual or expected, rises above the Fed's target in the next year or two, it will tighten policy. However, the Fed's track record is so bad that the most likely scenario is that it will get it wrong no matter what it does.

The dollar will continue to float, and we will remain on a fiat paper money standard. The emerging dilemma in late 2009 was a continuation of CPI deflation and a fragile economy on the one hand while asset inflation on the other hand was strengthening to the point of creating fears of another bubble. The Fed has presumably learned the lesson that benign neglect of asset inflation is dangerous, yet premature tightening when the economy is fragile and flirting with deflation courts disaster. If such conditions continue, the Fed will be back to a Scylla and Charybdis choice.

A third key issue for central bank control has been the proliferation of nonbank financial institutions and new financial instruments. Together, they have generated credit growth far in excess of the banks and all too frequently this has gone unnoticed by the authorities. Figure 5.3 shows the trend in the ratio of nonbank assets to bank assets since 1950, and the relative shrinkage of bank assets is clearly evident. In 1950, nonbank assets were about half the size of bank assets. By 2008, they were two and a half times larger. They have shrunk dramatically since the crisis, however, but that may prove temporary. The Federal Reserve has direct control over banks only through the reserve requirement ratio. When the Federal Reserve squeezes bank reserves, credit growth outside the banks often accelerates. Moreover, the capital requirements on nonbanks are far lower than on banks. This has been

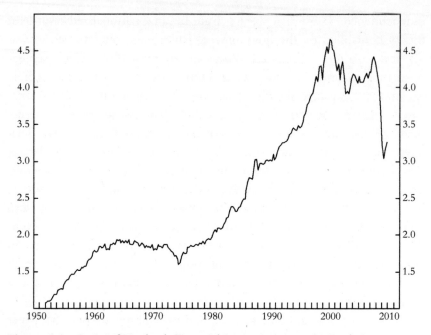

Figure 5.3 Ratio of Nonbank Financial Institution Assets to Bank Assets
Source: Chart courtesy of BCA Research Inc.

a huge issue for the central bank because it forces the Fed to focus on targets such as interest rates and price inflation that are notoriously difficult to model. The recent financial collapse has diminished this problem somewhat, as many nonbank financial institutions have been decimated and some survivors hastily became banks to get access to Federal Reserve protection.

In short, the difficulty of central bank control of money and credit is not going away. If anything, it will become more difficult and more complex. Central bankers will be feeling their way along, making decisions by the seat of their pants in a dangerous and difficult economic, financial, and political environment.

Federal Deficits, Inflation, and Crowding Out

There is a natural tendency for people to associate large and growing government deficits with accelerating price inflation, currency collapses, and ultimately too many zeros on banknotes along the line of the Zimbabwe experience shown in Figure 1.2 in Chapter 1. This view is derived from the experiences of Latin America and many other countries. It has not been true of the United States (excluding the South's continental currency collapse during the Civil War). The record shows that in the United States there has been no direct link between fiscal deficits, high ratios of government debt to gross domestic product (GDP), and inflation. Even during the high inflation years of the 1970s, the U.S. government debt-to-GDP ratio never went beyond 30 percent. Much higher ratios after World War II and in the 1980s did not lead to big percentage changes in the CPI. In fact, the opposite occurred.

The question now is whether this is about to change. Will the Great Reflation experiment push the United States toward the stereotypical Latin American experience? The answer will depend on the Federal Reserve and the pressure on it to monetize the massive deficits once recovery is under way.

During a balance sheet recession, central banks can print a lot of money and finance very large government deficits at very low interest rates without risking higher price inflation. Their actions should be seen as antideflationary and are necessary to offset the collapse in spending and credit demand caused by the sudden rise in private savings needed to rebuild balance sheets. The crunch comes later when the recession is over and private credit demand starts up again. That is when the Fed will have its true independence tested, and the outcome is far from certain for several reasons. First, the Fed's credibility has been seriously compromised by the many disastrous mistakes it has made almost from its beginning in 1913. It created the asset bubble in the 1920s; it played a key role in the 1930s collapse; it caused the 1970s high price inflation; and it fostered the credit and asset bubbles from 1984 to 2008 that led to the recent market collapse, recession, and 10 percent unemployment. Partial redemption came with the astute bailouts and radical lending after the crash, but then it is always easy in the short term for a central bank to write checks on itself, because it *is* the money. The checks don't bounce.

The Federal Reserve, with compromised credibility, is not in a good position as we move into the next stage of economic recovery. It will be walking a very fine line between nervous foreign central banks and private holders of U.S. dollars and Treasury bonds on the one hand. On the other hand, there are populist politicians facing an angry electorate, which is distrustful of governments and Wall Street. These people are suffering from large income, job, and wealth losses, and are reeling from the unexpected and shocking collapse in housing prices. The government will be increasingly tempted to cater to populist, interventionist sentiments. The authorities badly need growth to reduce unemployment, and the central bank will not be permitted to get in the way and risk aborting economic recovery prior to the next election. This will be the test as to whether the fiscal deficits will be linked much more directly to inflation than they have been in the past. We will then see whether the United States starts down the Latin American track.

At this point, we need to introduce the concept of *crowding out*. It refers to how fiscal deficits impact the economy, financial system, interest rates, and inflation. When the government spends money, it must compete with the private sector to get its hands on whatever it is trying to buy. That could be anything from tanks for the military and salaries for government workers to purchases of equity in banks to bail them out. The term *crowding out* refers specifically to how the government extracts resources from the private sector to pay its bills and what the consequences are.

The concept of crowding out will be extremely important in the years ahead because the federal government, as discussed in Chapter 4, has been increasing, and will continue to increase dramatically, its demands on the financial and productive resources of the nation. When there is a temporary surplus of both, following an economic slump and a related rise in the private sector's saving, there is generally little or no difficulty for the federal government. All of that changes when the economy begins to recover. At that point, the private sector is also trying to expand by spending and borrowing more. The battle for increasingly scarce resources begins, and tension in the markets increase. However, the government is by far the largest and most powerful entity in the economy. It will therefore not be denied its demands. This raises the important question as to how the process of forced resource transfer to the government works and what is the collateral damage to the private sector.

There are several ways the government can extract extra resources from the private sector, none of them without consequences. First, it can raise taxes, but politicians usually get thrown out of office when they do so. The Obama administration will certainly attempt to raise tax rates, but may not be very successful at raising much more money. That effort, however, will surely create a nasty political backlash that opposition politicians will try to exploit. The American public is financially damaged and bitter in the current environment, and people feel that their leaders have already caused them too much pain. Moreover, as the Japanese experience demonstrated during its long recession, raising taxes can quickly undermine economic recovery.

However, even if the government doesn't raise taxes, people are not fooled by the deficits. They have to be financed out of new borrowings. People know that someone has to pay at some point and that could be them or the next generation. People and businesses begin to predict a rise in the tax burden in the future and adjust their spending accordingly. This is called *Ricardian equivalence*,[5] and to the extent to which it comes into play, it can have a negative effect on the economy in the near term because people will save more, either to pay future taxes, or just to hedge against increased uncertainty. It is generally believed that the higher the government debt ratio is, the stronger the Ricardian equivalence factor. In the extreme, a dollar of extra government spending may cause people to cut their spending by more than a dollar, and GDP could actually fall.

If people don't increase their savings in the face of higher government deficits, the increased government borrowing will force up interest rates to the point where marginal private borrowers can't compete. A rise in interest rates could be catastrophic, since the economy will likely remain fragile and vulnerable to any shock. Higher interest rates would also increase interest payments to foreigners and reduce capital spending, which lowers living standards in the future. It would raise the cost of servicing government debt, which would compound the escalating government debt-to-GDP ratio, further crowding out the private sector. Higher interest rates raise residential mortgage and other consumer credit costs, which creates more political backlash. Steeper commercial mortgage rates would be an unwelcome extra kick to the unfolding commercial real estate decline, discussed in Chapter 13.

A third alternative way for the government to try to extract an increased share of resources from the economy is to use extensive controls on things like wages, prices, and interest rates. People expect this in wartime and acquiesce. Controls were used effectively by all countries during World War II. In the postwar period, the U.S. government tried wage and price controls in the early 1970s and credit controls in the early 1980s. Both were disasters and will not likely be used again in peacetime, short of a calamity extreme enough to galvanize public support.

The fourth way for the government to increase its share of resources would be to create additional money by selling bonds to the Federal Reserve and the banking system (i.e., monetization). Experience has shown that some countries have even used force to make central banks give them currency to pay their bills. California, which is effectively broke, fortunately lacks a central bank so it can't print money. Its solution was to create IOUs and use them to pay its bills, an alternative to central bank money printing. Argentina at the end of 2009 tried to raid the central bank's foreign exchange reserve to pay its bills and fired the governor when he refused. These are extreme cases and highlight the sort of financial dramas that can occur when governments run out of the ability to pay their bills.

In short, deficits create problems; and big deficits, if not brought under control, create big problems. There is no easy way, beyond the short term, for the government to extract extra resources from the economy without having serious consequences. When the economy is depressed and the government's fiscal capacity is ample, the consequences are minimal and reversible if the government runs surpluses (puts resources back into the economy) after the economy recovers. This was John Maynard Keynes's prescription—balance the budget over the business cycle with deficits in recessions and surpluses in booms. It was perverted by his followers, who had other agendas and did not shrink from the idea of chronic deficits.

Unfortunately, the United States has run large chronic deficits for most of the period since 1980 when Ronald Reagan and his supply-side advisers pushed fiscal deficits into the stratosphere. This has had two major consequences. One was that the U.S. government entered the balance sheet recession with an already large debt-to-GDP ratio of

45 percent, restricting fiscal capacity to safely run additional deficits in the future.

Figure 5.4 shows the trend of private U.S. savings as a percentage of GDP since the early 1980s. The progressive collapse is evident, although the crash and recession of 2008–2009 have pushed the savings rate back up as occurred after the previous recession, reflecting the public's effort to reduce debt. It remains to be seen whether this also will be reversed.

The second problem with the Reagan deficits was that they were so huge that they began to absorb a growing share of the dwindling supply of private savings. This is shown in Figure 5.5. In 1980, the government was taking almost no private savings. By the late 1980s and early 1990s, the government was taking up to 60 percent of private savings. The Clinton era reversed this for a while as the government actually ran surpluses; but the Bush Administration deficits caused the government to absorb increasing amounts of private savings again, even taking more than 100 percent by the end of 2008.

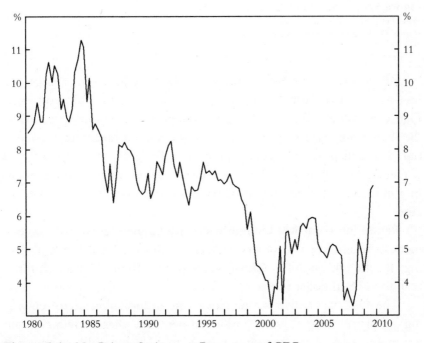

Figure 5.4   Net Private Savings as a Percentage of GDP
Source: Chart courtesy of BCA Research Inc.

Figure 5.5 U.S. Saving/Investment Collapse
Note: Four-quarter moving average of budget data.
Source: Chart courtesy of BCA Research Inc.

All economics textbooks focus on the link between savings and investment. The latter is the key to future growth and prosperity. Figure 5.5 shows that, as the government has increasingly absorbed the dwindling stock of private savings, investment (excluding residential) has collapsed in a series of cycles. By 2009, investment as a percentage of GDP had fallen to close to zero from around 6 percent in 1980. Even this number is paltry compared to China's 45 percent currently.

Figure 5.6 compares United States and Chinese gross fixed investment in recent years. China's has been accelerating, the U.S.'s declining. By the end of 2009, China was investing about 25 percent more than the U.S in dollar terms.

The U.S. experience is a textbook case of the public sector crowding out private sector savings and investment, and thereby reducing the productive base of the economy relative to what it would have been if savings had remained at more traditional levels. Chronic deficits mean

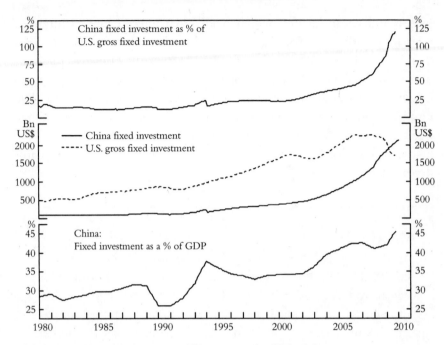

Figure 5.6 Fixed Investment: China versus the United States
Note: China fixed investment for 2009 is estimated by BCA Research Inc.
Source: Chart courtesy of BCA Research Inc.

lower living standards in the future. The United States has unfortunately jeopardized its growth potential, which is the key to reducing deficits in the future with as little pain as possible. Without the incremental growth, there will be that much more pressure on the Federal Reserve to assist in the financing of those deficits in an inflationary way— excess money printing.

The astute observer must wonder why the government was able to crowd out the private sector and reduce the productive base of the economy below trend without a rise in interest rates or inflation of prices of goods and services. Over the past 27 years inflation and interest rates actually fell. The answer lies primarily with China and also some other developing countries. China became the manufacturing work-shop of the world over this period, and with its very low wages, very high productivity, and enormous savings and investment, it was able to supply the United States with both cheap goods, which held down prices, and cheap savings, which held down interest rates. Moreover, China and other developing countries bought dollars by the trillions, thereby financing the vast increase in U.S. imports. However, it was a pact with the devil. The United States got only an artificial and temporary boost to its standard of living and wealth based on borrowing. The result was an increase in indebtedness to foreigners; a loss of economic freedom ("I owe my soul to the company store"); and a relative decline in the productive base of the economy, which future living standards depend on.

Conclusion

When there is inflation, there is always too much money and credit. The old line "Money makes the wheels go around" is certainly true, and when the economy has fallen off a cliff, the central bank's job is to make sure there is enough of the green stuff around. But if the central bank prints too much money for too long, the economy and financial system become very unstable. Large government deficits both complicate the job of central bankers and destroy the wealth-creating power of the economy by absorbing private savings and crowding out capital investment. The latter is the source of future income and wealth. Massive budget deficits into the future will mean continued anemic investment and, at best, anemic income and wealth gains.

In the short term, fiscal deficits and extreme monetary expansion are necessary to help the private sector repair balance sheets, but they cannot, by themselves, raise U.S. living standards, except temporarily. The United States has already started down the track toward lower living standards and wealth, a track that was temporarily reversed by the credit and asset bubble of recent years. That is over. Wealth is still 17 percent lower than at the peak in 2007, in spite of the post–March 2009 rally in stocks.

Jacques Rueff famously said that the United States as the reserve currency country can run [international] "deficits without tears."[6] That was true for many years. It no longer is.

If the Federal Reserve continues to monetize U.S. fiscal deficits for too long, excess money creation could once again lead to another, temporary feel-good asset inflation and potential mania; but the ultimate consequences would be even more tears once the bubble pops, as they all do. In the next chapter, we discuss bubbles and manias.

Chapter 6

Financial Manias and Bubbles

[O]ne thing is certain, that at particular times a great deal of stupid people have a great deal of stupid money. ... At intervals, the money of these people—the blind capital, as we call it, of a country, is particularly large and craving; it seeks for someone to devour it, and there is a "plethora"; it finds someone, and there is speculation; it is devoured, and there is "panic."
—WALTER BAGEHOT, "ESSAY ON EDWARD GIBBON," 1856

As the Great Reflation worked its way through 2009 and into 2010, it was evident that numerous asset prices had risen so sharply that many investors were wondering whether we were in the early stages of yet another financial mania. Financial manias are seductive because they hold out the prospect of fast money for the nimble. However, they are bubbles and don't last. When they burst, as we learned in 2008 and 2009, they destroy untold wealth and have the potential to bring down the entire financial system.

Financial manias and bubbles, as Professor Kindleberger stated in his famous *Manias, Panics, and Crashes,*[1] are hardy perennials and there is every indication that they will continue to be. All investors, or would-be investors, would be negligent if they did not make a serious effort to understand them, to recognize them, and to be ready to take action when they see the signs that they are getting out of hand. While such signs are always evident in a full-fledged mania, it is fascinating to note that almost everyone gets trapped and pays a very heavy price.

There have probably been more financial manias in the past 50 years than in any other period in history. More recent experience shows that they seem to be getting more extreme, as are the nasty consequences. Manias and bubbles are an integral part of the Age of Inflation because they are caused by too much money and credit.

A financial mania is an asset inflation that goes to an extreme, as we discussed in Chapter 1. Mania implies irrationality on a wide-spread scale. Some of the best descriptions of manias come from social psychologists, those who study crowd behavior.[2] They point out that intelligent people usually act rationally at the beginning of a mania, but gradually lose contact with reality. Toward the end, they join with enthusiasm in mass hysteria, infected by the prospects of quick wealth and oblivious to the known risks of catastrophic loss.

A bubble, in this context, refers to the rise in price of one or more asset classes, driven by mass excitement, which goes to such an extreme that valuation becomes absurd when viewed through the lens of even minimal common sense. Well-known examples abound. In 1989, the Japanese emperor's grounds were worth more than all the real estate of California. The price of gold in 1980 rose to almost $1,000 per ounce, compared to $35 per ounce only 10 years before. During the last stages of the tech bubble in 1999, corporate loss making was a badge of honor and stocks sold at hundreds of times the previous year's loss. Upstart companies run by kids with not much more than ideas were suddenly valued more highly than great companies with solid earnings, thousands of employees, and decades of solid performance.

Manias: Preconditions and Displacements

Financial history is replete with colorful examples of financial manias and bubbles, dating back to very early times. One of the interesting lessons is that the basic story behind each mania is always similar, although the details and objects of speculation differ from time to time. They have ranged from tulips (Holland in the seventeenth century) to canals (United Kingdom and United States in the eighteenth and early nineteenth centuries), railroads (United Kingdom and United States in the mid to late nineteenth century), and automobiles (early twentieth century). The perennials are real estate, equities, commodities (energy, food, gold, silver, copper), and office buildings. Emerging markets have always held attraction for speculators. North and South America were objects of huge speculation in the nineteenth century, as China, India, Brazil, and Russia are now.

Almost all manias have certain financial preconditions to grease the wheels. These are a fall in both price inflation and interest rates, accommodating monetary policies, and easily obtained credit. Other background factors are usually present as well. One is latent greed, a readiness to take on more risk to enhance incomes or simply to get rich. An additional factor is an absolutely low level of interest rates (as opposed to a falling trend) and, paradoxically, a low rate of profit.

As Professor Kindleberger has said frequently, "John Bull can stand many things, but he cannot stand 2 percent." John Bull is your everyday Englishman, and the phrase refers to his distaste for low returns and tendency to get seduced into taking more risk to get a higher return. This is particularly relevant in today's world when savers get 0.25 percent on their short-term funds and are driven to seek higher returns.

When interest rates are very low, two things happen. The first is that people try to get a better return by investing in riskier, higher-yielding assets. The second is that they can borrow cheaply so that leverage increases, which also enhances returns so long as the asset being bought is either rising faster than the rate of interest or yielding more. For example, if you could borrow at 2 to 3 percent and invest in bonds at 5 percent, you could make a lot of money. The same goes for gold. In the first 11 months of 2009, the price of gold rose by about

50 percent, providing fortunes for those speculating with borrowed money. In 2009, it was easy to see the tremendous incentives to speculate when interest rates were so low, and that is why many people are worried that the seeds of the next mania may already have been sown.

However, the factors just mentioned are only necessary conditions, but not by themselves sufficient to cause a mania. For that you need what Hyman Minsky calls a "displacement,"[3] a development that is fundamentally so new and exciting that it captures the imagination of large numbers of people. It is often based on technology, innovation, or the opening up of new trading opportunities. Frequently, they are linked. Examples are canals, railroads, steamships, the telegraph, and the Internet. New industries such as radio, automobiles, electricity, and chemicals in the 1920s were key displacements. More recently, the extension of mortgages to subprime borrowers lit a fuse under the U.S. real estate market, pushing it to extraordinarily overvalued levels, discussed in Chapter 13.

Deregulation of industries or whole economies triggers manias. Globalization has brought to the attention of investors immense new investment opportunities in places like China. In a mania, people become braver and more adventuresome. In recent years, investments have shifted to places like Africa, Mongolia, and Central Asia, areas that are much higher on the risk spectrum. Capital flows into riskier markets accelerated sharply, both in the mid 1990s and in 2006 and 2007. These flows are occurring again in late 2009 and 2010. Stock markets in places like China, India, Russia, and Brazil are up on average by more than 100 percent from their low points in early 2009.

Frequently, the displacement has occurred as a result of innovation in financial technique. Examples are the conglomerate, go-go period of the 1960s, the leveraged buyout (LBO) frenzy of the 1980s, private equity and hedge funds in the 1990s and beyond, and the new math applied to securitization and derivatives in the early 2000s.

Displacements as a result of fear have paradoxically opened up areas for speculation. Examples would be gold and silver in the 1970s as the fear of hyperinflation and economic collapse gripped many people. The short-lived panic flight to 30-year U.S. Treasuries after the crash of 2008 pushed prices up by 38 percent, driven by the widespread fear of another depression. And the run into gold in the latter part of 2009 suggests growing fears of a dollar collapse.

Characteristics of Manias

Displacement plays a crucial role in all manias. It inspires undue confidence and optimism in investors who target asset classes deemed to be the beneficiaries of the displacement. The widespread acceptance that a new era has arrived is used to justify high and rising prices. What starts out as investment over time turns into speculation. One of the most common characteristics of the late stage of a true mania is that people do not believe they are speculating, regardless of the buying frenzy and the prices being paid. They become convinced that something new and enduring has happened and they had better jump on the bandwagon for fear of being left out.

The time element needed to build this bulletproof confidence is an important ingredient in most manias. Generally, the displacement has been in place for a number of years before it catches the public's attention in a major way. The rising price trend of the eventual objects of speculation can be traced back far enough so that people really believe a new era has unfolded. This creates the feeling of legitimacy and credibility to back their extreme optimism. The recent U.S. housing bubble is a good example. Prices had risen steadily, though moderately, through the postwar period after 1950 in nominal terms with never a significant setback. Prices began to rise faster than trend in the late 1990s and the feeling became widespread that the bull market would actually last forever. Again, bravery and lack of respect for risk went to an extreme along with prices prior to the top in 2006–2007.

In general, the legitimacy of the new investment opportunities created by the displacement nearly always proves to be correct. To capture the imagination of millions of people, the story must be really good. Canals, railroads, steamships, the automobile, and the Internet did change the world dramatically by opening up huge new opportunities. The problem is always that too many people use too large a proportion of their wealth to speculate on the new objects, frequently relying on excessive leverage. When prices start falling from the inevitable overvalued extremes, panic ensues because speculators suddenly see their wealth wiped out and can't repay their loans.

A common, although not universal, characteristic of manias is that the objects of speculation are extremely difficult to value. A classic example was gold and silver in the 1970s. Promoters used the argument that if just one Chinese in 10 bought a Krugerrand, it would create additional demand for 100 million ounces of gold at a time when annual production was less than 50 million ounces.

In the mid-1960s, after a prolonged bull market, a number of studies extrapolated past supply and demand trends for common stocks and concluded that there would be a chronic shortage just as the market was forming a secular top. Prospective scarcity is always great fuel for a mania, and the 1968 peak was not to be reached again until the mid-1980s. Concept stocks, such as those based on the Internet or a prospective new drug, are always hard to value accurately. Once a few transactions take place at ludicrous prices, as occurred in the late 1990s, people start justifying almost anything.

In the go-go stock market of the late 1960s and 1970s, the so-called one-decision stocks—those that you would never sell because of their high and solid projected growth—became extraordinarily overvalued. Virtually any price (60 to 80 times earnings was not uncommon) was justified if you could project growth at 15 percent per annum forever. However, common sense in a mania is always in short supply. Nothing can grow at 15 percent forever. In the bear market of 1973 and 1974, the stock prices of this group were crushed, but most of the companies continued to prosper. The problem was the ridiculous prices that were paid.

There are examples when the objects of speculation have had great stories but no real intrinsic value. The tulip mania in Holland in the seventeenth century was one, although people at the time thought that the rarest species had unlimited value and paid ridiculous prices for them. Subprime mortgages in the United States, and repackaging of them into mortgage-backed securities with complex derivatives, also turned out in many cases to have little or no intrinsic value. The original mortgage borrowers frequently had no income and no assets, and the inflated value of the house was often worth less than the mortgage even at the time of purchase. Fraud, dishonesty, conflicts of interest, and aggressive promotion are common in all manias and play an important role in creating the appearance of value when, in fact, little or none exists. Ponzi schemes thrive in an environment of fast money, easy credit, and greed. The Bernard Madoff and Allen Stanford Ponzi schemes could never have flourished in a more conservative climate.

Another common characteristic of most manias is that, toward the end, prices start to rise nearly vertically. Figure 6.1 shows this pattern for five recent manias. The peak of each mania is indexed at 100 so that the run up to the top and the subsequent declines can each be compared. Common sense says that exponential rises are unsustainable and a collapse cannot be far away. The reality is that confidence and optimism follow the same near-vertical pattern. Conviction becomes increasingly unshakable the faster prices rise. People accelerate their borrowing and tend to concentrate their capital in the assets rising the fastest. Warnings from credible authorities are disregarded. Rising interest rates and tightening monetary policy frequently go unheeded for months or years.

A central role is frequently, if not always, played by financial institutions. In a mania, they increasingly tend to shift their asset and liability structure in the direction of more risk and less liquidity, which, in the words of Kindleberger, "in a more sober climate they would have rejected."

Manias occurred long before central banks existed, so they are not a necessary ingredient. However, as the history of the past 200 years

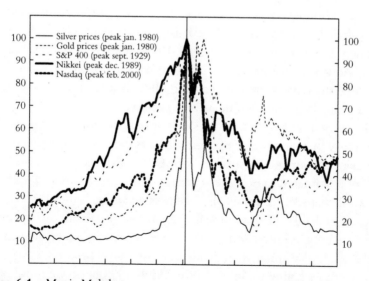

Figure 6.1 Mania Meltdowns

Note: Vertical line marks peak. Data shown six years before and six years after the peak.
Source: Chart courtesy of BCA Research Inc.

has shown, central banks can play an important role in supporting a mania, fanning the flames of speculation, and even creating a mania.

As we discussed in the previous chapter, money and credit do not look after themselves very well, and central banks have a sorry record in figuring out how to get the monetary control mechanism right at any particular time and the impossibility of keeping it right. As Kindleberger has so astutely observed, "When the government produces one quantity of the public good, money, the public will proceed to make more, just as lawyers find new loopholes in tax laws as fast as legislation closes up old ones."

Manias often get started in the aftermath of the previous burst bubble when central banks turn sharply to ease, pump money into the system to bail out financial institutions, and actively encourage the use of credit to restart the economic engine.

Central banks can also play a similar role when they try to resist upward pressure on their currency by buying the reserve currency, or under the gold standard, buying gold. In either case, central banks' growth in reserve assets adds to commercial banks' reserves, as explained in Chapter 5. In practice, it is difficult to sterilize the expansionary effect of these inflows, and money and credit growth accelerates. China has been a classic recent example, as shown in Figure 6.2. In 2006–2007, the Chinese bought $600 billion and their money supply and stock market exploded upward. Under the partial gold standard, U.S. gold reserves increased 130 percent from 1914 to 1924, leading to a huge surge in credit and stock prices in the 1920s until the bubble broke in late 1929.[4] The same story has started to repeat in 2009 in several countries that are experiencing large increases in currency reserves.

Whether a central bank initiates ease or responds to upward pressure on its currency by buying reserve assets, it greases the wheels and supports and eventually encourages speculation, however unwittingly. In an environment of low interest rates and low inflation, the preconditions for a mania are set. All that is needed is the displacement and some "animal spirits."

Central banks play a critical role in the aftermath of the mania when the bubble bursts and panic ensues. They can either help to pick up the pieces by using their lender of last resort powers or make the crisis worse by failing to do so. In the 1929–1933 period, central banks, including the Fed, conspicuously failed to provide liquidity when it was needed. In fact, they did the opposite, raising interest rates and tightening

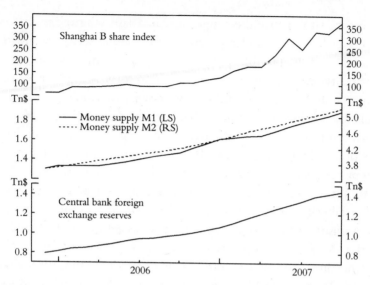

Figure 6.2 China: Stock Prices, Money Supply, and Foreign Exchange Reserves
Source: Chart courtesy of BCA Research Inc.

liquidity. This gave the banking system an additional push toward collapse. Many believe that this was a principal cause for the depth, length, and breadth of the Great Depression.

Having learned this lesson, central banks changed their behavior in the postwar period. They have repeatedly come to the rescue of endangered financial institutions, some would argue too readily. Following the crash of 2008–2009, central banks, acting in their lender of last resort capacity, have pulled out all the stops and flooded their economies with money. They have bailed out almost all large financial institutions, with the notable exception of Lehman Brothers. These actions have aborted a potential depression, but the long-term consequences will be known only in the fullness of time.

Another characteristic of true manias is that they tend to last much longer than most people think. Many are the stories of speculators who, sensing an impending end, sold too soon, only to see prices keep rising. Unable to stand the thought of forgone profits when all around people are getting rich, they pile back in again with even more money in order to make up for the cost of their early exit. As Kindleberger so aptly said, "There is nothing so disturbing as to see a friend get rich."

History shows that the longer a mania lasts, the more dangerous it is. Prices have time and momentum to become seriously inflated as the number of people infected grows and the mania takes on an aura of normality and permanence. It is common for vast numbers of people to commit all their savings and borrow heavily to acquire the objects of speculation. These objects are often used as collateral for loans made by financial institutions. As the frenzy heats up, the underlying balance sheets of people, businesses, and banks deteriorate steadily. Continually rising prices become necessary for the debt to remain viable.

At some point, ominous signs develop—a bankruptcy, a major fraud, a faltering of prices, a shock from out of the blue. Confidence and optimism start to erode. A few lucky ones get out, but denial is very powerful. Most are too paralyzed, mesmerized, or complacent to sell. "Buy the dips" becomes a common mantra. Once the initial drop in prices accelerates, disbelief prevails. People wait for the rebound to sell. However, with only sellers and no buyers, rallies are short, weak, and on low volume. It becomes almost impossible to get out. As the saying goes, the elevator always descends fully loaded, and the speed of decline in prices, once momentum builds, is faster than the rise.

Liquidity disappears. It is like the proverbial fire in the movie theater. Prices typically drop 30 to 50 percent in a matter of days or weeks. Bids on riskier assets, such as the stocks of small companies, disappear altogether. Once the transition from mania to distress has occurred, panic and crash follow quickly. However, the true economic consequences linger on, often for years.

We have been experiencing some of these as a result of the most recent episode, and they will probably be with us for a very long time.

Table 6.1 The Aftermath of Financial Crises

	Decline/Increase	Duration
House Prices	−35%	6 years
Stock Prices	−55%	3.5 years
Unemployment	+9%	4 years
Gross Domestic Product	−9%	2 years
Government Real Debt	+86%	3 years

SOURCE: Carmen Reinhart and Kenneth Rogoff, "The Aftermath of Financial Crises," paper presented to the American Economic Association meeting, January 3, 2009.

Reinhart and Rogoff,[5] in an important study on the aftereffects of severe financial crises in a number of countries, drew some general conclusions. These are summarized in Table 6.1 and show that the impact of financial crises is both deep and long-lasting.

The Next Mania

The history of manias and bubbles over the past 200 years shows clearly that there is a cyclical pattern. The timing is not precise but there is sufficient regularity to be noteworthy. Wars of the twentieth century and the Great Depression of the 1930s have understandably complicated the pattern somewhat. However, the pre-1914 and post-1960 periods show enough similarity to suggest that some sort of natural rhythm may be present.

The rationale for such a rhythm is not difficult to understand. The first is economic. Each crisis, following a burst bubble, causes economic activity to decline. This brings down interest rates, frequently to very low levels because of deleveraging and central bank monetary expansion. The former reduces the demand for credit; the latter increases the supply. Liquidity, after the panic has receded, rises sharply, while price inflation and interest rates fall. This stimulates spending and profits, but also asset prices as the new liquidity must eventually find a home.

A second rationale is psychological and is important in the spacing between a crisis and the next mania. Burst bubbles and panics cause a large loss in personal wealth. Revulsion sets in and people become conservative to a degree that is proportional to their previous recklessness. As time passes and they see markets rising, people start to lose their fear and begin to focus on trying to get back the money they lost. The longer the time interval since people have made money, the more intense their desire to exploit a perceived opportunity and the greater their newfound courage as bad memories fade. In addition, new classes of speculators appear who do not have firsthand knowledge of the last crisis. Tolerance for risk, once again, becomes a function of how fast the markets are rising.

At this point, the necessary conditions are in place for the next mania. As soon as the displacement is evident, speculation will then proceed to the irrational once again, assuming the money and credit fuel are present. The regularity of manias over 200 years suggests that roughly 7 to 10 years is the time required to complete the cycle of renewed liquidity expansion, psychological adjustment, and discernment of the displacement.

Table 6.2 lists the dates of the onsets of the major crises together with the approximate duration of time from the previous crisis. Numerical precision is not possible. Frequently, there is more than one mania occurring at the same time, with peaks often two to three years apart in the same mania. Sometimes the peak of the mania occurs well before the crisis, sometimes almost coincidentally. Subjectivity has been used to include manias that are large and global with severe afteraffects. We have excluded numerous small ones that are better thought of as

Table 6.2   History of Financial Crises

Year of Onset	Duration (Months)
1799	4
1809	13
1816	12
1826	10
1837	9
1847	10
1857	10
1866	9
1873	7
1882	9
1890	3
1907	8
1920	9
1929	8
1973–1974	5 or 6
1979–1980	5 or 6
1987	7 to 10
1990	7 to 10
1997–1998	7 or 8
2000–2002	10
2008–2009	8

Source: Charles P. Kindleberger and various others.

overly optimistic bull markets. However, for our purposes, generality is adequate.

From the end of the eighteenth century, there have been 21 distinct manias and crises, or approximately 10 per century. We did not count the almost 35 years between the end of the Great Depression and 1973, the first of the unfolding postwar crises that had monetary and banking implications. There were, however, earlier signs of financial trouble, marked by the sterling devaluation of 1967, the gold crisis of 1968, and the spectacular bankruptcy of the Penn Central railroad in 1970. Adding up the remaining number of years and dividing by the 21 crises give an average interval of nine years between the end of one financial crisis and the peak of the next mania. Fifteen of the 22 crises fall within a range of 7 to 11 years.

Based on this 200-year experience, the probabilities strongly suggest that another mania will start to unfold in the next year or two and form a peak sometime in the 2015 to 2019 interval, assuming that the worst of the recent crisis is behind us. The first precondition—liquidity expansion—is already in place and is unprecedented in magnitude. The second precondition—optimistic psychology—is still in the early stage of recovery, stimulated by the dramatic rise in many asset prices from the March 2009 lows. However, this is not yet a mania. With the exception of gold and real estate in some areas, prices of most major assets are still well below the peaks of 2008.

The third precondition is the displacement. It is almost always a product of long wave forces, particularly toward the end of the down wave and the beginning of the next upswing. In Chapter 3, we discussed the long wave and some of the well-known displacements in previous long cycles. We mentioned the role of canals, railroads, steamships, automobiles, electricity, chemicals, and technology. The deregulation and rapid growth of China, India, and other developing countries are clearly a major new force in the world. That, together with full implementation of technology into the information age, will almost certainly serve as displacements for the next mania, along with some others such as alternative energy, which society won't get a full grip on for some time.

The role of the displacement is critical because it creates the "new era" thinking that generates the excitement and optimism that all manias need. The displacement also creates the new targets for speculation—the assets and asset classes that will be beneficiaries of the displacement and to which people can impute whatever value they wish, oblivious to reality. For example, China and some other emerging markets have a number of positives going for them that don't exist in the advanced industrial economies. A short list would contain the following: undervalued exchange rates and strong currencies, strong fiscal positions, highly liquid economies, solid banking systems, strong underlying economic growth, low world interest rates, low inflation, huge labor force, strong work ethic, advanced product technology, pent-up demand, and underinvestment by global money managers.

Extraordinarily high savings and investment ensure continued growth, particularly vis-à-vis the advanced countries where savings and investment have fallen sharply. The case is compelling and it would not be difficult to imagine much greater capital inflows to their markets from the developed countries. Long-term prospects in the developed economies may remain relatively dismal due to the lingering effects of the financial crisis and the extension of the long wave economic decline discussed in Chapter 3.

Strong growth in countries like China had a profound impact on the demand for, and price of, many commodities before the crash. There is every likelihood that the demand will resume, fostered by prospects for an increase in inflation expectations and a weak dollar. Increased fears of eventual monetary debauchery in the United States stemming from the Great Reflation would almost certainly feed into monetary demand for gold, silver, and other precious metals.

Some people rely on two arguments against an early return to mania-like conditions. First, the banking system remains traumatized and, for the most part, still undercapitalized. This will surely delay any return to reckless lending. However, that is always the case after a major crisis, and repair often does occur much faster than most expect. By the second half of 2009, some banks were already earning record profits and bonuses. Top hedge funds and private equity firms were also on a roll again with funds under management building up rapidly and headhunters kept busy. The steep positive yield curve (short-term rates far below long-term rates) is likely to last at least a couple of years. Most banks will be minting money and rebuilding capital rapidly, in part because they borrow from depositors at very low rates and lend or invest the money at much higher rates. Therefore, repair of balance sheets of financial institutions may not delay the beginning of the next asset inflation by much.

Reregulation is the second argument against an early return to speculation. At present, the proposals for new regulation are a work in progress, with lawmakers battling each other, regulators battling each other, and lobbyists resisting all change. It is not clear (at the time of this writing) what the new regulations will be, who will administer them, and whether there will be proper accountability—something sorely lacking prior to the crisis. However, one thing is clear from history. If enough liquidity is created, it will find a home in some asset class somewhere in the world that is beyond the reach of regulators.

The great elasticity of credit has been evident since the Bullion Committee Report of 1810 brought it to the public's attention. If the desire to borrow and to speculate is present, entrepreneurs and ingenious new financial practices will find a way to accommodate that desire. Perhaps the most egregious example of elasticity of credit and the difficulty of controlling money was seen in Kuwait in the late 1970s and early 1980s. Speculation in stocks and real estate occurred outside the banking system through the use of postdated checks requiring no cash balance and no bank loans. After the crash, precipitated by an attempt by someone to cash a check, it was found that there was almost $100 billion in worthless checks outstanding. This tale should be a reminder that people will always find a way to speculate if the desire and monetary fuel are present.

Conclusion

The authorities never set out to create manias deliberately. They do like to reflate asset prices after a crash because that helps to repair balance sheets. But once the process of reflating asset prices starts, and if other preconditions are present, the next mania is just around the corner if some new displacement is present to create the optimism and the greed. Regulation is relatively impotent, as the past 200 years of history will attest.

(continued)

To repeat Professor Kindleberger's words, manias are a hardy perennial.

The avalanche of new money created by the Great Reflation, the near-zero returns on short-term money, and the contagious effect of sharply rising asset prices since the panic ended suggest that we may be off to a good start for the next mania. If so, we are only in the very early stage. It would take several more years before it really flowers. However, a new uncertainty now exists: whether the Fed and other central banks will start to target asset price inflation and, if so, when.

Part II

THE MARKETS: PREPARING FOR THE NEW INVESTMENT ENVIRONMENT

Chapter 7

Asset Allocation: Investing in a Turbulent World

The greatest enemy of a good plan is the dream of a perfect plan.
—CARL VON CLAUSEWITZ[1]

T he Great Reflation is an *experiment,* a point we cannot emphasize strongly enough. The program was thrown together piecemeal in response to a great crisis, much as people stick fingers into holes in a leaking ship. There is never much thought of the future when the ship is sinking. As in all experiments, the consequences and final outcome are unknown and investors are faced with great uncertainty and risks that cannot be remotely quantified.

Wealth preservation over the next five years should be the single most important investment objective of almost everyone. This requires a plan, serious study and thought, patience, objectivity, prudence, and a strong resistance to running with the herd. There is a lot of money sloshing around the world as a result of the Great Reflation, and periodically this will find a home in various asset markets, pushing prices to unsustainable levels, as we discussed in the preceding chapter. However, the underlying footings of the economy will remain weak, and asset prices cannot levitate indefinitely on hope and momentum alone. Severe shakeouts will be a fact of life. Gains will be difficult to keep, and losses easy to come by. Living standards and wealth could be under pressure for years.

The bubble of 1982 to 2008, as described in Part I, was created by wildly excessive money and credit inflation and fiscal excesses. Much more of the same can hardly be expected to restore health, except temporarily, nor can it be expected to create enduring prosperity and wealth.

An important conclusion from Part I is that all financial markets will become increasingly volatile and unstable compared to recent years. The collapse of the private-sector debt supercycle and the beginning of a public-sector debt supercycle will inevitably change the way the economy works, alter investment returns, and sustain risk at a very high level. U.S. living standards, excluding the beneficiaries of the bubble, have been under pressure for some years. The crash of 2008–2009 in house prices and the stock market reduced household net worth at one point by about $14 trillion, or almost 25 percent. Pension funds have been decimated and, as a result, retirement incomes will prove disappointing or worse for many millions of people.

This outlook, while somber, should not be taken as a doomsday scenario. The economy and incomes will grow again and markets will recover. However, sustained prosperity and gains in wealth will be difficult to come by and at best will be relatively muted compared with the credit-juiced asset inflation from 1982 to 2008.

Almost all investors are in a more precarious financial position than before the crash and will have to be far more disciplined, knowledgeable, and respectful of risk than they have been. The simple buy-and-hold investment strategies that worked in the postwar period up to 2000 cannot be counted on. Since then, the Standard & Poor's 500 Index has been on a roller-coaster ride, with declines of 48 percent and 57 percent and a rally of 102 percent in between.

The stock market recovery from the low in 2009 has also been explosive and has helped to restore overall household wealth positions somewhat, but sustainability is another issue. Huge question marks overhang the market because of its dependence on artificial support from the government and the Federal Reserve. The experience of the past 10 years could well be the template for the next 10 but with an important difference: The long wave discussed in Chapter 3 suggests that the downward phase has resumed. Moreover, there will be no private credit boom to support growth and generate high returns. In fact, what little credit growth there has been since the crash comes from government and Federal Reserve support, particularly in the mortgage market. In 2009, federally guaranteed mortgage lenders accounted for virtually all of the net new mortgages, and the Fed had bought close to $1.25 trillion in mortgage-related securities for its own balance sheet. This is not a picture that suggests an early return to a healthy economy and financial system that will be self-sustaining on their own.

The approach laid out in Part II of the book will help investors manage their assets more effectively than most people have been able to achieve in the past 10 years and, in particular, cope with the difficulties and uncertainties of the turbulence that lies ahead as the Great Reflation experiment plays out. In the following chapters we examine the main financial markets that investors will be using to try to accomplish their goals. Markets will be volatile, perhaps enormously so, and investors will need objective tools to make disciplined decisions. Otherwise, the cards will be stacked against them.

Asset Allocation

Asset allocation is simply an attempt to bring a rational process to the ever-present problem of what investors should do with their money to achieve their goals. Investors have three main decision points: which assets to hold, in what proportions, and when to change those proportions. Investors need to have realistic expectations, but very few do. Most people want high returns and no risk but that is not how the world works. Risk and return go up and down together. There are proven techniques that will maximize expected return for a given risk, or minimize risk for a given expected return, and that is how investors should think about investing. The concept is straightforward, but the application and execution require some effort. In Part II of the book, we try to simplify the process as much as possible so as to make it useful for most investors.

Sophisticated institutions use complex, computer-driven models, but it remains far from clear that their results are better than those achieved using a simplified approach. Lack of discipline and a strong tendency of most people to feel more comfortable running with the herd are the real enemies of good investment performance, not the lack of complex models.

The starting point for all investors is to establish goals. For individuals this is a subjective process and should be done with family members and trusted advisers. Institutional investors have boards of trustees and directors whose job is to set goals. Second, investors need to decide which asset classes they should focus on and to understand the risk and returns they can expect from each. Third, they need to understand the correlations (the degree to which they move together) among the different asset classes they hold so they can benefit from the risk-reducing potential of diversification (i.e., not putting all your eggs in one basket). Fourth, investors must be aware of the characteristics of a good portfolio. These are derived from the individual holdings in the portfolio and how they interact with each other over time in the real world of market fluctuations, economic cycles, and inflation.

Each investor has needs that are unique to some extent. One size does not fit all when it comes to portfolios. However, there are some general points that apply universally. A good portfolio will have sufficient liquidity to take care of cash needs and the absorption of capital losses, and also will take into account the time horizon and risk tolerance of the investor. The portfolio will have sufficient liquid reserves and cash flow, if possible, to avoid the need for selling securities at an inopportune time. The less cash flow that investors have, the more liquidity they should hold. All portfolios got stress-tested in the recent crash, and far too many people found they had insufficient liquidity and cash flow and had to dump securities at a time of general panic. That is a position in which you should never find yourself. The smart ones had liquidity and bought in the panic at fire sale prices.

The portfolio must be able to protect against general price inflation (loss of purchasing power) and currency depreciation. It must be
diversified across and within asset classes to reduce risk. For example,
you don't want all your money in stocks. And the position you do
have in stocks should be diversified by industry, size, and geogra-
phy. The assets that are expected to produce either income or growth
should be purchased and held only when they provide good value.
Otherwise, there is too high an exposure to capital loss or income
disappointment.

For most people, in normal times, three legs to the portfolio stool
will do the job well—stocks, bonds, and short-term liquid assets.
These can be held directly or in the form of mutual funds or other
types of pooled funds.[2] With a judicious mix of these assets, investors
can get income, growth, and liquidity. They are overwhelmingly the
most important financial assets for most people, and that should be
their primary focus. The problem currently is that we are not in normal times. Safe liquid assets yield almost nothing, and a portfolio of
stocks, bonds, and short-term liquid assets does not provide proper
protection against a decline in the purchasing power of money. As a
result, many investors are once again reducing liquidity and speculating in perceived inflation hedges like gold and commodities. We will
return to this theme later.

Owning a quality house or other form of property can provide
a fourth leg to the portfolio stool and make it more solid because it
will provide protection against inflation in the long run. A house,
purchased at a sound valuation, properly financed over a reasonable
term, and providing principal and interest payments over the life of the
mortgage, creates forced savings. By retirement, the mortgage should
be paid off (assuming that the temptation to borrow with home equity
loans against rising values is avoided). In such a case, the homeowner
would have a large, inflation-protected asset and be debt free. This would
provide a wonderful cushion in old age with no mortgage servicing costs
at a time of reduced cash flow.

There are other asset classes definitely worth consideration for
portfolios that can provide a more optimal mix to attain risk and return
objectives. These are discussed in the following chapters.

Competing in the Financial Jungle

The investment world is populated with millions of very smart people who are attracted to the high potential rewards. Also, the game is exciting and intellectually stimulating. They are all striving to get better than average returns, which is arithmetically impossible. Since the total returns available are set by the market, the small number of very successful investors means that the great majority will get below-average returns. Commissions, fees, and other transaction costs (which can be a huge percentage of total returns) further diminish what most people will actually receive. For this reason, there are many experienced investors who argue that it is impossible for almost everyone to beat the averages consistently.[3] Those who share this belief should follow a purely passive strategy by allocating their investable money among low-fee index funds or exchange-traded funds (ETFs). However, this approach still does not solve the problem of when to increase or decrease exposure to any one asset class. For example, in a stock market mania like the one in the late 1990s, investors end up holding far too much in that asset class at the top of the market unless they rebalance their portfolios aggressively. Rebalancing means selling on the way up so that your overall exposure remains close to what you originally wanted. In today's world of enormous volatility, successful investors will be those who reduce exposure to assets that rise too fast and have become overvalued and risky. This way they can hope to cut exposure prior to major market declines.

We believe that an intelligent, disciplined approach, as outlined in the following paragraphs, will provide investors with concepts to develop the tools necessary to compete successfully in the financial jungle.

However, there is an important caveat. There is no simple how-to cookbook. Investors must be prepared to put in the time and energy. They must think independently and avoid the mass hysteria of the frequent asset manias that have proven so tempting but dangerous for many. As the old saying goes, "Don't confuse a bull market with brains." Investors need to equip themselves with basic tools for success. These include common sense and an understanding of the nature of the environment in which they are investing. Part I has outlined just how unstable, volatile, and complex this environment will be.

The Great Reflation experiment will mean that the Age of Inflation will continue, but with unprecedented new twists that will have implications for all asset markets. There will be changes (i.e., increases) in taxation, U.S. dollar problems, more bubbles, more financial crises, and threats to retirement income. The specter of debt deflation and fears of general price inflation will reappear all too frequently.

The fragile state of the economy and financial system will continue to require inflation of money and credit, heavy government intrusion into the private sector, and frequent resorting to subsidies and support programs. This will continue to distort relative prices of labor, goods, services, and assets. It will sustain the economy in an artificial state and will compound instability and make it almost impossible to understand what is real and what is not.

The issue for investors is how to navigate in this artificial, anchorless world of fiat paper money and, in particular, how to avoid the massive losses of wealth that come from being on the wrong side of instability and how to augment wealth by being on the right side.

Stocks for the Long Run

Stocks, also called equities, are shares in a company's assets and profits. Chosen well, they can provide both growth and income. Over long time periods, stocks have been extremely rewarding, generating on average about 9 to 10 percent yearly returns. After adjusting for price inflation but not taxes, the return has been between 6 and 7 percent, depending on the starting and ending points. At that rate, money doubles every 10 to 12 years. However, it has to be emphasized that we are talking about very long periods, say 40 to 50 years. Figure 7.1 shows total inflation-adjusted returns on the S&P 500 with a trend line back to 1885. It is evident that the long upward trend, which averages about 6.5 percent per annum, is broken periodically with major declines. There are also periods when the market is flat for a number of years and periods when it rises sharply. The latter are called secular bull markets, and since 1885 there have been four—1885–1910, the 1920s, 1950–1968, and 1982–2000. During the last three secular bull markets, returns have been more than twice the long-term average.

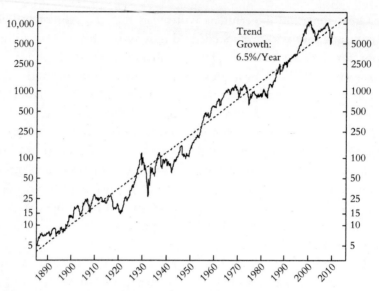

Figure 7.1   Real Total Return of the S&P 500, 1885–2009
Note: Deflated by consumer prices; dashed line represents long-term trend.
Source: Chart courtesy of BCA Research Inc.

The risk of owning stocks declines with time. For example, over intervals of 10 years, investors on relatively few occasions have experienced net losses and these have been small. This is shown in Figure 8.6 in the next chapter. Over much shorter periods, however, losses can be huge.

The very long-term data demonstrates that there is something inherent in a market-based capitalist society that generates consistency of returns over long periods. This is true across nations where long-term real returns have been roughly comparable to the U.S. returns.[4] The reason returns are so consistent over long periods is that business competition arbitrages excessive under- and overvaluation. For example, if share prices are overvalued in a particular industry and profits are very high, it will be easy for companies to raise money on the stock exchange, go into competition, and bring down the returns and valuations.

The starting point for most stock market investors is important because of the huge swings in valuation. They do not have the luxury of a 40- to 50-year time horizon. Even 10 years is a long time for many, and some fall into the "I don't buy green bananas" camp. Exposure should be minimized after long secular bull markets because they create huge overvaluation. For example, in Japan in 1989 the price-earnings (P/E) ratio on the Nikkei index was over 100, and in early 2000 in the United States, the P/E ratios on the S&P 500 and NASDAQ were 31 and 135, respectively. Conversely, exposure should be maximized after long secular bear markets when stocks have become very cheap. Jeremy Siegel[5] examines this issue and looks at the risk—defined as volatility of real returns—in owning stocks over varying holding periods, compared with bonds. At the 10-year mark, Treasury bills and bonds have more downside risk than stocks and less upside potential after adjusting for inflation.

It is clear that stock market risk declines the longer the holding period. With a 10-year holding period, stocks are actually less risky than bonds and, on average, provide a much higher rate of return after taxes and inflation. And, as pointed out earlier, over the past 130 years there have been only four 10-year periods that have shown negative returns. The strong evidence that stock market risk declines dramatically as the holding period lengthens is very important information for the disciplined investor. In particular, younger people and institutional investors, such as pension funds and endowments, that have very long time horizons should hold a much higher proportion of their assets in stocks relative to high-quality bonds. The appropriate ratio, however, has to be adjusted for the risk tolerance, time horizon, valuation, and liquidity needs of the individual or the trustees of an institution. It is one thing to think you have a long time horizon, but quite another to ride out a severe bear market with nonchalance because you trust the long-run risk and reward data.

Another important consideration for investors is which sectors of the stock market they should focus on. Ibbotson & Associates[6] has done extensive statistical measurement over varying time periods for three categories of stocks—large, midsize, and small companies. The relative size is based on the stock market value of the entire company (shares outstanding times the price per share). Ibbotson further subdivides these three categories into growth and value companies.

Growth companies are defined as companies with high price-to-earnings (P/E) and high price-to-book value (P/B) ratios. The value companies are defined as those with low ratios. These are relatively crude measures, but are broadly useful in looking at return performance over long periods. In practice, a true value investor looks at a number of variables that indicate whether a stock is inexpensive relative to its growth prospects. For example, a stock with a P/E of 15 is a much better value than a stock with a P/E of 10 if the former is expected to grow three times as fast.

Over long periods of time, the small-cap and mid-cap value companies outperform the other four categories by a very wide margin. These results are confirmed by data from Jeremy Siegel.[7] In a market as competitive as the U.S. stock market, these differences in return seem to conflict with the idea of markets being efficient.[8] There are several explanations for the occurrence. First, smaller companies are generally thought to be riskier and therefore should have higher returns. Second, smaller companies are less followed by analysts, brokers, and large money managers than big companies are and, therefore, are frequently overlooked despite good return-and-risk prospects.

Growth companies tend to be priced expensively, as they are generally at an earlier stage of development when sexiness and hope are given a disproportionate weight by investors. They tend to be priced on optimism[9] and as a result get badly hurt when news is disappointing. This happens frequently for less established, early stage companies with unproven technology and extensive competition. In fact, the worst category of stocks is small-cap growth.

In the asset allocation decision, small value companies should, based on this long-term evidence, have a disproportionate weight in the equity part of most portfolios. The proportion depends on two things—the size of the overall portfolio and risk tolerance of those responsible. Small companies are only a tiny portion of the equity universe, and hence very large institutional funds cannot put enough weighting in this area to make much of a difference to their overall returns.

Small companies are more volatile and can become excruciatingly illiquid over short periods of time in severe bear markets. Therefore, they are not a very suitable class for older investors of modest means who need liquidity and stability. However, these stocks can add tremendous value so long as investors take a long view, diversify, and consider their investments as akin to private equity. The more modest the portfolio, the greater the need to restrict the proportion of assets in small companies because of illiquidity. The risk of small company investing can be reduced markedly by focusing on balance sheet quality, cash flow, the experience of management, and how attractive the company is as a takeover candidate. In a world of instability and periodic debt crises, companies with such characteristics will not only be survivors, but also have the resources to capitalize on growth opportunities. Alternatively, they will be targets themselves for acquisition by others, providing liquidity events for their investors.

All portfolios should have exposure to larger companies. Fortunately, mid-cap value companies have shown returns over long periods that are only a few percentage points lower than small value companies. And these companies are generally quite liquid, though not as liquid as the large-cap companies. Investors should apply the same criteria as they do to small companies when choosing larger-cap stocks for their portfolios. However, it is more challenging to get good returns, because larger companies are widely followed by analysts and money managers, are often complicated to understand, and are usually priced efficiently and more expensively. That is why it is difficult for the average investor to add much value to the portfolio with really big companies. The positive is that because they are large, they are generally very liquid, pay a dividend, and have strong market share, brands, and ability to recover from adversity. However, big companies are not without risk, as demonstrated by General Electric and Citigroup, which fell 83 percent and 98 percent, respectively, in the 2008–2009 bear market, and General Motors and Chrysler, which went broke.

Bonds for the Long Run

As discussed in Chapter 9, we make a distinction between default-free bonds of national governments and all others. The latter, mainly bonds of corporations, state and local governments, and mortgages, have varying degrees of credit risk. This runs along a spectrum that goes from highly rated AAA bonds to far below investment grade securities often referred to as junk or high-yield bonds. We will return to this subclass later.

There are five main reasons why investors should hold very high-grade bonds such as Treasuries or close substitutes in a portfolio. First, they provide diversification away from an all-equity portfolio, and statistically such diversification, up to a point, has been shown to reduce risk disproportionately to the reduction in return.

Second, high-quality bonds of large issuers provide liquidity to a portfolio since they can be sold on a moment's notice in virtually any quantity at very close to the market price.

Third, from time to time, high-quality bonds have been in strong bull markets, which have generated exceptionally high returns with relatively low risk. When these opportunities arise, large allocations to such bonds can be made. For example, from 1982 to early 2009, 10-year Treasury bonds generated total returns (income plus capital gains) of 10.3 percent per annum, but with lower risk than the S&P 500, which produced almost the same return. There are times, such as from 1982 to 2009, when investors can make such large returns in high-quality bonds that the need for riskier assets in a portfolio is greatly reduced. The converse is also true; bond prices can decline for years in secular bear markets. There are also shorter-term cyclical trends in bond prices of roughly four to six years that can provide very attractive opportunities.

Fourth, quality bonds purchased at fair valuation lock in a solid income stream, which can be critical for investors facing a collapse in short-term interest rates. During 2009, many older investors with the bulk of their funds in the money market faced a catastrophic loss of income as short-term rates fell to less than one half of 1 percent from the prevailing 5 percent or so in 2007.

Fifth, Treasury bonds provide a hedge against an outright debt deflation collapse. During the darkest days of the financial crisis in early 2009, 30-year Treasury yields fell to 2.5 percent from 4.2 percent two months earlier, providing huge capital gains at a time of collapsing prices of stocks and lower-quality bonds. During the Great Depression of the 1930s, those holding highest-quality bonds had solid returns from late-1929 to mid-1933, while stocks fell 80 to 90 percent over the same period.

In short, quality bonds should have a place in virtually all portfolios. The proportion depends on valuation, the likely trend in general price inflation, the strength of business activity, and, as always, the investor's degree of risk tolerance. We discuss a few simple strategies in Chapter 9 for helping investors capitalize on opportunities arising from the purchase of bonds at an advantageous point in the cycle.

Bonds are notoriously bad investments during a period of rising inflation. For example, from January 1967 to the trough in October 1981, Treasury bonds fell in price by 65 percent. Fortunately, the government began issuing Treasury inflation-protected securities (TIPS) in 1998, and these provide high quality, liquidity, and income while protecting the investor from the ravages of future inflation.

The subclass of bonds that includes all those that have some degree of default risk can also play an important role in portfolios, depending on how they are priced in the marketplace. Higher-yielding, riskier bonds can and do fluctuate sharply. Price movements, particularly at the riskiest end of the spectrum, are correlated closely with equities. For example, in the recent crash, bonds with modest to high credit risk were effectively 100 percent correlated to the S&P 500 Index. These bonds have a place in most portfolios but only at times when their yields have much more than compensated for the risk of defaults. This happens in every business cycle recession, particularly when the economy is falling sharply and fears of bankruptcies start spiraling. Exposure at the appropriate time has demonstrated clearly that the actual risk in holding a diversified portfolio of these bonds is far lower than the perceived risk. Such mispricing is what generates the opportunity to create better returns without adding to risk.

Unfortunately, this is an asset class that is complicated, and most investors will need professional help in accessing it. Security selection in this area is complex. However, the average investor can get exposure to the sector via mutual funds, ETFs, and, if the portfolio is large enough, directly with a segregated or pooled account with a specialized manager.

Asset Allocation: Other Considerations

For most investors, stocks and bonds (of varying maturities) should be the two core asset classes of an investable portfolio. As we discuss in the following chapters of Part II, there are a variety of other assets that many investors might wish to include in a portfolio: real estate, gold, commodities, hybrid securities like preferred stock, convertible bonds, special vehicles based on derivatives, foreign stocks and bonds in developed and developing countries, venture capital, private equity funds, hedge funds, and many others, including alternative assets such as private equity, timber, and farmland. The list is long, and a full discussion of all these classes is beyond the scope of this book. Fortunately, there are a number of excellent books and other sources available for the interested investor.[10]

A number of large endowments, such as those of Princeton, Yale, and Harvard, shifted large proportions of their portfolios to these other asset classes in recent years. The outsized returns made their managers celebrities until mid-2008. However, successfully managing such portfolios is very complicated, and requires a large staff of professionals and a major investment of time, energy, and systems. Moreover, much of the high return in these portfolios was a result of hidden leverage and other high-risk strategies. The crash decimated many of them. The result for university endowments was cancellation of scholarships, building projects, and more. Other endowments similarly had to cut back on funding obligations.

It remains to be seen whether long-run performance is really that much better for these supposedly sophisticated endowments after adjusting for leverage and risk. This is not to say that there aren't a number of very successful money managers who use complex strategies, but they tend to be highly focused and disciplined and employ proven risk-control strategies.

Most investors are probably wise to keep their investments simple and confine themselves to what they understand and can realistically manage. Many investors delegate to professional managers and tend to choose those with previous hot performance. However, the data show that over time, something like 80 percent of managers underperform the market. There are a few great managers but most are closed to new and small investors. The search for the next great undiscovered manager is probably just as difficult as finding the next great stock.

Experience generally shows that as successful managers get bigger, their returns fall back toward the mean. Staffs grow and become hard to manage; more and more time is spent meeting with existing or potential clients. And as successful managers get rich, they start to focus on expensive cars, second and third homes, and other aspects of a wealthy lifestyle. Time spent on actual investing and risk control is sacrificed. The larger the pool of funds to manage, the more difficult it is to get great returns. When managers get really large, they effectively become the market and will be lucky to provide market returns less their expenses. It takes a truly exceptional manager of a very large portfolio to consistently beat the market after fees. Research shows that very few do.

Most asset classes, other than very high-grade bonds, have equity-like characteristics. They are either a physical asset or a claim on a physical asset. There are exceptions, such as pure market-neutral funds, but in practice, even those often do not protect against adverse market movements. The experience of the 2008–2009 market showed that there were essentially two classes of assets—risk and nonrisk. During the meltdown, money that had been put into risk assets such as stocks, high-yield bonds, commodities, and real estate were all decimated. Government bonds, gold, and the dollar went up as people sought a haven.

Gold, as we discuss in Chapter 11, is a perennial favorite with many investors. Its mystique goes back thousands of years and explains the continuing high level of interest in recent decades in spite of the fact that the price was less than 15 percent higher in late 2009 than it was in 1980.

Gold is a hybrid asset. It is part commodity, subject to supply and demand for things like jewelry and industrial and commercial products. It is also part money whose defining character is its *hardness,* which means it cannot be printed by governments, is not a liability of anyone else, and is universally accepted. The gold price went up during the recent meltdown because many feared a collapse in the banking system and paper money. As the crisis abated, the dollar and government bonds retreated back toward the levels prevailing before the Lehman Brothers collapse. Everything else rose. However, the retreat in gold prices proved temporary because investor attention began to focus on monetary inflation and very low short term interest rates. This showed that gold is a unique asset with properties that are sought after in varying conditions.

The close correlation among various risk assets was a nasty surprise to the many who had pursued highly complex asset allocation processes involving hoped-for diversification among numerous asset classes. The lesson, not surprisingly, is that historical correlations are not necessarily indicative of future correlations, particularly during stressful times when portfolio diversification is supposed to reduce risk. That is why in the short run, the most effective, safest, and noncorrelated asset is cash, held in bulletproof investments like U.S. Treasury bills.

For this and reasons of simplicity, we recommend for most people a portfolio allocation that is based on two principal components. One is assets that carry risk but have substantial prospective returns. Because capital values of these assets can fluctuate considerably, they should be considered as equity or quasi-equity. Basically, they are either a physical asset or a claim on a physical asset. The other component of the portfolio comprises assets that are not at risk and generate returns that will be safer but more modest. These assets include cash, short-term deposits, money market funds, government bonds, and very high-quality corporate bonds. Government-indexed bonds (discussed later) can be included if the purchasing power of money is at risk.

Asset Allocation and Inflation

For the most part, the category of assets at risk will provide a hedge against inflation over time. Some assets will do the job better than others. For example, commodities and commodity-producing companies are direct beneficiaries of inflation. Real estate provides good long-term inflation protection. Companies that are users of commodities, such as food manufacturers, utilities, and oil refineries, will be hurt by inflation. Experience has shown that stocks as an asset class (e.g., the S&P 500) perform poorly when price inflation is accelerating.[11] In the very long run, however, they do provide considerable protection against the decline in purchasing power of the currency, as demonstrated in Figure 7 1.

The category of assets not at risk will do badly during inflation because the income they generate is usually fixed, as is their capital value. For example, a 30-year bond with a 4 percent fixed interest payment will drop by 70 percent overnight if inflation suddenly went from zero to 10 percent and yields matched that rise. At the end of 30 years, the capital value of the bond would see its purchasing power also drop by over 70 percent if inflation averaged just 5 percent a year.

Treasury bills and bonds are the ultimate so-called safe assets because their default risk is assumed to be zero and they are extremely liquid. Moreover, they are the best hedge against actual debt deflation because the real value of the principal and interest payments will rise as the price level falls.

There are a number of hybrid assets that investors can use to their advantage in constructing a portfolio without adding undue complexity. Fixed income Treasury bonds are safe from default risk, but very vulnerable to inflation. As discussed earlier, there are Treasury inflation-protected securities (TIPS), which are indexed to inflation. Both the capital value of the bond and the interest payment are increased (annually) by the rise in the consumer price index.

Gold, as mentioned earlier, is also a hybrid asset—part money and part commodity. As money, it is always accepted and provides psychological and physical protection from a breakdown in the paper money system, particularly in times of war, revolution, draconian controls, confiscation, and harsh taxation. Being part commodity, gold also provides protection against inflation in the long run.

Hence, gold should be considered a safe asset but only in the long run. Its capital value can fluctuate enormously in the short to intermediate term. From the peak of close to $1,000 per ounce in early 1980, it fell almost 70 percent over the next 20 years, a warning to those who speculate in gold after the price has risen sharply.

In the environment we see ahead, investors would be well advised to hold some portion of their assets in both TIPS and gold, keeping in mind that the latter can be vulnerable when speculation is high. Additional exposure to inflation hedges can be achieved by tilting the equity portfolio more in the direction of companies whose underlying business is effectively hedged against inflation. The essential idea of an inflation hedge is to have exposure to, or a claim on, assets whose underlying value and cash flow will rise at least as fast as price inflation. However, investors must avoid overpaying. Good inflation hedges tend to get hyped and become extremely overvalued in an inflation scare. Gold at $1,000 per ounce in early 1980 was a classic example.

How much exposure to inflation hedges is appropriate will depend on a combination of the relative valuation of inflation hedges and prospects for the dollar and pressure on the central bank to monetize government deficits. The important thing for investors is to have the discipline to maintain a strategic core position of inflation hedges and to use common sense to avoid getting caught up in hysteria. Those speculating in housing in the early- to mid-2000s or commodities in 2007–2008 were badly burned, which should be a reminder to those getting carried away with inflation fears currently.

In general, the appropriate allocation to different asset classes is one of the most complex decisions that investors make. Each individual investor or institution must decide what is appropriate for their needs after careful consideration. There are many variables involved. Each investor's decision will be driven by such things as the size of assets, size and stability of income, degree of risk tolerance, patience, the number of dependents, and many other factors. As we have emphasized repeatedly, keep it simple and the results will be better. Those lacking the tools and experience to make such decisions should consult a trusted professional who is free of any conflicts (i.e., does not benefit from helping you in any way other than from a disclosed fee). Those who do not make the effort to put in place an appropriate asset allocation plan are destined to experience substantial shrinkage in their wealth. The plan doesn't have to be perfect, but it does need to be sound and well thought out.

Conclusion

Managing your assets efficiently and effectively will be much more important than it has been in the past. Most people fail miserably because they don't have a plan, don't have objectives, don't have discipline, and are not prepared to spend the time and effort required. This is a huge disconnect from reality because most people are counting on a secure financial base on which to retire and to pass on to beneficiaries.

The principles of asset allocation are straightforward, but the execution is not. This chapter was designed to provide a basic understanding of the principles involved. The following chapters in Part II look at the different asset classes and provide some tools for investors to help them to decide which allocations are appropriate for them.

Chapter 8

The Stock Market

Everyone ought to be rich.

—JOHN J. RASKOB
Ladies Home Journal, 1929.

Warren Buffett can testify to how you can get rich in the stock market. However, following the crashes of 2000–2002 and 2008–2009, not to mention 1929–1933, millions of people can testify as to how you can destroy your financial future if you don't know what you are doing.

Buffett not only happens to be a very smart man—extremely knowledgeable about the market, business, and the economy—but he also has a strategy, discipline, patience, and methodology that he sticks to. He avoids fads like the plague, looks for compelling value, does his own homework, and, above all, uses common sense. His approach is micro-based and focused primarily on company selection and owning a piece of the business he invests in for the long run.

Our approach is macro-based and complementary to his. Both require knowledge and discipline, but from different perspectives. As discussed in Chapter 7, our approach focuses, first, on how much of your investable funds you want to have in the stock market as opposed to which companies you should own. Second, it looks at whether you can add value by periodically changing your allocation to stocks when risks and valuation have altered significantly.

Equities, as an asset class, play a key role in investors' portfolios. If selected properly, taking into account risk and value, they can provide growth and the likelihood of dividends that will grow over time. Compounding total returns from dividends and capital gains over long periods sounds trivial but is one of the most important investment insights you can have. Investors who start young and invest their savings prudently in equities can expect to have a very substantial nest egg when they retire.[1]

Within the equity class, there are many choices and strategies. Investors can focus on large or small companies, value or growth companies, and foreign equities, in either developed or emerging markets. However, it is beyond the scope of this book to delve into equity sectors. For the interested reader, there are many good books on the subject.[2] The average investor should be aware that all these choices are easily accessible through mutual funds and low-fee exchange-traded funds (ETFs) if they are not in a position to do their own stock picking or invest in foreign stock exchanges.

In this chapter, we focus on ways to make decisions on how much of the investor's portfolio should be in stocks as a whole, otherwise known as the "policy" target exposure to equities. What this means is that an investor would have a policy of holding, on average, a given percentage of the portfolio in stocks. That number could be 30 percent, 50 percent, or higher, depending on how aggressive and long-term the investor is. The important thing is that, whatever the number chosen, it must be derived from a careful understanding of risk and return objectives. One common way of calculating an appropriate target for individual investors is to subtract their age from 100. Thus, a 50-year-old could have 50 percent in equities, a 70-year-old could have 30 percent. However, individual circumstances must be taken into account with any given rule.

Most investors do not have a rigid policy allocation but rather a range of plus or minus some percentage around the target. Rebalancing of equity exposure is triggered when it moves to either extreme. For example, if the equity target is 70 percent, plus or minus 5 percent, then the investor will sell equities when they become 75 percent or more of the portfolio. Conversely, the investor will buy when equities fall to 65 percent or less. The experience since 2007 shows how this can work to the investor's advantage. Stocks would have been sold during the late stages of the bull market and rebought at much lower prices after the crash, producing better performance than a buy-and-hold approach.

Recent experience has also demonstrated that stocks have become extremely risky over the short to intermediate term. An investor in the example just cited would still have experienced devastating losses in 2008–2009, particularly if the investor had tried to rebalance quickly. Liquidity could have been dissipated far too soon before the bottom was reached. On the other side of this are investors who had too much risk exposure at the top of the market and were forced to sell at the bottom. Being underinvested when the rally starts compounds poor performance.

Using a few simple techniques, investors can expect to improve their overall investment performance by pursuing a policy that deliberately reduces or increases their equity exposure in a range that brackets their policy target. For example, using a target of 70 percent total equities, it could make sense to think of a range of, say, 50 to 85 percent with the expectation that, over time, exposure will average 70 percent. In a risky, expensive, and volatile market environment, investors could drop their exposure to 50 percent temporarily and rebalance from there. After there is a fundamental improvement in the risk/return profile of the market, they would move back up to 70 percent or even to the 85 percent exposure that is the top of the range.

The tactical issue is knowing when changes to the equity allocation should be made. That is the purpose of this chapter, and it draws on the analysis in Part I of the book, which looks at the macro factors affecting risk in the market. We focus on the U.S. market to avoid complexity, but the basic principles hold for stock markets in all countries.

Stock Market Cycles

Table 8.1 shows bear and bull markets since 1835, including dates, percentage decline or rise in the subsequent bull market, and the

Table 8.1   Bear and Bull Market Cycles in the United States, 1835–2009

Market Top	Market Bottom	Declines		Subsequent Rises	
		Months	%	Months	%
Oct. 2007	Mar. 2009	17	57	N/A*	N/A*
Mar. 2000	Oct. 2002	31	49	60	101
Jul. 1998	Oct. 1998	3	20	17	304
Jul. 1990	Oct. 1990	3	20	93	67
Aug. 1987	Dec. 1987	4	35	31	233
Nov. 1980	Aug. 1982	21	28	60	62
Dec. 1976	Mar. 1978	15	19	32	73
Jan. 1973	Oct. 1974	21	48	26	73
Nov. 1968	May 1970	18	36	32	48
Feb. 1966	Oct. 1966	8	22	25	80
Dec. 1961	Jun. 1962	6	28	44	86
Aug. 1956	Oct. 1957	14	22	50	267
May 1946	Jun. 1949	37	30	86	158
Nov. 1938	Apr. 1942	41	46	49	62
Mar. 1937	Mar. 1938	12	55	8	132
Jul. 1933	Mar. 1935	20	34	24	121
Sep. 1932	Feb. 1933	5	39	5	106
Sep. 1929	Jun. 1932	33	86	3	394
Jul. 1919	Aug. 1921	25	32	97	40
Nov. 1916	Dec. 1917	13	33	19	39
Dec. 1909	Dec. 1914	60	29	23	65
Sep. 1906	Nov. 1907	14	38	25	60
Jun. 1901	Oct. 1903	28	22	35	111
Jan. 1893	Aug. 1896	43	32	58	22
May 1887	Dec. 1890	43	22	25	39
Jun. 1881	Jan. 1885	43	36	28	140
May 1872	Jun. 1877	61	47	48	62
Apr. 1864	Apr. 1865	12	27	85	271
Dec. 1852	Oct. 1857	58	65	78	47
Aug. 1847	Nov. 1848	15	23	49	87
May 1835	Jan. 1843	92	57	55	64

*Cycle not yet complete.

Note: A bear market is defined as any decline of 15 percent or more in the all-share index. The base for the Standard & Poor's 500 Composite is 1941/1943 = 10.

duration of each. Over the whole 174-year period, bear markets have averaged −37 percent, bull markets 114 percent. The duration has averaged 2 and 3 1/2 years, respectively, for bear and bull markets. Over the post–World War II period, the data are not much different.

The purpose of tactical shifting of equity exposure is to try to capture as much of this lost money—the percentage decline from highs to lows—as possible by a timely reduction in exposure and timely increase in exposure to participate in the rally off the lows. If exposure is not increased in an optimal way, the money saved in the bear market may be more than offset by underexposure in the next bull market. The holy grail is, of course, to sell everything at the top and reenter at the bottom. However, the holy grail is never found, nor is such pinpoint market accuracy. It is impossible to sell at the high and buy at the low, which is why most investors should never be totally out of the market or totally in. However, market declines on average of 37 percent afford the possibility of doing much better than a simple buy-and-hold strategy, riding the cycle up, down, and back up again. This is particularly true in a secular bear market when declines are generally much bigger and prices can remain depressed for years. The issue is whether there are sufficiently reliable tools to give investors confidence that they have a reasonable chance of doing significantly better than a simple buy-and-hold strategy. We believe the answer is yes.

There are two other reasons to employ a disciplined policy of tactical reallocation of equities. By shifting part of the portfolio into safer, more liquid, and better-performing assets prior to major market tops, the investor is in a much better position, after a market decline, to make portfolio shifts into sectors that have emerged with better risk/return prospects. Many investors have ridden poor-quality equity positions down through the bear market and, when the time comes to increase overall equity exposure, are unable or unwilling to do so, remaining locked into losing positions.

The other rationale for tactical reallocation is simply to reduce risk. Most investors go into bear markets with too much equity exposure as a result of complacency or greed. If investors do not rebalance and/or lower equity targets during bull markets, their equity exposure becomes excessive at or around market tops. Bear markets march to their own drummer. When they start, it'is not possible to know how deep they will be and how long they will last. The severe ones are so painful that the average investor, whether individual or institutional, becomes psychologically traumatized. Stress and sleepless nights are common. Capitulation and margin calls at or near the end of the decline are also common, forcing liquidation at the worst possible time.

Investors who are out of step with the market compound their mistakes by frequently missing the recovery after a steep slide. Having liquidity and a good, stress-free frame of mind during major sell-offs is conducive to aggressive reallocation to stocks when values are compelling and forced sellers are creating bargains.

We have sketched in Figure 8.1 an idealized, trend adjusted, smooth business cycle to explain stock market cycles better. It is oversimplified and cuts through the complexity and noise of the real world, particularly the highly uncertain one of today.

Our starting point is the favorable sweet spot in the business cycle marked at point A. That is the time when investors should be starting to move toward their maximum equity weighting. It occurs after the economy has gone into recession, inflation expectations have fallen, demand for credit has slackened, and the central bank is in a position to ease policy by expanding bank reserves and lowering short-term interest rates far below long-term rates. Note that point A comes before the end of the recession when most people are fearful and the news is discouraging. The recession trough is marked with an x.

Around point "A" is a confusing time and difficult for most people to take on risk. They are reacting to what they read in the press, watch

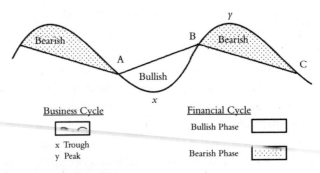

Figure 8.1 Idealized Business Cycle

on television, or see in the world around them. The sweet spot is typically a time of high and rising unemployment, falling profits, fear of bankruptcies, and increasing home foreclosures. Negative stories in the press abound, as scary news sells well. The classic example is the cover of *BusinessWeek* magazine in 1979 entitled "The Death of Equities." It was not the absolute low of the long bear market, but it was 12 years into the decline and not a bad time to be increasing equity exposure to participate in the greatest secular bull market in history.

More recently, an article dated February 26, 2009, by Peter Cohan was titled "Bill Gross [the market guru of the current period], the $747-billion Bond Man, Declares the Death of Equities." That was just a few weeks before the March lows and the start of one of the biggest market rallies in history.

One of the most common mistakes investors and forecasters make is to project where they think the economy is going, then assume the stock market will follow. In 2009, many investors and economic gurus missed the March bottom because they remained bearish on the economy. The reality is that the stock market leads the economy, not the other way around. Often there appears to be a disconnect between the two because of complex leads and lags between them.

The stock market is a forward-looking, discounting mechanism. It incorporates well-publicized information. Shareholders are part owners of companies whose value is determined, not by today's rate of profit, but by the earning power of enterprises many years into the future. At the sweet spot—point A—long-term, experienced shareholders recognize that the worst is over and values are attractive. Liquidity at this point is improving, and probabilities favor economic recovery within six to nine months. At the margin, the sophisticated buyers start to dominate the sellers. Prices stop falling as the ingredients to create the next upcycle are put into place. Frequently the end of a bear market comes about not with a stabilization of prices but rather with a dramatic reversal, called a selling climax. Prices reverse to the upside quickly and sharply, often gaining many percentage points within days. For example, selling climaxes occurred after the lows in 2009, 2002, 1998, 1987, and 1982, averaging 27 percent over 48 days. That is why investors should never be totally out of the market and should be prepared to start buying before they are sure a final bottom has occurred.

As time passes, the market moves into the second stage of the bull market (the area marked AB in Figure 8.1 is the total portion of the cycle that is bullish). The news brightens, companies start to report better results, and unemployment begins to fall. At this point, it is widely recognized that the next recovery has started. General confidence improves, driving stock prices even higher. The final or third stage of the boom is when everyone is confident that business and profits are good. Rising prices have gone on long enough to create widespread optimism among investors and business managers. Overvaluation develops and is ignored. Prosperity is projected to last indefinitely, and the media have become cheerleaders again for the bull market because greed is back and good news is now selling well. Prices at this point have moved far above long-run intrinsic value. During the third and last stage of the boom, major excesses are created. These sow the seeds of the next downturn, during which time they will need to be purged.

The peak of the economic upswing is marked by point y. Prior to that and during the first half or so of the downswing in the cycle (the bearish phase), marked by the area BC in Figure 8.1, business and financial conditions become unfavorable. Most companies suffer, some much more than others. Profits have become disappointing, cash flow has diminished, credit has become tight, and interest rates and costs have risen. Spending on plant, equipment, and new hiring, which became excessive during the boom, must be reversed to restore profitability and eliminate distortions. Smart shareholders begin to reduce equity exposure at point B, anticipating that the cycle has moved into the late stage and that financial and economic stress will soon occur. They anticipate that other shareholders will also be selling, either out of distress or because they also will be fearing a bear market. John Maynard Keynes said this best using his famous analogy of a beauty contest:

> "It is not a case of choosing those faces that, to the best of one's judgment, are really the prettiest, nor even those that average opinion genuinely thinks the prettiest. We have reached the third degree where we devote our intelligences to anticipating what average opinion expects the average opinion to be. And there are some, I believe, who practice the fourth, fifth and higher degrees."[3]

During the negative phase of the cycle, selling builds up from those who focus primarily on short-term momentum and the daily news. As a result, markets, as a whole, generally get caught in a self-feeding decline, taking prices well below long-run intrinsic value before the bear market is exhausted.

As Table 8.1 shows, the fall over these shorter cycles is mostly in the 20 to 40 percent range. Declines tend to be much larger during secular bear markets, which are those that span several short cycles and can last for many years. The defining characteristic of a secular bear market is that over a lengthy period of time, stock prices are lower than they were at the beginning. These very long bear markets are clearly visible in Figure 8.2 and are indicated by the movement of stock prices from highly overvalued levels to extremely undervalued ones. Since 1885, there have been four, counting the current one. The earlier three lasted 14 years on average. The current one is 10 years old at present. The jury is still out on whether March 2009 marked the secular low.

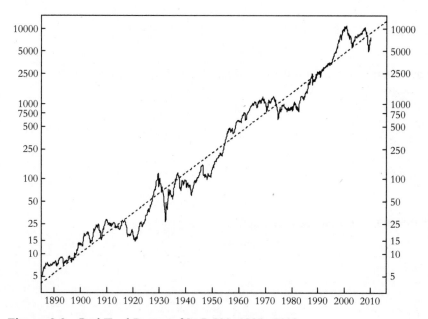

Figure 8.2   Real Total Return of S&P 500, 1885–2009
Note: Deflated by consumer prices. Dashed line represents long-term trend.
Source: Chart courtesy of BCA Research Inc.

Some examples of cyclical bear markets within a secular bear market since 1929 are shown in Table 8.2.

Table 8.3 shows cyclical market declines within secular bull markets. They can be steep, particularly when the market is substantially overvalued (e.g., 1962, 1987) and therefore there is still a strong incentive to cut exposure prior to these declines, even though new highs will occur in the next recovery. However, it is far more important to reduce exposure going into a secular bear market. It is evident that the declines can be far more severe and last much longer than during secular bull markets. Recoveries in secular bear markets can be explosive if they start from very oversold levels, but frequently peak early and are marked by a failure to make highs above the previous peak. Cyclical bear markets during secular bull markets lasted about one-third as long as cyclical bear markets during secular bear markets lasted.

Clearly, there is a strong case for investors to try to minimize losses from bear markets. Buy and hold with fixed allocations is just too risky,

Table 8.2 Cyclical Market Declines in Secular Bear Markets

	% Decline	Duration (Months)
1929–1932	89	34
1937–1938	49	12
1973–1974	44	21
1981–1982	24	16
2000–2002	48	31
2007–2009	57	21
Average	50	23

Table 8.3 Cyclical Market Declines in Secular Bull Markets

	% Decline	Duration (Months)
1956–1957	19	18
1961–1962	27	6
1987→	35	4
1990	21	3
Average	26	8

particularly in secular bear market environments. This is particularly relevant now. Even through the great overvaluation culminating in the early 2000 top has been mainly eliminated, as discussed later, it is not yet certain that the secular bear market is over. One characteristic of secular bear markets is that the bottoming process can take years and prices can move to extreme undervaluation. For example, at the low in 1982, the P/E ratio on the S&P 500 was 7.9 and the dividend yield was 5.8 percent. By March 2009, the P/E ratio on the S&P was 28 and the dividend yield was about 2 percent, both showing valuation significantly less attractive than at the stock market low in 1982. However, the high P/E ratio was distorted by the collapse in profits and really needs to be normalized. Even doing that leaves it high relative to the 1982 low.

It is important to note that it is entirely possible that, even though the post–2000 secular bear market may not be over, prices do not necessarily have to make new lows. Valuations could continue to fall if earnings, dividends, book values, and other metrics improve while stock prices could remain in a trading range or move slightly higher.

Tactical Stock Market Reallocation

Ideally, investors should cut back to the low end of allocations going into the risky phase of the cycle (point B in Figure 8.1) and move to the top end of allocations when entering the sweet spot of the cycle (point A in Figure 8.1). Executing these tactical moves in a timely way in the real world is, of course, far more difficult than simply observing past cycles and back-testing.

Tools can be created from different methodologies to use as a guide for investors to help in the execution of increasing or decreasing exposure in a way that enhances returns and cuts risk. In order of importance four of them are:

1. Money, credit, and liquidity
2. Valuation
3. Psychology
4. Statistical (technical) analysis

Tool 1: Money, Credit, and Liquidity

Money, credit, and liquidity changes[4] are the driving force behind all cyclical stock market movements. They are the lifeblood of the economy. They are also extremely important in driving all other asset markets such as bonds, short-term interest rates, currencies, gold, real estate, and commodities.

The modern financial system is highly complex and global in nature, making it difficult to use only nationally published data. Single indicators, which can be reliable for several cycles, will frequently fail in the next. For that reason, it is important to use several different indicators to derive a consensus as to what is happening to liquidity pressures. The purpose is to generate reliable signals as to when liquidity is getting sufficiently tight to make the risk of a bear market very high, and conversely, to generate signals as to when liquidity flows are about to shift to the expansionary stage that leads stock market recoveries.

It is worth keeping in mind that we are looking for leading indicators of the market. Most economic measures, like profits, employment, inflation, retail sales, changes in inventories, and consumer and business confidence, are coincident to lagging indicators and are revised frequently and substantially. Hence, they are not very useful for anticipating change. Most financial indicators of liquidity have leading characteristics and are not subject to the same degree of revision because they are either market observed, like interest rates, or they are reported by financial institutions to the Federal Reserve or some other government agency where accuracy is extremely important.

Here we look at four useful financial measures. There are countless others that analysts can create and combine in ingenious ways. Our purpose here is not to provide a system of indicators to use blindly but rather to show interested investors the usefulness of the approach, provide an understanding of the powerful impact liquidity changes have on markets, and hopefully to provide encouragement to make this approach an important part of their market research.

One of the most important indicators is the yield curve. It is the difference between short-term and long-term interest rates. We generally use the difference between 10-year Treasuries and the 90 day Treasury bill

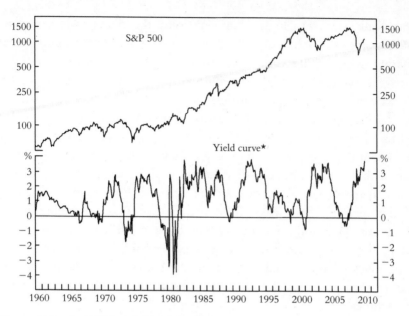

Figure 8.3 S&P 500 and the Yield Curve
*10-year Treasury bond yield minus 3-month Treasury bill rate.
Source: Chart courtesy of BCA Research Inc.

rate, shown in Figure 8.3. The yield curve is an exceptionally powerful indicator of liquidity changes and the state of the economy over the course of the business cycle. When the economy goes into recession, two important things happen: The central bank eases monetary policy and aggressively tries to lower short-term interest rates. At roughly the same time, the demand for credit begins to decline. The combination of the two—increased supply of liquidity and falling demand for credit—pushes short-term rates down relative to long-term interest rates. The yield curve indicator rises sharply as a result, signaling a positive environment for equities. Conversely, at the top of the business cycle, the central bank is reducing the supply of liquidity while the demand for credit tends to accelerate, pushing short-term rates up relative to long-term rates. As a result, the yield curve indicator drops toward or below zero, signaling tighter liquidity and a negative environment for equities.

The second important financial measure is banking liquidity. It is calculated by taking a ratio of bank holdings of securities relative to total bank assets. The logic is the same as for the yield curve. In periods of recession, the demand for bank loans, following a peak, tends to fall sharply, while at the same time the central bank is pumping reserves into the system in order to reduce interest rates and stimulate the growth in money supply and spending. The banks buy securities to replace falling loan demand so as to increase their earning assets as a whole. This indicates that bank liquidity is improving. Toward peaks in the economic cycle when liquidity is being stressed, business demand for bank loans is very strong, either to finance inventory, because credit markets have tightened, or because cash flow has weakened, or a combination of the two. Central bank policy is also tightening at this point. Therefore, when bank liquidity according to this measure is falling, banks liquidate their investments. As bank loans rise relative to bank investments or total bank assets, the banks are becoming less liquid, an indication that the investment environment is becoming hostile for equities.

A third indicator to watch is simply the rate of change of bank business loans. We always include changes in commercial paper because of its close substitute for bank loans. When the business loans plus commercial paper series spikes upward toward the end of an economic cycle, it is usually a sign of stress and an approaching bear market. Conversely, after it has fallen sharply, the financial and economic situation has generally become much more liquid.

A fourth indicator is the interest-rate differential between riskier bonds and Treasuries, discussed in Chapters 7 and 9. The spreads increase sharply when the market perception of risk and financial stress is rising. The result is a reduced flow of liquidity to the riskier part of the corporate sector where access to money is critical. When the spreads narrow, risk conditions are improving and the flow of funds to the corporate sector is picking up.

Figure 8.4 shows the S&P 500 and the three measures of liquidity just discussed. In practice, we look at those and the yield curve. The four indicators together give a broad perspective on what is happening in the financial system. Of the four, the yield curve is the most consistently useful in portraying overall financial ease or tightness.

Referring to Figures 8.3 and 8.4, the reader can see the broad relationship between periods of easy and tight liquidity and market

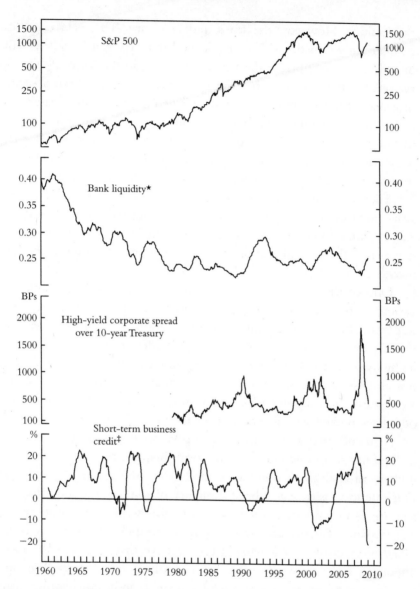

Figure 8.4 S&P 500 and Measures of Liquidity

*Investments/bank credit.

‡Commercial and industrial loans plus nonfinancial commercial paper.

Source: Data provided by Merrill Lynch. Chart courtesy of BCA Research Inc.

fluctuations. However, the leads and lags vary. The yield curve can be quite early sometimes. Looking at the last 10 years, it became positive in early 2001, well before the bottom in stocks in the fall of 2002. The reason it was so early is that the stock market had entered a secular bear market from extraordinarily overvalued levels, discussed later. The astute investor would have been looking at a variety of other factors, including credit spreads as indicated by the yield of junk bonds versus Treasuries in Figure 8.4. It was still widening dramatically, telling the investor to be patient and that the yield curve was very early.

The yield curve remained very positive for most of the next five years, indicating too much liquidity was being created, a tip-off that excesses were building in the financial system. The yield curve became negative in the second half of 2006, giving ample warning of the bear market to come.

One of the important lessons is that investors need to look at a variety of different money and credit indicators, each of which conveys important but somewhat different information. It is only in this way that the investor can develop a thorough understanding of the dynamics at work surrounding major turning points. And, as discussed later, it is also essential to use indicators other than in the money and credit area to gain a comprehensive and accurate assessment of whether the odds have moved significantly in the direction of a bull or bear market.

As mentioned earlier, there are many other indicators of changes in liquidity in the economy, some more helpful than others. A comprehensive analysis of them all is far beyond the scope of this book. Our intention is to give a brief summary of some of the indicators we feel are most important for investors to follow. There is one perennial favorite of many analysts—the money supply. These analysts are called monetarists, particularly if they believe that money is the most important indicator to forecast the economy and markets. We find that, in general, it is not very useful as a single indicator because of its instability. The money supply is most useful as a supplementary indicator. There are several measures of money supply—the monetary base (M0), M1, M2, and even higher according to how broad the definition is. Frequently they move in different directions, further complicating the life of the monetarist. There are some excellent books on the subject of money, monetarism, and markets that interested readers are referred to in the Notes.[5]

To summarize at this point, the basic concept is that investors should be bullish on stocks when liquidity is improving, particularly on a rate-of-change basis. This occurs when bank business loans are being liquidated, bank investments are rising relative to bank assets, short-term interest rates are falling relative to long-term interest rates, and money flowing into the riskiest bonds is increasing relative to the flow into the least risky bonds.

The theory also works in reverse: When the various measures of liquidity are deteriorating, the environment becomes hostile for stock prices and a bear market is on the way.

Would-be money and credit followers, it must be emphasized, should always remember that there is no standard set of indicators that can be used to generate mechanical buy and sell signals with any degree of precision. But it must be said that closely following indicators of liquidity, of which there are many more than we have space to discuss here, will provide invaluable insights into when exposure to equities should be maximized or minimized. The indicator approach provides objectivity and discipline. However, the process is as much art as science. It requires sound judgment, big picture thinking, common sense, and keen curiosity to understand what is actually occurring in the financial system below the surface. Those who do follow this approach will have an edge over most investors.

Tool 2: Valuation

Stock market valuation at extremes can tell investors a lot about risk, but not necessarily indicating turning points. Stocks can become expensive and then go on to degrees of overvaluation that boggle the mind. We discussed in Chapter 6 how, in a mania, the process of overvaluation can go on for a very long time and crowd hysteria can take prices to ridiculous levels.

In the great unwinding of the excesses of an asset bubble, prices generally go far below long-run equilibrium values and can remain depressed for years. A good example was seen in the late 1970s and early 1980s. Stocks fell to the point where dividend yields and P/E ratios were 5.3 and 8.5, respectively, and they remained cheap for years.

For the rare person who can remain rational and independent of crowd hysteria, extremes are not hard to spot, as we show later, although trying to time a reversal with any degree of precision is impossible.

Periods of over- and undervaluation are an integral part of the investment cycle. It is crucial to monitor these to gauge when risk is increasing unacceptably so that action can be taken. Conversely, when values have improved sharply in a bear market, risk is much lower and potential returns higher. Investors should then increase exposure. It is unfortunate but true that most investors act pro-cyclically: Their courage increases as the market rises and it falls when the market is declining.

In assessing valuation, it is worthwhile for investors to be clear on a few concepts. The value of a company is derived from the cash it generates, which is available to shareholders or for growth-enhancing investment. That cash is then discounted back to the present at a risk-adjusted rate of interest. The same is true of the market as a whole. The higher the price paid for a stock relative to future earnings, the greater the hope of investors, but the lower the realized return must be in the future. The higher the price paid due to increased optimism, implicit or explicit, the greater the chance of disappointment when upward momentum ceases and the balance between buyers and sellers in the market starts to shift toward the latter. This is usually caused by a squeeze on liquidity. Valuation, whether of individual companies or of the market as a whole, is critical for investors. The bigger the overvaluation, the more vulnerable it is to a liquidity squeeze and the bigger the fall when it comes. It follows that major undervaluation will then develop. However, there is a lack of symmetry. Expansionary liquidity will not necessarily turn a cheap market upward very quickly. That is the source of the old stock market saying, "You can lead a horse to water but you can't make it drink."

Here we look at just a few valuation measures that we think are important. The dedicated analyst will probably look at many others.

Trends in the long-run realized rate of return after inflation have been very helpful in highlighting periods of extreme secular under- and overvaluations. Figure 8.5 shows the inflation-adjusted total return

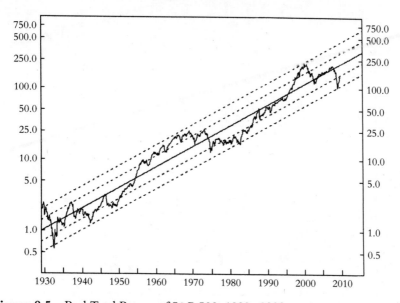

Figure 8.5 Real Total Return of S&P 500, 1929–2009

Note: Deflated by consumer prices. Dashed lines represent one and two standard deviations about the mean. Stock market data before 1926 from Cowles Commission.

Source: Chart courtesy of BCA Research Inc.

(dividends plus capital gains) of the S&P 500 since 1929. The average annual return has been slightly under 7 percent, but there has been a great roller coaster ride along the way. Also shown in Figure 8.5 are bands of one and two standard deviations above and below the trend line. This makes it easy to spot the three periods of great overvaluation—1929, the late 1960s, and the 1990s. Periods of extreme undervaluation are also easy to spot—1932, the early 1940s, 1950, the late 1970s and early 1980s, and early 2009.

Figure 8.6 shows 10-year rolling returns back to 1880. Rolling returns are calculated by taking, for example, the returns for each of the first 10 years and averaging them, and then doing the same for years 2 through 11, 3 through 12, and so on. As can be seen in Figure 8.6, the 10-year annualized return recently fell below −5 percent. That is what shareholders would have realized had they bought the index and held it for the last 10 years. The remarkable thing is that there have been only five other periods since 1880 when returns were either negative or close to it. If investors had bought at each of the previous 10-year-low

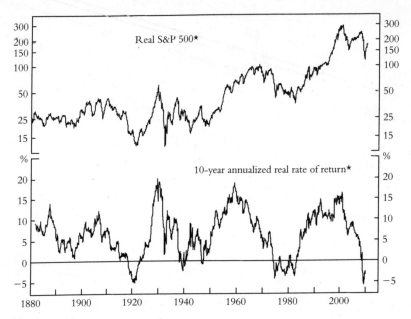

Figure 8.6   S&P 500 and 10-Year Annualized Real Rate of Return
*Deflated by consumer prices.
Source: Chart courtesy of BCA Research Inc.

readings when they were negative, they would have had average annualized returns of about 13 percent over the following 10 years, about double the 6.4 percent long-run returns over the whole 130-year period.

The 1974–1982 period is unique because there was a zig-zag pattern for eight years before a true bottom to the secular bear market was formed. This provides a lesson that may be relevant now. Even though the 10-year rolling return got to −5 percent in the first quarter of 2009, we can't be sure yet that we won't experience a repeat of the 1974–1982 period. Value itself does not tell you about turning points. For that reason, the investor needs a variety of tools. However, increasing exposure in the market when value is compelling will eventually be very rewarding, just as heavy exposure when values are terrible will produce dismal returns or losses.

Regression to the mean (i.e., markets always return to the long-run average after they overshoot or undershoot) is an important concept in financial markets and valuation in particular. When returns are too high for too long, which is shown as the area above the trend line, penance must be served by returns falling far below the trend line. This observation, while obvious with hindsight, is not properly taken to heart by most investors during the euphoric upswings. The tendency for most investors is to get more bullish the longer returns are above normal and to get more bearish the longer they are below normal. The disciplined investor with a keen eye on history will do the opposite.

A third long-term valuation measure is shown in Figure 8.7. It was introduced by Professor James Tobin, the Nobel laureate, and is called Tobin's Q; it demonstrates the power of regression to the mean. These data are published quarterly by the Federal Reserve Bank. It is calculated by using replacement book value (to take into account the effect of inflation on company balance sheets) of the nonfinancial corporate sector. Book value is then compared with the total stock market value of the same companies. If, for example, the stock market value is the same as the book value figure, Tobin's Q is zero (i.e., there is no premium). If stocks rise 50 percent above book value or fall 50 percent below, then Tobin's Q would be +50 or −50, respectively.

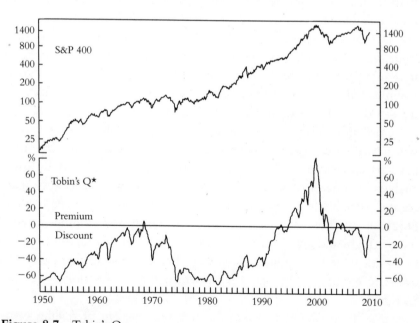

Figure 8.7 Tobin's Q
*Premium/discount of equity market value against current-cost book value.
Source: Chart courtesy of BCA Research Inc.

At the market peak in 2000, Tobin's Q was 70, far higher than anything seen in the postwar period, clearly indicating massive over-valuation. At the low in March 2009, Tobin's Q was −40, indicating very significant undervaluation. However, stocks were not as cheap in early 2009 as in the late 1970s to the early 1980s, and in the 1950s, according to this measure. In those two periods, stocks were selling at times at more than a 60 percent discount.

There are a variety of other measures of value that investors can employ to gauge undervaluation and overvaluation of stocks. Several different measures should be employed because they do not all necessarily arrive at the same conclusion. This can be confusing for investors, but it is also the real world. At any particular point in time, one measure may be giving a more accurate reading than another. The successful investor will understand the environment well enough to know which ones to pay attention to.

Some of the other important valuation measures are outlined next. By examining how these measures move over time vis-à-vis the stock market, investors can develop the knowledge and confidence to use them effectively.

The price-to-earnings (P/E) ratio is a widely used measure of value, and is particularly popular for valuing individual stocks. However, it is subject to drawbacks, as is any other measure. Earnings can be manipulated by creative managers or altered by changes in account-ing standards. Earnings fluctuate widely over the cycle, rising sharply in booms and collapsing in recessions. As a result, using a single recent year's earnings can often make stocks look cheap at the top of the mar-ket and expensive at the bottom. Some try to avoid this by using analysts' estimates of future earnings, but these are notoriously inac-curate, particularly around turning points. To minimize some of these problems, we use a five-year moving average of past earnings to even out the highs and lows over the business cycle. This also captures earning revisions, which are usually downward because management tends to overstate earnings. The result is shown in Figure 8.8 along with the S&P 500.

Since 1926, the P/E, using the five-year average of trailing earn-ings, has averaged 15 with sharp fluctuations to either side. Readings at or above 21 (overvaluation) were reached on nine occasions, and readings at

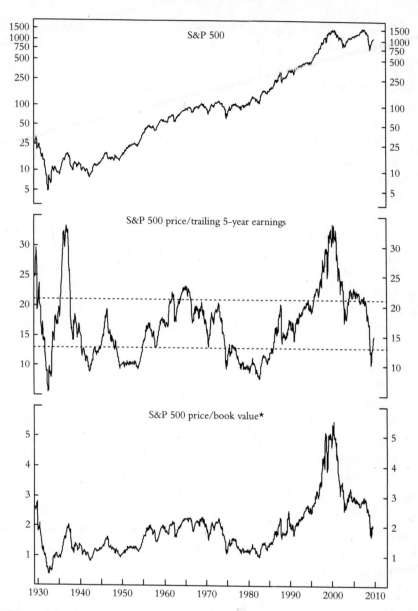

Figure 8.8 S&P 500 and Measures of Value

*S&P 400 price/book value prior to 1977.

Source: Chart courtesy of BCA Research Inc.

or below 13 (undervaluation) were reached on seven occasions, including March 2009. Again, the period 1974–1982 stands out as one where P/E ratios remained low for years. Very high P/E ratios can also exist for lengthy periods. Valuation readings can be quite early, demonstrating that the astute investors will use a variety of other market indicators to refine their overall approach to changing allocations to the equity market.

There are still other measures of value that can be useful and provide somewhat different readings from those just mentioned. Figure 8.8 also includes price-to-book value. This incorporates a balance sheet measure whereas the P/E ratio is based on company income statements. Book value is the accountants' valuation of the net assets of the companies included in the particular index used. This measure avoids some of the problems of earnings distortion but is certainly not distortion-free itself. In addition, it does not take into account the fact that there is an upward bias to the ratio as manufacturing and other heavy industries have shrunk relative to technology, financial, and other service industries. These have much less fixed capital in plant and equipment and hence could be expected to have a higher ratio of price to book value for a given dollar of earnings.

Other popular measures of value not shown are the price-to-sales ratio and the dividend yield. The former does not seem to provide information that is substantially different from the measures discussed, although many find it very useful for individual company valuation. The dividend yield can give misleading signals at times. It needs careful interpretation because of changing institutional arrangements. Prior to the 1960s, stocks were bought primarily for dividends, and payouts from profits were high. After 1980, companies began to cut dividend payouts and use extra cash to buy back their stock, which provides more value to taxpaying shareholders. The result was that shareholders got less cash but more capital appreciation.

Tool 3: Psychology

Psychological traits of investors have long been a fertile area for the analyst, financial historian, and social psychologist in trying to understand how and why markets move. Economics and financial theory have been based on the assumption of the so-called rational man, who, by acting in his own self-interest, causes markets to behave efficiently and optimally. Milton Friedman, another famous Nobel Prize winner, even claimed that speculation would be self-stabilizing! In the real world, the rational man is frequently nowhere to be seen, and speculation has proven to be anything but stabilizing.

There is a lengthy literature on crowd behavior and manias, some of which are listed in Chapter 6 Notes. More recently, behavioral finance[6] has become popularized as a field of study. The conclusion from all of this work is that investors will not do well by following the crowd, particularly around turning points. Seasoned investors point out that to be successful, you will need to have a contrary opinion of the market. David Dreman[7] has been the foremost authority on the subject.

The basic idea beyond contrary opinion is that most investors cannot control their emotions and as a result alternate between moods of excessive greed and fear. They fail to exercise discipline, patience, and common sense. They fail to employ sound and proven strategies, even though there are countless books that have repeatedly stated and proven that these are essential qualities for success. Studies in behavioral finance and contrary opinion explain a lot about investor psychology.

For our own purposes, we are interested primarily in utilizing indicators that show when crowd psychology is at an extreme. These indicators are useful because, when the emotions of investors are at an extreme, it is only a matter of time before the market changes direction, usually quite dramatically. It is a proven fact that when the vast majority of investors hold the same opinion, it is invariably wrong and the market is at an important turning point.

There are a number of indicators that reflect investor opinion. We will focus on just three. Figure 8.9 shows the S&P 500 and the percentage of investment advisers who are bullish or bearish. The shaded areas show bear markets. Most people wrongly think that professional opinion is better than nonprofessional opinion. The reality is that the former is subject to emotions just as much as the latter. Professionals become too bullish toward the top of the market and too bearish after a big fall. Fortunately, they are sufficiently consistent to provide a good contrary indicator.

Customer margin debt is also shown in Figure 8.9. This is a measure of the amount of money individuals have borrowed to buy stocks.

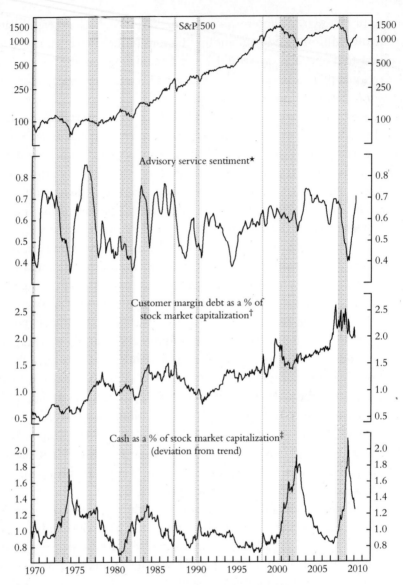

Figure 8.9   S&P 500 and Measures of Sentiment
*Source for data: www/investorsintelligence.com.
†As a percentage of Dow Jones Wilshire 5000 Index.
‡Cash in money market funds and savings deposits.
Note: shaded for S&P 500 bear markets.
Source: Chart courtesy of BCA Research Inc.

As the market goes up, people become more bullish and buy with borrowed money. Hence, it is a good measure of emotional extremes of the individual.

The two indicators showing professional and nonprofessional opinions have provided some excellent signals although they are by no means perfect— nothing is. But as an adjunct to other indicators, they are very useful.

Another important measure of psychology is the amount of cash people hold: the more bullish, the less cash; the more bearish, the more cash. Figure 8.9 also shows the ratio of cash, defined as the total funds in money market accounts and savings deposits to stock market capitalization. Good signals were given at the market peaks of 1973, 1980, 1987, 1990, 2000, and 2007. The market troughs of 1974, early 1982, late 1987, 1990, 2002, and 2009 are also easily identified.

Another measure of the psychology prevailing in the market is media coverage, and some analysts[8] have created useful indicators, although the concept is necessarily somewhat subjective. At or approaching peaks, the media have enormous coverage of the bull market because the percentage of the population interested in stocks rises sharply. When media coverage reaches an extreme, it is a bad sign for the future trend of the market. Bullish forecasters get the most press. When the bullish atmosphere generated by the media reaches a fever pitch, investors should be reaching for the sell button. Conversely, at or around the bottom, and usually for a while longer, positive media coverage of the market all but ceases. Stories focus on the dreary macro picture—rising unemployment, bankruptcies, falling profits, recession, the bear market, and why stocks should be avoided. However, these are all lagging indicators and investors should be starting to buy.

Tool 4: Statistical (Technical) Analysis

The tools discussed so far—money, credit, and liquidity; valuation fundamentals; and psychology—often do not help much with timing. They indicate risk and the preconditions for a change in trend. There are tools that statisticians, also called chartists or technicians, use to help with timing directional change in the market. For the most part, these people do not rely on fundamental analysis but tend to use only charts and market data. Our approach is eclectic, and we think investors can benefit from using charts as a supplement to fundamental indicators. Frequently, the latter do not say much within a time frame that is useful to most investors. Most of us do not want to be a year or two early or late in altering allocation to equities. Using charts can be very helpful in sharpening the timing.

There are many technical systems in use today, some driven by very sophisticated computer algorithms and models. There are also many books written on the subject. It is beyond the scope of this book to go into this topic. The reader is referred to some excellent sources in the Notes.[9]

One simple and widely used statistical measure is the moving average of stock prices. The average can be calculated over any time period. We generally focus on three- and nine-month periods. The objective is to smooth the data so that underlying trends become more obvious. Calculations are made as follows for, say, a 13-week moving average. You average the closing weekly price for each of the past 13 weeks. This creates the first data point. By dropping the first week and adding the 14th, a second point is calculated and the process is continued, giving rise to the *moving* average. Figure 8.10 shows the S&P 500 and the two moving averages over four different time periods. The top two panels show how the moving averages can be used as a tool to time the market bottoms of 2009 and 2002 in a timely way. The bottom two panels show how the moving averages could have been used to time the market tops of 2007 and 2000 prior to the major part of the declines.

In examining Figure 8.10, turning points in the market become much more apparent to the eye. The basic idea is to look for a reversal in trend, which is confirmed by both the faster (three-month) and slower (nine-month) moving averages. The recent examples shown in Figure 8.10 are relatively clear. However, the use of the moving averages can be deceptive. The reality is that a lot of so-called noise exists around the trends and it is important to establish buy and sell rules. For example, the investor could have a rule that he buys every time the three-month average rises above the nine-month average. But as soon as trading rules are established, whipsaws occur. These are the short-term reversals that cause needless buying

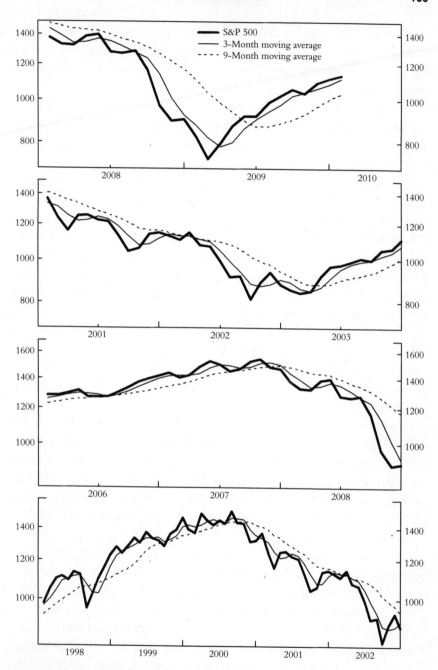

Figure 8.10 S&P 500 and Moving Averages
Chart courtesy of BCA Research Inc.

and selling. To prevent this, filter rules have to be established. For example, you could use a rule that the three-month moving average has to be at least 1 percent above or below the nine-month moving average before a signal is given.

Markets trend most of the time, either up, down, or sideways. The objective is to create a trend-following indicator that will signal reversals in a timely way while avoiding needless whipsaws. Achieving that objective is far more difficult than it would appear, and there are many ingenious techniques that have been tried over the years. Investors have to experiment to develop systems with which they are comfortable.

Academic studies do not support the idea that profitable buy-and-sell strategies can be developed that will generate profits, after transaction costs, that beat a buy-and-hold strategy consistently. However, these studies generally look only at the moving averages. Using moving averages to *supplement* other tools changes everything, which we explain in the next section, called "Using the Tools."

The deviation from a long-term moving average can also be helpful in highlighting periods when the market has become overbought or oversold. When this occurs, it means that the market has probably moved unsustainably to an extreme in the short term and is subject to a reversal.

In bull phases, however, markets tend to remain overbought for some time, and in bear phases the opposite is true. The crucial point is that at major turning points, the deviation of the market from its trend often becomes extraordinarily large. This is common at market tops in a mania and is called a market blow-off, as in volcano. Examples are the 1929 and 1987 market peaks, as well as the 2000 peak in the NASDAQ, which reflected the tech bubble.

At market bottoms, the opposite occurs when there is widespread fear. This is called a selling climax and, for the brave, is an extremely profitable time to invest. Some examples are 1962, 1974, 1982, 1987, 2002, and 2009. An important caveat is that in major bear markets, there are often two or more selling climaxes before the absolute low is reached. This occurred in the recent crash with a low in November 2008 and a lower low in March 2009. However, those who bought around the low in the late fall of 2008, had they survived the trauma of the February and March 2009 sell-off, would have been well ahead a few months later. Market analysts have developed some rules, such as a market reversal must have a nine-to-one ratio of rising to falling stocks to be sure that a selling climax has formed a convincing bottom.

Using the Tools

We have outlined briefly and somewhat simplistically four different sets of tools to provide ideas to help investors alter their allocations to equities when market conditions warrant it. Our basic point is to show what is possible for investors in developing their own programs. We have not set out to present a definitive model for investors to use. That would require a book in itself.

The four basic tools we described are money, credit, and liquidity; valuation; psychology; and statistical (technical) analysis. To give an example of how an investor might integrate the four sets of indicators, let's look at what was happening just prior to the 2000 and the 2007 market tops.

We chose these because they are recent and the subsequent bear markets were traumatic. Any investor in his right mind would have been very happy to have sharply reduced equity exposure prior to these declines.

By early 2000, the yield curve and high yield spreads were signaling tight money. The P/E ratio (five-year average) and dividend yield were at 34 and 1.1, respectively, and Tobin's Q was at 70, by far the highest level ever recorded. Clearly, it was an extraordinarily overvalued stock market. The cash held in money market funds plus savings deposits relative to the market's total value was the lowest in 25 years. The percentage of bullish advisers was close to 70 percent, a very high reading. Those measures plus the mania in technology stocks clearly signaled extremely bullish psychology and therefore a severe warning sign. Finally, the S&P 500 broke decisively below its nine-month moving average in March 2000. In short, if there ever was a well-signaled bear market, that was it.

The 2007 market top was also signaled clearly in advance. Liquidity indicators had deteriorated sharply by early 2007. The yield curve was negative and the high-yield spread had begun to rise sharply from a low level. Valuation measures showed overvaluation, although nothing like 1999. The P/E ratio and dividend yield were at 23 and 2, respectively, both negative indicators, and Tobin's Q was at the zero line, showing stocks were neutrally valued. While down sharply from the 1999 peak, that reading was still at the level of 1968, which was the start of the previous secular bear market. Psychology was rampantly optimistic. Investment advisers were overwhelmingly bullish, and the cash hoard indicator had dropped sharply. Although well above the 1999 level, it was still extraordinarily low compared with the previous 30 years. Finally, by mid-2007, the S&P had decisively peaked and broken sharply below its nine-month moving average by mid-year. In summary, an objective reliance on the indicators would have warned of an impending bear market, although not the crash that subsequently occurred. To have seen that coming, you would have had to be a close observer or participant in the mortgage and other debt markets. That is where the real excesses and bubbles were to be found.

Conclusion

The basic purpose of this chapter was to show that an eclectic approach, using just a few well-known market indicators, can provide investors with the confidence and tools to alter equity exposure in a timely way. Investors need a disciplined program to help them accomplish this if they want to avoid the gut-wrenching market declines that we have seen in the past 10 years. Millions of people have experienced dramatic losses in their net worth. In addition, pensions have been devastated. To build a solid nest egg for the future, investors will have to avoid further big hits to their net worth. They will have to have the equity component of their overall wealth aligned with market risk and opportunities for return.

Stock market investing is difficult and can be very dangerous. The approach outlined in this chapter can be used, if applied with discipline and common sense, to greatly help in *The Battle of Investment Survival*, the title of a stock market classic by Gerald Loeb.[10]

Chapter 9

Interest Rates and the Bond Market

Bonds are certificates of Guaranteed Confiscation.

—Franz Pick[1]

W hen it comes to bonds, investors will want to know whether the Great Reflation will eventually become the Great Inflation. If that were to happen, bond values would evaporate as they did in the 1960s and 1970s. A 30-year bond lost over 70 percent of its value during those two decades. However, if the Great Reflation fails to resuscitate the economy and Japanese-style deflation were to take hold on a sustained basis in the United States, then Treasury and other very high-quality bonds would be valuable assets.

As pointed out in Part I of the book, the Great Reflation poses very serious risks for bonds in the long run. However, in the time frame of most investors, say one to three years, deflationary pressure as measured by the consumer price index (CPI) will be strong enough to dampen potential upward pressure on interest rates.

The mathematical relationship between bond yields and bond prices is inverse. When one goes up, the other must go down.[2] Should the outlook for general prices change from deflation to rising inflation, bond prices would fall. There are techniques (discussed later) that will provide investors with ways to protect them from inflationary losses in the fixed income markets. However, as Figure 9.1 indicates, this is not

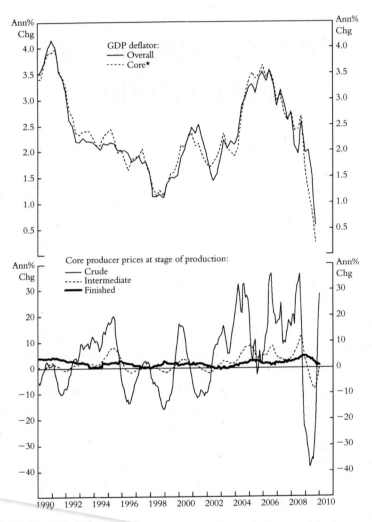

Figure 9.1   U.S. Inflation
*Excludes food and energy.
Source: Chart courtesy of BCA Research Inc.

likely to be a risk anytime soon. Some measures of price inflation in late 2009 were even negative and others were close to it.

In Chapter 7 we discussed the critically important role that bonds play in investors' portfolios. Bonds are also referred to as fixed-income securities because the great majority of them carry a rate of interest that is fixed until the bond is paid off at the end of its life. Maturities can vary from a matter of days to 30 and 40 years, and are available all the way along the maturity spectrum. When the financial world was stable before 1914, there were some bonds issued with a maturity of 100 years, such was the confidence of investors in the long-term purchasing power of money.

The financial world of today could hardly be called stable, and that is unlikely to change for years, if not decades. As a result, investor confidence in the future is volatile and fragile. Fortunately, investors face a multitude of choices in deciding which fixed-income securities best fit their needs for liquidity, safety, and income. However, everyone faces the classic risk/reward trade-off. The shorter the term to maturity and the higher the quality, the lower the return. For example, the highest-quality short-term securities are U.S. Treasury bills. They have maturities that range from one day to one year. The 3-month yield was close to zero at the end of 2009. Treasury bonds of 30-year maturity yielded 4.4 percent, while, at 10 years to maturity, AAA corporates yielded 3.5 percent and lowest-quality corporate bonds, also called junk bonds, yielded 9.5 percent for 7-year maturities. These are shown in Table 9.1.

Table 9.1 Yields on Selected Fixed-Income Securities, December 31 2009

	Yield (%)
3-Month Treasury Bills	0.03
3-Month Commercial Paper	0.20
10-Year Treasury Bonds	3.40
30-Year Treasury Bonds	4.40
AAA Corporate Bonds*	3.50
BBB Corporate Bonds*	5.50
High-Yield Corporate Bonds†	9.50

*Approximately 10 years to maturity.

†Approximately 7 years to maturity.

Table 9.1 highlights some options and shows just how difficult the risk/reward trade-off is for investors in today's environment. For example, those with a portfolio of $5 million, a sum generally considered much more than adequate for retirement, would receive a return of only $10,000 per year if it were completely invested in 3-month commercial paper. To get higher returns, the investor is forced into longer-term maturities, and therefore pressured to take on the risk of higher inflation and capital losses. Price inflation is effectively zero today. If it were to jump to just 3 percent overnight and was matched by a similar jump in yields, the 30-year Treasury bond would lose about 36 percent of its capital value, dwarfing the current 4.4 percent yield on the bond.

The investor can also improve returns by reducing quality to, say, BBB (reasonably high quality), and shortening the term to maturity to, say, 10 years. The return is 5.5 percent, as shown in Table 9.1, but the risk from exposure to higher inflation, while reduced, is still present and the risk from credit default and credit downgrades is raised, particularly if the Great Reflation doesn't work and we go into deeper deflation. Historical experience shows that the default rate on BBB bonds is rarely over one percent and averages about one quarter of 1 percent over long periods. However, there is a good deal of uncertainty whether default rates will be the same in tomorrow's unstable world.

The prospect of more financial turbulence than we have experienced in recent years means that the average investor should probably tilt his portfolio more in the direction of safety and liquidity and less in the riskier direction of chasing higher returns. The many who have suffered massive wealth losses as a result of the crash in stocks, house prices, and pension fund assets simply cannot afford another major decline in net worth. The net private savings rate in the United States has risen from under 3 percent to over 5 percent recently. Investors will have increased funds to put to work, much of those funds in the fixed-income market. Moreover, the aging of baby boomers in the years ahead will increasingly tend to tilt many portfolios toward the safer area of fixed income and liquid securities. However, the paltry returns available on the most liquid and safest securities create a huge dilemma forcing investors into a riskier world if they want to improve returns. All of this means that fixed-income assets will be of much greater importance and concern to most investors in the future.

The message to investors is that they will have to become much more knowledgeable about the bond market, much more involved, and much more active in deciding what to hold, how much to hold, and when to make changes in maturities or quality. The purpose of this chapter is to serve as an introduction to these issues. There are many great books and financial services that are available to those prepared to put in the time and energy to learn.[3] However, there is no substitute for experience and hands-on involvement. It must constantly be kept in mind that Wall Street is a sophisticated manufacturing and marketing machine that will always have unlimited products to sell to you but with the primary motivation being to maximize the bonuses of Wall Street salespeople and the share prices of Wall Street firms, not the wealth of investors. This is particularly true in the current environment of extraordinarily low returns on short-term, safe assets. Investors will have to be wary and avoid the temptation to look for higher returns on obscure products with large hidden fees and risks. Those without great expertise should always seek the advice of disinterested professional advisers—those who are never in a conflict of interest situation.

Some Background on Interest Rates

It is important for investors to have some sense of the key economic role that interest rates play. Only with this understanding will they be able to make effective decisions concerning the fixed-income component of their portfolios.

To start with, investors should understand that interest rates have an important job to do. In many ways, they are the most important set of prices in the economy. On the surface, they allocate the supply of credit available to those wanting to borrow. When the supply of liquidity rises relative to the demand for credit, as was true in 2009, interest rates fall to low levels. When demand for credit increases relative to supply, interest rates will rise. However, the real world is much more complex and a host of other factors are involved in the determination of interest rates. In an unstable world, not surprisingly, interest rates will be volatile. The shortest end of the credit spectrum is the money market. The central bank has almost complete control over the risk-free rate of Treasury bills in the zero to three months maturity spectrum because it can buy or sell them in virtually unlimited quantities. As the maturity spectrum lengthens on Treasury securities, interest rates generally are higher, reflecting greater uncertainty. The fact is that, at a moderately long term to maturity, the ability to buy and sell bonds without moving prices declines. In addition, the longer the time horizon, the more uncertainty there will be that future price changes of bonds will work in investors' favor.

Longer-term Treasury bills and bonds are determined by expectations of what short-term interest rates will be in the future.[4] These expectations will be shrouded in uncertainty, but clearly related directly to what people think inflation is likely to be. However, no one *knows* what inflation will be, particularly for the distant future. As a result, people tend to extrapolate the recent past into the future, which will always be misleading around major turning points.

In the complex environment of today, uncertainty is particularly high because the powerful forces of deflation are in an epic struggle with the equally powerful forces of reflation. We don't yet know which will win, and this will continue to cause unprecedented volatility in expectations. Government intervention in all the credit markets has short-circuited the link between expectations and the actual level of interest rates. This can only be temporary, as it has created artificial markets that never last for long. The distortions are an unfortunate fact of life in the short run, and because of the importance of interest rates, this has major distorting consequences for all asset markets and the economy.

Interest rates are a key component in the mechanism of adjustments to imbalances in the economy and financial system and will move, sharply at times, to eliminate them. For example, they rose dramatically to kill inflation in the late 1970s and early 1980s, and the same will happen again if the Great Reflation ultimately becomes the Great Inflation. The central bank cannot control longer-term rates in the way it can control very short-term interest rates except in the near term and only with massive intervention. Interest rates, it cannot be emphasized enough, are a critical factor driving all financial and nonfinancial market prices and investors need to understand the various forces moving them.

The important factors that determine interest rates were discussed in Part I. To review, some of these include the level and change in private-sector credit demands, the rate of profit or return on capital in the economy, the direction of stock prices, fiscal deficits and whether they are growing or shrinking, the overall government debt to gross domestic product (GDP) ratio and its trend, the size and direction of the current account deficit, international capital flows, and prospects for the currency. Last and most important is the rate of price (CPI) inflation and its expected trend. The next section looks at ways for investors to develop tools to help understand and anticipate interest rate movements.

Tools for Interest Rate Forecasting

In the real world, factors determining interest rates are not independent. They interact in such a complex way that even the most knowledgeable and experienced fixed-income analysts have great trouble making consistently useful forecasts.

A recent example will make this point clear. An apparently logical interest rate forecast gone wrong occurred in the 2006 to mid-2008 period. The United States was running very large budget and current account deficits; the U.S. dollar was falling to new lows; the economy and short-term business credit demand were powerful; gold, energy, and most other commodity prices were exploding upward. Given all these known bearish factors, most forecasters at the time were calling for much higher interest rates. In fact, the opposite occurred. In early-2006, the 10-year Treasury bond peaked at around 5 percent and fell in a series of steps to a postwar record low of 2 percent in the first quarter of 2009.

Why did the typical forecast go so wrong? The obvious answer is that there were other factors affecting interest rates that were bullish for bond prices (lower interest rates) and that more than offset the bearish factors that most analysts were looking at. Some of these were the growing forces of world deflation and the flood of savings into the United States from China and some other developing economies.

We have used this example in order to show investors that there is an approach that cuts through the complexity of trying to assess the myriad factors affecting interest rates and provides a better chance of being on the right side of the trend.

For most investors, there is little or no point in spending a huge amount of time trying to be better than the professionals at analyzing all the macro factors that they look at. The key is to look at a few things that really matter and incorporate them, along with common-sense judgment and a healthy dose of contrarian thinking, into developing a view on where interest rates might be heading.

Here are some of the few time-tested bond market tools we rely on. First and most important is valuation. Figure 9.2 shows a bond valuation index together with the U.S. Treasury 10-year bond back to 1965.

This is published regularly by the Bank Credit Analyst and it is an excellent tool, based on several factors. We publish it here with kind permission.

A study of Figure 9.2 shows that many excellent signals of extreme over- and undervaluation have been given over the past 45 years. However, like any valuation tool, it cannot be relied on to indicate turning points. Markets can become very undervalued, as in 1980–1981,

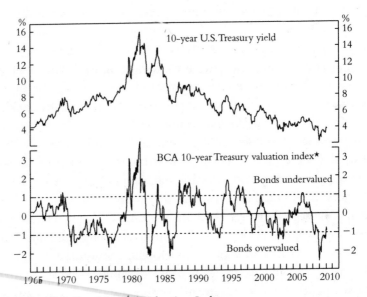

Figure 9.2   U.S. Bond Model Valuation Index
*Index takes into account the long-term trend in U.S. inflation and real bond yields.
Source: Chart courtesy of BCA Research Inc.

and stay that way for many months. But the index then did tell you that from a longer-term perspective, a great opportunity was developing. Moreover, if bonds are really cheap, the market is already anticipating very bad news. Therefore, it requires much worse than expected news to knock prices even lower.

Second, we want to know the likely direction, magnitude, and timing of economic and price inflation pressures. This is not particularly difficult, and objective indicators can be very helpful. Inflation tends to lag and be sticky. Figure 9.3 shows the consumer price index and two measures of economic slack—capacity utilization and unemployment. Figure 9.3 also includes unit labor costs. The latter series adjusts wage increases for productivity gains to get a measure of actual increases in labor costs. For example, if a firm has to pay 10 percent more in wages but productivity of each worker rises 10 percent, then there is no increase in unit labor costs.

Interest rates and inflation generally rise in the second half of business expansions, and changes in the unemployment rate and capacity utilization are pretty good indicators of that stage of the business cycle. If they are indicating that the economy has moved into the latter stage of the business cycle and unit labor costs are rising, then the odds favor a rise in interest rates. Figure 9.3 shows that conditions were positive for interest rates in late 2009. Inflation was falling and negative, and both measures of the economy were showing a lot of slack.

Third, we want to know what bank lending to businesses and bank liquidity are doing. These were discussed in the previous chapter and are shown in Figure 9.4.

As can be seen, during 2009 bank lending to businesses (including changes in commercial paper) collapsed, and bank liquidity, as indicated by commercial bank purchases of securities, was rising. These patterns are consistent with very low interest rates and a lack of pressure to raise them. Investors should watch these series closely to see when conditions might change and become adverse for interest rates.

Fourth, we want to have as clear a sense as possible as to the secular trend of interest rates. When it is down (see Figure 9.2), as it has been since 1982, there is a major tailwind behind bond prices. Mistakes in timing can be made up over time. Conversely, when the secular trend is bearish, as it was from 1950 to 1982, losses cannot be made up.

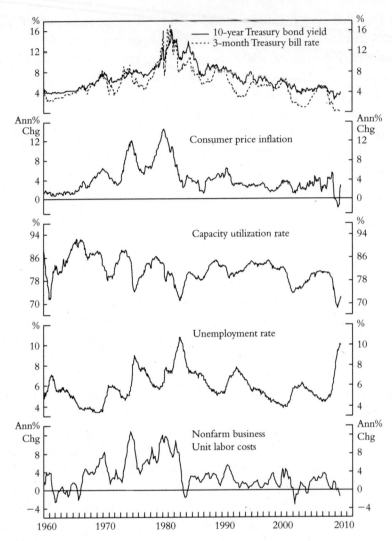

Figure 9.3   The Economy, Inflation, and Interest Rates
Source: Chart courtesy of BCA Research Inc.

Cyclical increases in rates can be huge when driven by rising inflation and time is an enemy. It was during that period, when socialism, central planning, Keynesianism, unions, and budget deficits were on the rise around the world and central banks went soft on inflation. Most of these factors reversed after 1982, unleashing the greatest bond bull market in history.

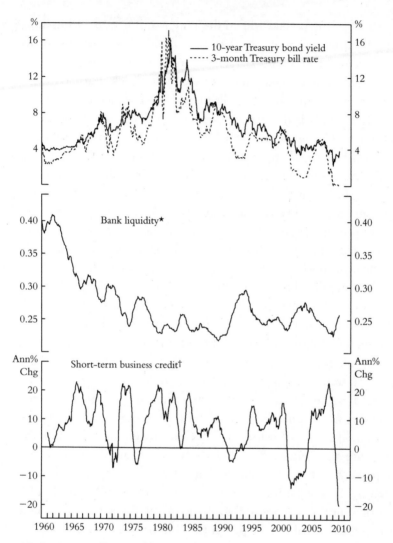

Figure 9.4   Interest Rates and Measures of Liquidity
*Investments/bank credit.
†Commercial and industrial loans plus nonfinancial commercial paper.
Source: Chart courtesy of BCA Research Inc.

Bond Investing for the Future

The overriding question for bond investing is whether the positive forces driving the secular bull market of 1982 to 2009 are ready to reverse.

Part I of the book outlined the potential inflationary implications of a public debt supercycle in the years ahead. There are many who are convinced that President Barack Obama and the Democratic Congress are determined to take the United States back into a much more socialist, interventionist, and ultimately inflationary world. Long-term political swings of this nature are well documented by John Sterman and others who worked in the MIT System Dynamics Group,[5] and we discussed this in Chapter 3. They trace the long-term swings in U.S. politics from left to right and back since 1790. The most recent swing to the right began in 1980 with Ronald Reagan, and a reversal in 2008 seems to have occurred, triggered by the disgrace of George W. Bush and his policies, the collapse of financial markets, a deep recession, and deep disillusionment with free market economics. Historically, 30 years of right-of-center policies is a long time, and a swing to the left of center would be predicted by those adhering to long wave analysis.

If so, and we believe this view is credible, it is bad news for the long-term trend of bond prices and interest rates. That prospect would be reinforced by the large fiscal deficits, massive indebtedness to foreigners, the likelihood of a continued fall in the U.S. dollar, the lagged effect of unprecedented monetary stimulus, and prospects that the Federal Reserve will have to tighten policy after the economy recovers. However, we emphasize the long term. According to experts like John Sterman, the economy needs a decline in real rates to start the next long wave upswing; U.S. real Treasury yields are pretty low—around 1.4 percent—using an expected inflation rate of 1.5 percent as predicted by Treasury inflation-protected securities (TIPS) bonds. However, the real return on corporate BBB bonds is still above 5 percent, an above-normal rate, and about 10 percent on high-yield bonds.

Since troughing of the long wave is always associated with very low interest rates, opportunities in the corporate bond market should remain good for a few years, barring another major collapse in the economy, which seems unlikely at the time of writing.

There are some tools and guides that the average investor can use to access the opportunities in the corporate bond market that occur from time to time. As mentioned before, there is an entire spectrum of bonds with risk slightly above Treasuries at one end, to bankrupt or near-bankrupt company bonds at the other end. Figure 9.5 shows three

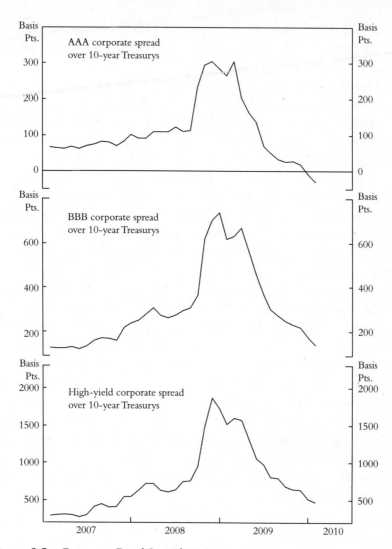

Figure 9.5   Corporate Bond Spreads
Source: Chart courtesy of BCA Research Inc., data from Merrill Lynch.

of these risk classes in terms of interest rate spreads vis-à-vis Treasuries over the past three years. At the height of the financial panic, these spreads ranged from 300 basis points on AAA bonds to 2,000 basis points on high-yield bonds.

From the low in prices earlier in the year to December 31, 2009, the annualized return on the AAA bonds was almost 30 percent and on the high-yield bonds it was 69 percent. The return on the S&P 500 over the same period was 65 percent. Clearly, riskier bonds can add value to a portfolio if the timing is right.

A simple tool that investors can use to assess the timing factor is based on the fact that yield spreads move in cycles. They are narrowest (market is underpricing risk) in the latter part of a business cycle upswing. As a recession deepens, the market moves to the opposite extreme. Investors become increasingly concerned with loss, and start to overprice risk. In the previous two cycles, the spread on high-yield bonds peaked at around 10 percentage points above 10-year Treasuries, producing very big future returns. The peak in spreads was far higher in the current cycle, and the returns, as mentioned, have been stellar. The difficulty for investors is knowing when the process of under- or overpricing of risk is near an end. No one wants to catch the falling knife. One simple tool is to use a trend-following device like a moving average of three or nine months. Figure 9.6 highlights the trend reversals of the past two cycles, and investors could have used this to execute fairly timely buys and sells in this asset class. It shows that if investors had timed their move into high-yield bonds when the three-month moving average broke below the nine-month average, they would have generated enormous returns over the next 12 months.

Investors should keep in mind that the real world of higher-yield bonds is complex. However, the average investor can play successfully in this area, but only by applying some effort, thought, common sense, and analysis. If possible, the investor should seek the help of a trusted, experienced bond adviser.

Inflation-Adjusted Bonds

Inflation-adjusted bonds can be a very powerful supplement to bond portfolios. Both the capital value and the semiannual interest payments are increased by the percentage rise in the consumer price index. Figure 9.7 shows how they have performed. Real, inflation-adjusted yields have averaged around 2 percent, but total returns can be much higher if investors buy when real yields are high and then, subsequently fall, because they can also realize capital gains.

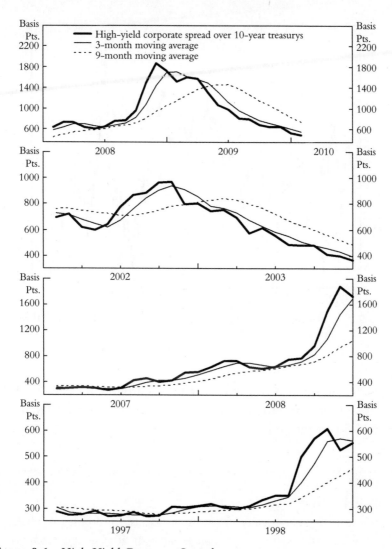

Figure 9.6 High-Yield Corporate Spreads
Source: Chart courtesy of BCA Research Inc., data from Merill Lynch.

Inflation protection eliminates one risk but there is another that reflects potential increases in real yields when capital losses can be incurred. As shown in Figure 9.7, these can be quite large and therefore investors should be aware that the returns can be poor if they acquire these bonds when the real interest rate is low. For example, in

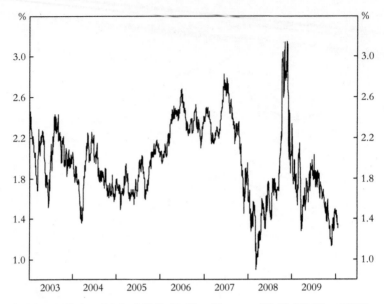

Figure 9.7   Inflation-Linked U.S. 10-Year Treasury Yield (10-Year TIPS)
Souce: Chart courtesy of BCA Research Inc

late 2009, the implied real interest rate was around 1.4 percent. If the real interest rate were to double to 2.8 percent, the investor would lose about 11.5 percent on the price of the bond.

Conclusion

Investors have basically three main decision points in bond investing: the first two are the length of an average term to maturity and the quality of the bonds they wish to hold. How well or how badly bonds will contribute to investors' portfolios in the future will depend on getting these two decisions right. In this chapter we discussed the factors that go into both decisions.

The first is getting the trend of interest rates right. Exposure should be at the high end of the policy target range when interest rates are expected to fall and at the low end when interest rates are expected to rise. Frequently, bullish and bearish forces will offset each other and investors should stay close to their benchmark target. In late 2009, bullish and bearish factors roughly offset each other, suggesting that investors should be neutral (i.e., hold their bond exposure to the target ratio). Falling inflation, the threat of deflation, huge excess capacity in the economy, and very low short-term interest rates offset poor valuation, the potential negatives from large fiscal deficits, and disturbing long-term prospects for inflation. Treasury bond yields were relatively stable through the second half of 2009, tending to drift slightly upwards. Investors should track the trend closely by watching the moving averages for a signal that bond yields are likely to break one way or another. When that occurs, investors can reassess the fundamentals and decide whether to change the target allocation.

The second decision point—how much quality risk to take on—is critically affected by the tug-of-war between the forces of reflation and deflation. In the near future, it is likely that reflation will win but not to the point of triggering an increase in general inflation. As a result, credit spreads are likely to be stable or contract further. Therefore, the corporate bond area will remain a fertile area for investors to acquire better returns. Again, it will be important to follow closely the trend to see when conditions change, either for the better or for the worse. The economy will remain fragile and vulnerable to another deflationary shock until deleveraging is well along and the economy can sustain growth without artificial life support from the government. Therefore, investors should not be complacent about risks when they opt for lower quality.

The third decision point is whether to opt for inflation-adjusted bonds (TIPS), either because inflation is expected to rise or inflation-adjusted yields are well above the long-term average. At 1.4 percent return, they are not very good value.

Chapter 10

The U.S. Dollar

Paper money is only as good as the people who print it and they are under constant pressure to print more of it.
—WILLIAM REES-MOGG[1]

The Great Reflation means that the supply of freshly printed dollars will continue to rise sharply and persistently for years. We outlined in Part I why the demand for dollars is very unlikely to follow and could even decline. As most people know, if you increase the supply of something faster than the demand, the price falls. In this case, the dollar will fall against other currencies.

Many Americans will wonder why that matters. When UK Prime Minister Harold Wilson devalued the pound sterling by 14 percent in November 1967, he quipped that "the pound in your pocket wouldn't change [value]." Well, it did, and a series of crises followed that eventually took the pound down another 60 percent at its lowest point. Moreover, in terms of purchasing power, the pound "in your pocket" did lose a lot of value—95 percent, in fact, since the 1967 devaluation. For years after Wilson's devaluation, UK stocks and bonds fell sharply.

This example should serve as a warning to anyone that a steep slide in the dollar would not be a trivial matter, as it would play havoc with all U.S. financial markets. Beyond that, it would have more add-on effects because the U.S. dollar is the key currency in world trade and central banks use it for the bulk of their reserve holdings. If they dump the dollar, an *eventual* possible consequence of the Great Reflation, there would be global financial chaos. We emphasize *eventual* because just the fear of chaos will prevent dollar dumping in the short term and maintain the nervous dollar stalemate that has prevailed for some time. But in the long run, no one in their right mind will want to hold dollars if they think their value will drop sharply.

Some Background on the Dollar

Once again, a little historical background is important in understanding where the U.S. dollar is likely to go in the future. For most of the period from the late eighteenth century until 1933, the U.S. dollar was pegged to gold at $20.67 per ounce. Except for the U.S. Civil War and 14 years after, fluctuations in the U.S. dollar against other currencies mainly reflected problems with the other currencies, not the dollar. For this reason, confidence in the dollar's solidity and integrity built steadily and persistently, even after President Franklin Delano Roosevelt devalued the dollar against gold in March 1933. He raised the U.S. commitment to buy gold to $35 per ounce from the former $20.67, a devaluation of 40 percent. Before doing so, he confiscated all American holdings (including silver) at the old price. In spite of this treachery and all the currency instability in the 10 years of depression, the dollar continued to maintain a strong international reputation, primarily because other countries had torn themselves and their finances apart during the two world wars.

In 1948, the United States held over 700 million ounces of gold, equal to 72 percent of the world's gold stock, and was running a huge balance of payments surplus, keeping the dollar in short supply and hence valuable. The Bretton Woods international monetary system, put in place at the end of 1945, was based on the dollar's convertibility into gold at $35 per ounce. Other major currencies were pegged to the dollar.

Everyone needed and wanted dollars, as it was considered "as good as gold." As a result of its long-term track record, the dollar earned a reputation that made it the reserve currency of choice and it replaced the pound sterling, which had been the primary reserve currency for centuries.

By the 1960s, the dollar's reputation began to tarnish, and some central banks decided they would rather have gold instead of dollars. This change in attitude gained force and finally pushed the United States to abandon the link to gold in August 1971, float the dollar, and impose wage and price controls and import surcharges. These supplementary policies were meant to reduce the flow of dollars onto the world's exchange markets.

The date of August 1971 is historic in the sense that it was the first time since the Civil War that the United States formally rejected external monetary discipline. This ushered in the modern era of the dollar, and it has not been a happy experience.

As pointed out in Part I, the U.S. dollar has been on a roller coaster ride and declined substantially against the world's strong currencies. Figure 10.1 shows the dollar's performance against some of them, as well as gold and commodities. The dollar's internal purchasing power has declined by a huge 80 percent; it has declined by 97 percent against gold and 75 percent against a basket of commodities. There has been unprecedented volatility in U.S. stocks and fixed-income markets with frequent manias and crashes.

All investors need to understand the issues that will determine whether the dollar's past performance will continue into the future. A look at what happened during that 40-year period provides good insights as to what to look for in gauging where the dollar's exchange value will be heading in the future.

Determinants of the U.S. Dollar

The U.S. dollar is still overwhelmingly the most important currency in the world in spite of its disastrous performance. It has been supported by the fact that serious economic and financial problems exist in most other countries and there is no viable substitute. Yet that is no reason for complacency.

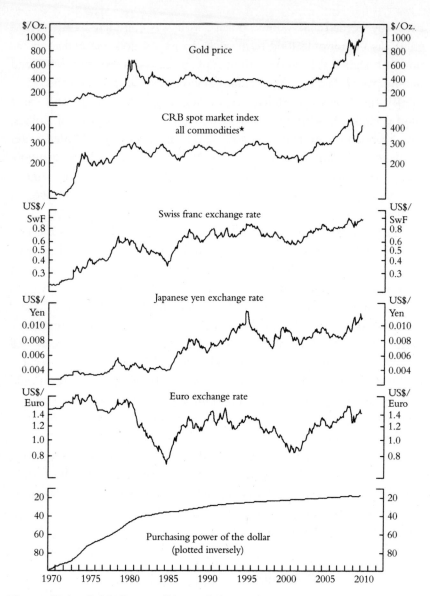

Figure 10.1   Gold, Commodities, and Currencies
*Source for data: Commodity Research Bureau.
Source: Chart courtesy of BCA Research Inc.

The value of the dollar, like that of other currencies, is determined by supply and demand on the foreign exchanges. However, it
is a currency that is fundamentally different from all others for three
main reasons. First, most international commodities and other globally

traded goods are quoted in U.S. dollars, most international contracts are written in U.S. dollars, and payments are made in U.S. dollars. Second, central banks hold most of their international reserves in currencies and by far the largest component is dollars. At the end of 2009, dollars held by the various monetary authorities around the world totaled about $4 trillion. Third, the United States has the largest, most liquid capital market in the world and relatively good governance, backed up by the rule of law.

Because the dollar is so important to so many people, the Great Reflation experiment has created a growing sense of unease that its future performance may be even more disastrous than its performance has been during the past 40 years. When President Nixon abandoned gold backing in 1971, his most ominous words were "We're all Keynesians now." His meaning was clear. Henceforth, the United States would focus economic policy only on domestic considerations such as unemployment, jobs, and growth. External pressures would take a backseat. All U.S. Treasury secretaries go through the ritual of saying that the United States has a strong dollar policy. What they mean is that their policy is to say that they have a strong dollar policy. After 1971, the U.S. dollar, unbacked by anything other than promises, was set free to float, and its long-run value against other currencies would henceforth depend on which countries inflated the fastest.

The U.S. dollar has particularly important bilateral relationships with a few currencies. These would include the Canadian dollar, the euro, the pound sterling, the yen, and the Chinese renminbi. Those currencies are heavily traded in foreign exchange markets. There is an enormous volume of trade and capital flows among countries issuing those currencies, and collectively they hold a large percentage of world reserves.

However, it is not our purpose to delve into all the complexities that determine bilateral exchange rates, because any one exchange rate is determined by the developments in the two countries on opposite sides of the exchange rate and by a host of other factors. Our focus is on the long-run external value of the dollar generally. We can get a good sense of this by looking at what is called the trade-weighted U.S. dollar index (TWI). It is calculated by averaging the main currencies, weighting them by the proportion of U.S. trade with each particular country. It is shown in Figure 10.2. However, it is important to note that the TWI can move only against currencies that float, which includes most of the

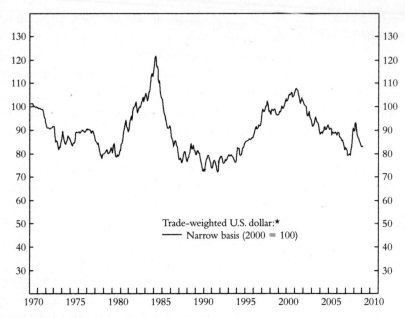

Figure 10.2   Trade-weighted U.S. Dollar
*Source for data: JPMorgan Chase & Company.
Source: Chart courtesy of BCA Research Inc.

developed world's currencies. Some of these have been quite weak, and as a result, the TWI is only about 20 percent below its level in 1970.

To determine whether the dollar is weak against those currencies like the renminbi that either don't float or are heavily manipulated, you have to look at the volume of dollars countries buy on the exchange market to keep their currencies stable against the dollar. Foreign central banks have bought about $4 trillion worth of U.S. dollars, shown in Figure 10.3, on the market since 1970, to either slow or stop the dollar's fall. This has created a huge dollar overhang on the market. This would not be such a big problem if the United States ran a current account surplus in its trading with other countries. However, it has been running very large deficits.

When the United States runs a current account deficit, as it has done all the time since 1980, it puts an excess supply of dollars onto the world market. This excess can be augmented, reduced, eliminated, or even reversed by private net capital flows (for portfolio or capital investment reasons) into the United States. The term *net* refers to the

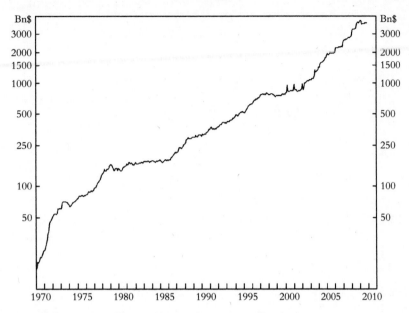

Figure 10.3   U.S. Dollar Holdings of Foreign Official Institutions
*Source for data: Federal Reserve Board.
Source: Chart courtesy of BCA Research Inc.

difference between capital inflows and outflows. Figure 10.4 shows the
U.S. current account balance alone and net of the long-term capital
flows since 1970. It can be seen that the United States was not far out
of balance until the early 1980s, but since then, coinciding with the
buildup of the private debt supercycle, there has been a progressive
deterioration. After 2001, the United States moved into massive overall deficit.

For fuller understanding, we must factor in an added complicat-
ion—the desire of central banks to hold more reserves. If they have confidence in the reserve currency role of the dollar, they will want to add
to their holdings over time. As world trade grows, countries want larger
reserves to cover temporary imbalances in their own external financial
positions. For most of the postwar period, foreign central banks have
wanted to add to their dollar holdings. In particular, after the crisis in
developing countries in 1997 and 1998, most of their central banks
decided to hold a lot more dollars because they had confidence in it.
However, there is the well-known paradox that comes with being a

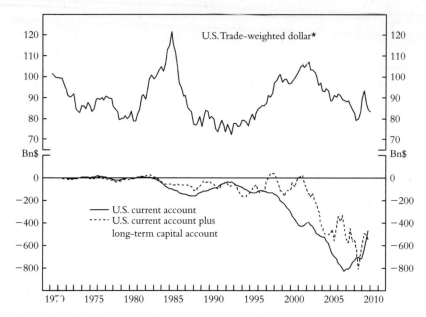

Figure 10.4   U.S. Current Account and the Dollar
★Source for data: JPMorgan Chase & Company.
Source: Chart courtesy of BCA Research Inc.

reserve currency country. It has to run a deficit to create a sufficient amount of its currency for countries that want to hold it. However, that very process undermines the long-term viability of the reserve currency—in this case the dollar—by creating too many of them.

There is another side to being a reserve currency. In the dollar's case, it has given the United States a free ride for far too long in running balance of payments deficits financed automatically by foreign central bank purchases. For corporations, it would be called vendor financing. The buyer never has to pay. For a country, it is called seigniorage, and it is the ultimate free lunch for a reserve currency country like the United States.

The downside of this free lunch, like all free lunches, is that it creates bad habits. The United States has been able to pursue policies that have been far more inflationary than they would otherwise have been. This habit was aided and abetted by two other seemingly free lunches. One was the dramatic industrial growth of low-wage, high-productivity developing countries like China. The other was the extraordinarily high volume of savings in these countries relative to their ability to invest locally. The result was that the United States was able to finance huge fiscal and balance of payments deficits with falling inflation and interest rates. This was too good to be true. The disequilibrium of this arrangement led directly to the crash of 2008–2009. The U.S. dollar, under considerable pressure, had fallen sharply prior to the Lehman Brothers collapse. It did rally briskly for a short while during the panic but then resumed its downward course after the panic subsided. This has raised concerns that a major new decline may be in the works.

The Dollar's Future

There is one overriding reason why concerns over the U.S. dollar's future value are justified. Foreign central banks, as we pointed out before, have acquired almost $4 trillion, whether out of need or to keep their currencies stable against the dollar. Monetary authorities are traditionally conservative by nature and do not want to lose money on their dollar reserves, nor do they relish the prospect of disruption to their export industries, which lose competitiveness when their currency rises. The United States has a near-zero interest rate policy and is running fiscal deficits so large that government debt will soon equal 100 percent of gross domestic product (GDP). Such behavior is totally inappropriate for a reserve currency country, and whatever confidence in the dollar that still exists cannot last without a major change in policy.

At the current trade-weighted exchange rate of the U.S. dollar, it is almost certain that the massive fiscal deficit, discussed in Chapter 4, together with monetary and other forms of stimulus, will lead to renewed widening of the current account deficit, as it always does, when the economy recovers from recession. Big fiscal deficits cause imports to rise much faster than exports.

Before the crisis, the external deficit was running at $800 billion per annum. Even assuming GDP growth of just 2 percent per annum, well below the long-run average, and significant spending retrenchment on the part of the consumer, the deficit could easily widen to over $1 trillion, unless the dollar were devalued sharply against other currencies.

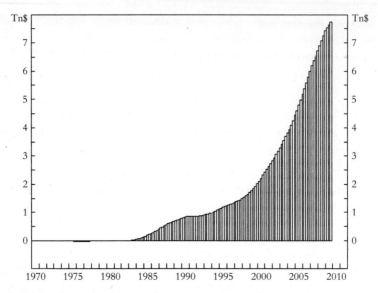

Figure 10.5   U.S. Cumulative Current Account Deficit
Source: Chart courtesy of BCA Research Inc.

A current account deficit in any one year is not particularly serious, but the United States has been running them for almost 30 years. These have accumulated to $7.5 trillion, as shown in Figure 10.5. These accumulated deficits end up as financial claims on the United States and are reflected in the holdings of foreign central banks.

To get a more complete picture of the U.S. external position, we have to take into account capital flows between the United States and foreign countries. The United States is a large investor abroad, buying stocks, bonds, and businesses, and investing directly in production and other facilities in foreign countries. The latter do the same in the United States. Figure 10.6 shows the trends for both U.S. assets held abroad and foreign-held claims on the United States. Both have risen a lot in recent decades, but the crucial point is that the net difference between the two has moved dramatically against the United States.

The United States used to have a net positive balance, but the inflationary policies from the 1960s onward have swung the difference to a negative $3.5 trillion. This means that, if you look at the U.S. external balance sheet, its liabilities are $3.5 trillion more than its assets. For an individual or corporation, a negative net worth implies that you are on

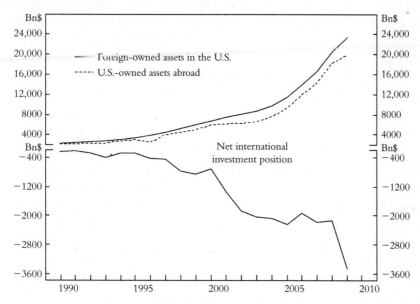

Figure 10.6   U.S. Net International Investment Position
Note: Valued at current cost.
Source: Chart courtesy of BCA Research Inc.

the way to bankruptcy court. However, governments have monopoly taxing powers and this sustains hope that they will honor their debts. In the U.S. case, the situation is made more precarious than the raw figures suggest; U.S. assets are largely held by the private sector and are, for the most part, not very liquid. However, most of the U.S. liabilities are very liquid. Central banks could, in theory, try to liquidate their trillions of dollars quickly. Moreover, privately-held foreign claims in stocks and bonds are also in the trillions of dollars and could be dumped in a panic. And if that were to happen, Americans could also panic out of dollars, adding greatly to the excess supply.

From a long-term perspective, it is clear that the dollar faces serious trouble. We believe the trend will continue downward. The dollar is already in huge surplus on world markets, and the Great Reflation can only add trillions more. Foreign central banks are very nervous over the future value of the dollars they hold in reserves. The U.S. current account deficit is chronically so large that only a sharp fall in the real (inflation-adjusted) value of the dollar can be counted on to reduce it. Finally, since the 1960s, the United States has never concerned itself with the dollar's external value and never imposed financial discipline when called for by external pressures. This undermines confidence in the U.S. dollar and, over the long run, declining confidence in the dollar will result in a phasing out of its role as a reserve currency, hopefully on a gradual basis.

Most investors, however, are concerned with the short- to intermediate-term outlook. While downward pressure on the dollar is obvious, a dollar crisis in the near term is not. The great dilemma for foreign central banks is that they are faced with the "too big to fail" problem—they hold too many dollars. If they try to switch out of even some of them, they risk a U.S. dollar collapse. The Treasury and corporate bond markets would also be in trouble because foreigners are heavy investors there as well. A dollar collapse would have two unwanted effects on foreign central banks: It would trigger large foreign exchange losses on their dollar holdings, and push their currencies up, possibly quite dramatically. The result would undoubtedly be another global financial crisis.

The United States also has a lot to fear from a dollar collapse—inflation, a spike in interest rates, and inability to fund fiscal deficits. If it occurred, it could easily trigger the much-feared double-dip economic downturn and another housing and banking collapse. For these reasons, there has been a sort of stalemate in the currency markets. In a globally deflationist, fragile economic world, no one wants their currency to go up. Some central banks are more sensitive than others to this problem. This is why some, like China, have been pegging their currencies to the dollar. (In November 2009, China announced it would go back to a policy of allowing some appreciation of the renminbi.) Other countries' currencies float fairly freely, like the euro, yen, pound sterling, Canadian and Australian dollars, and Norwegian kroner.

A critical question is how long this two-tier monetary system can last, because it is obviously creating large distortions, disequilibrium, and inflation in those countries that have pegged their currencies to the dollar. Some, like China, have argued that it will last a long time. It has been dubbed the revived Bretton Woods system or Bretton Woods II. It is the de facto successor to the Bretton Woods I system, which lasted from 1945 until 1971. Proponents of the revived system[2] argue that the emerging market countries with large populations, particularly China, will hold their noses and buy dollars. They want to keep their currencies cheap until all their underemployed, low-productivity labor is absorbed into high-productivity advanced industries. At that point they will have caught up to the West and will be free to let their currencies float upward if need be. That was the course Japan took after World War II. It kept the yen super cheap until it caught up with developed countries, then let the yen float up sharply.

This argument had a lot of empirical support until the crash of 2008–2009. With the United States engaged in unlimited bailouts, deficits, and monetary easing, China and other big dollar holders have experienced growing unease at the prospect of large dollar losses and sharply rising domestic asset inflation. The crash and its aftermath have produced a huge shock to confidence in the United States and its economic system, currency, and policy makers. Nonetheless, while large dollar-holding countries have done a lot of complaining, the fact is that they have continued to buy huge quantities of dollars. Some countries with floating currencies have also begun to take action to stop the dollar falling against their currencies. There is a final point which supports the prospect of an orderly erosion of the dollar as opposed to a collapse: There are no good currency alternatives into which countries can shift large amounts of their reserves. This is unlikely to change, possibly for 10 to 20 years.

Conclusion
The outlook for the dollar remains bearish over the long term, driven by continued U.S. current and capital account deficits, which will add to the massive excess supply of dollars already on the world markets. Investors should continue to bet on a continuation of the long-run decline, driven by unprecedented U.S. reflationary policies, including near-zero interest rates. However, investors should not bet on a dollar crisis and sharp fall in the short term, but rather a persistent erosion and the occasional countertrend rally. In a world of deflation and fragile economies, almost everyone wants dollar stability.

Chapter 11

Gold

When the paper system collapses, the survivors will dig in the rubble and they will find gold.

—William Rees-Mogg[1]

A continuing theme running through this book is whether the Great Reflation will turn into the Great Inflation and whether the U.S. dollar is headed for the dustbin of history along with the Zimbabwean dollar or the Reichsmark, as we discussed in Chapter 1. There are a lot of people who either believe it will happen or at least think it has a sporting chance. The run-up in the gold price to over $1,200 per ounce in late 2009 and extensive media publicity have added a significant degree of credibility to those who are already persuaded, or on the edge of believing, that the worst is inevitable for U.S. inflation and the dollar.

Has Gold Mania II Already Started?

Gold is the new poster boy, both for the bubble excesses of 2002 to 2008 and more recently because of the much-feared consequences of the Great Reflation. Gold skyrocketed from $280 per ounce at the end of the year 2000 to $900 per ounce before the crash, and to over $1,200 in late 2009. This amounts to a quadrupling of the price in nine years or 17.6 percent per annum compounded. With the exception of crude oil and the Shanghai stock index, gold has outperformed every other major investment class over this period, including commodities, the S&P 500, U.S. bonds, and the Morgan Stanley Capital International (MSCI) index of world stock prices. Figure 11.1 shows gold and these other asset classes back to January 2000, at which point they are all indexed to 100 for easy comparison.

This dramatic outperformance of gold over almost all major asset classes has naturally caught the attention of a lot of people, particularly after the September 2009 breakthrough of the $1,000 per ounce ceiling set almost 30 years ago. Gold in that earlier bull market had risen from its postwar pegged price of $35 under the first Bretton Woods system, an 18-fold gain as can be seen in Figure 11.2. This was a true mania that was initiated by fear of runaway price inflation and a collapsing dollar.

Many people are now betting that another mania in gold is under way. Figure 11.3 shows the path of the gold price from 1968 to 1980 with the current trajectory that started in 2001. At both starting points, prices are indexed to 100 to make comparison easy. The first gold mania lasted approximately 12 years, although from 1971, the year President Nixon freed gold from the dollar, the mania could be said to have lasted less than nine years. By way of comparison, the current gold run is about eight years old. Counting from the end of 1967, the first gold mania saw the price rise about fourfold in the first eight years, roughly the same as the gold price has done over the eight years since 2001. Clearly, the two are tracking pretty closely. Whether the current wave will continue to do so is another story, to be discussed next.

At this point, it is clear that investment demand, which is classified as demand other than for the arts, jewelry, and industry, has soared. Well-known hedge funds have loaded up on gold and gold shares, but probably more important, the general public is pouring money into gold mutual funds, exchange-traded funds (ETFs), and gold commodity futures. For as little as a thousand dollars and a low entrance and management fee, the so-called small investor can play. Leverage is readily available. Some

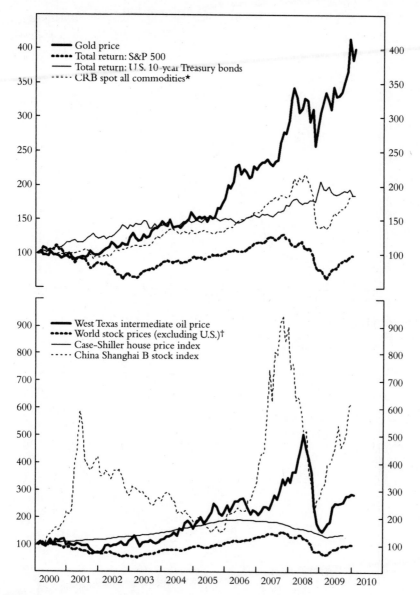

Figure 11.1 Gold and Selected Assets

*Source for data: Commodity Research Bureau. All series rebased to January 2000 = 100.
†Source for data: Morgan Stanley Capital International.
Source: Chart courtesy of BCA Research Inc.

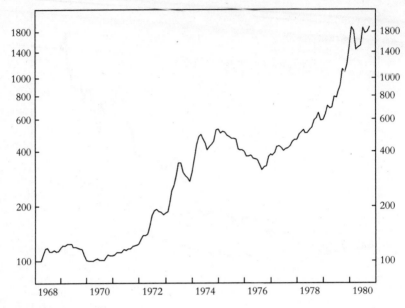

Figure 11.2   First Gold Mania, 1968–1980
Note: Gold price rebased to January 1968 = 100.
Source: Chart courtesy of BCA Research Inc.

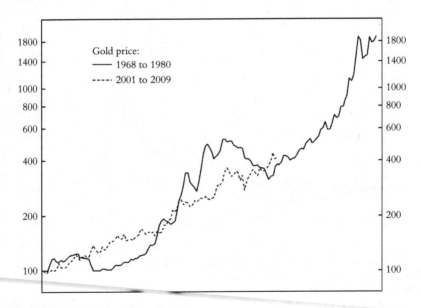

Figure 11.3   A Tale of Two Manias
Note: Both series rebased to 100 at start of mania.
Source: Chart courtesy of BCA Research Inc.

funds offer investors two or three times leverage on their initial investment, with the use of debt providing the extra kicker. This promises
investors double or triple the return that a fully paid gold position would
give. Naturally, it works in both directions; losses are doubled or tripled
as well. The minimum gold commodity futures contract is for 100 troy
ounces, which, at $1,200 per ounce, is U.S. $120,000, but the investor
has to put up only 5 percent or about $6,000.

Hedge fund purchases of gold are not reported but are probably
huge as well. New gold products appear almost daily. Individual
investor purchases of gold ETFs have exploded in the past five years
from 200 tons to over 1,400 tons (one metric ton = 32,151 troy ounces),
as Figure 11.4 shows. And this particular ETF series accounts for only
75 percent of all gold ETFs.

In short, the gold products are available, demand has heated up
dramatically, and a supportive story or "displacement," in Kindleberger's
words—a potential monetary debauchery and an eventual collapse in the

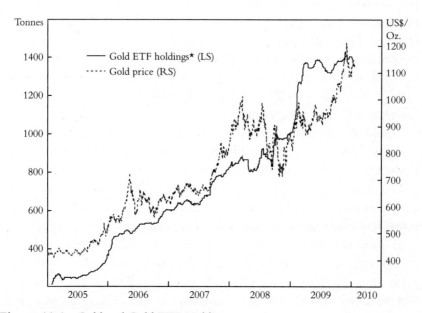

Figure 11.4   Gold and Gold ETF Holdings
*Source for data: Exchange-traded gold, Barcay's Capital.
Note: ETFs are stock-exchange-traded funds with very low fees and operate like mutual funds.
Source: Chart courtesy of BCA Research Inc.

U.S. dollar—exists for those who want to believe it. Not unrelated to that motivation for buying gold is recent central bank action. Both the People's Bank of China and the Reserve Bank of India have recently bought gold, the latter from the International Monetary Fund (IMF). The Indian central bank has also indicated that it has an appetite for more. In addition, central banks and sovereign wealth funds have been diversifying away from the dollar, acquiring shares in commodity producers and making loans for resource development and acquisition—in effect, acquiring a hedge against price inflation and dollar devaluation. The irony of central banks buying gold and inflation hedges while creating lots of paper money and acting as massive lenders of last resort has not been lost on sharp-eyed observers of the financial scene.

This chapter looks at gold from the perspective of the age-old tradition of insurance against wealth destruction and also from the perspective of gold as an investment and a target of manic hysteria. Both intersect for two main reasons. The investment/mania aspect relies heavily on the insurance motivation for justification. However, gold can provide cost-effective insurance only if the price is not too high, but we never know if the price is too high until after the fact. The essence of a mania is the creation of irrational valuation that destroys the notion of insurance, and this becomes particularly relevant when the price comes down from elevated levels. Gold fell from almost $1,000 per ounce in 1980 to a low of $280 per ounce 20 years later, making for a very unhappy investment experience.

Gold is a form of disaster insurance in which the premium rises, along with people's fears, to a level that may significantly overstate the probabilities of the occurrence of the disaster that gold is supposed to protect against. It would be similar to a situation in which your insurance company thought that the probabilities of your house burning down had doubled but it quadrupled your premium. The problem with gold, however, is a bit different. No one can establish the probabilities of monetary disaster in advance, and no one can say what is the right price for gold. That is one of the things that makes gold so interesting and attractive. It can never be subjected to a statistical calculation of value like an income-producing asset, nor can an actuarial calculation be made of the risks that gold is supposed to protect against. It can't be analyzed like most commodities, which have long-run cost curves that eventually are reflected in supply and demand balance. Almost all the gold ever mined is above ground and potentially available at a price. Investment demand swings dramatically relative to the annual output from mines and the off-take for industry and the arts. In addition, a lot of gold used in jewelry is disguised investment demand and can come back on the market if the price is high enough or if economic conditions deteriorate.

The key question for investors is how to approach gold against this backdrop. Should they play what surely looks like a developing mania, either by believing the story of dollar debauchery or believing that enough other people will believe it, which could take the price a lot higher? Or should they take a more sober, conservative view and continue to think of holding gold as an insurance policy?

Why Gold Has Enduring Value

The real price of gold (i.e., after inflation adjustment) has fluctuated enormously since the end of the gold standard in 1914. These fluctuations have become even more extreme since the first Bretton Woods system collapsed in 1971 and the official price of gold was freed. In spite of this volatility, gold has retained its special mystique based on a track record that goes back thousands of years. The properties that have made gold so attractive are well known. It is indestructible, it is revered for jewelry and the arts, and its high value-to-weight ratio makes it easy to store and portable—critical qualities in wartime. It is not a liability of anyone. It is easily transferable outside normal banking channels and hence useful to avoid the grasp of predatory governments. It cannot be blocked in time of war or sanctions against regimes that are out of favor. People have used it for tax-free inheritance planning for centuries. It is useful for hiding wealth, which is important in many countries. But, above all, it has provided long-term protection against destruction of wealth by maintaining its purchasing power over very long periods compared with paper money. For these reasons, gold has built a track record of trust over thousands of years in preserving wealth, and this is not going to disappear anytime soon, if ever. People who own gold for wealth preservation are long-term holders. They own gold for insurance and hope they don't need it.

Gold as a Monetary Standard

Gold (along with some other precious metals) has been used as a monetary standard since the Greek and Roman eras, and well before then as well. Its monetary function altered somewhat after early experiments with paper money. Virtually all of these ended up in disaster and, as a result, gold's role evolved into one of legal backing for paper issued by central banks, as we discussed in Chapter 1. Gold backing limited the quantity of paper a central bank could issue to the point where paper was considered "as good as gold." That was the theory. The practice was not always the same. Countries and empires come and go, and so do paper currencies. As William Rees-Mogg famously remarked, "Paper money is only as good as the men who control it and they are under constant pressure to print more of it."[2]

That observation explains why governments are generally so hostile to gold. When people see governments succumb to the pressure of money printing, they buy gold to escape the consequences—rising prices, currency devaluation, and often controls on foreign exchange conversion. Money printing doesn't work if the public can escape the consequences, which, one way or another, reflect the government's need to extract resources from the public to cover its expenditures that cannot be financed by taxation and bond issuance. Essentially, those hostile to gold are the soft money lobbyists, socialists, and others in favor of government centralization of power, control, and redistribution of wealth. This school of thought is generally unsympathetic to the ideals of personal liberty and free markets. That is why those who believe in economic freedom are usually the strongest supporters of gold and the most distrustful of governments.

Governments that adhered to the gold standard[3] made their currencies convertible into gold at a fixed price and held gold as backing to guarantee convertibility. Hence money was as good as gold as long as people trusted governments to follow the rules of strictly controlling the issuance of money according to their gold holdings. As a result, the gold standard did a remarkable job in maintaining the purchasing power of money during the 200 years up to 1914, as well as maintaining a high standard of personal and economic liberty. Figure 11.5 shows the purchasing power of the pound starting from 1717, when the United Kingdom went on the gold standard, until 1914, the start of World War I. It can be seen that UK consumer prices rose quite sharply during the Napoleonic Wars, when the United Kingdom had gone off gold. However, after the restoration of gold in 1815, prices came back down so that by the early-1900s they weren't much different from 200 years earlier! The stability came to an end in 1914 with the outbreak of World War I when countries could no longer stay on the gold standard and finance their war efforts at the same time. Great instability followed in the 1920s and into the 1930s. In March 1933 President Roosevelt closed the gold window, confiscated private Americans' holdings of gold and silver, and imposed draconian penalties for disobeying the new law ($10,000 fines and/or 10 years in prison). He then promptly raised the price from the

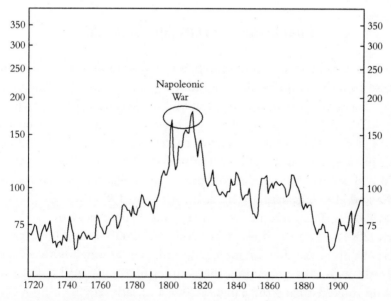

Figure 11.5 Stability of UK Prices under the Gold Standard, 1717–1914
Source for data: The *Economist*.
Source: Chart courtesy of BCA Research Inc.

long-standing $20.67 to $35 a troy ounce. Quasi-stability in the U.S. monetary system lasted until President Nixon broke the final link between the U.S. dollar and gold and set it free to float. Prior to that, the Federal Reserve had a legal requirement to hold a certain percentage of gold against the currency it issued. However, only foreign central banks had the right to convertibility—not U.S. citizens, for whom it remained illegal to hold gold until 1975.

The modern era of gold began in 1971 when the gold price, fixed for almost 40 years at $35 per ounce, was set free. Over those 40 years, the inflation-adjusted value of gold had fallen by about 65 percent. Gold was obviously a poor inflation hedge and, as a result, had become much undervalued by the time formal discipline on the Federal Reserve was removed. Gold entered its first truly global bull market in 250 years, totally unhinged from the gold standard. There had, of course, been bull runs in individual currencies of belligerent countries when they temporarily suspended the gold standard during wars. Examples were the Napoleonic Wars, the American Civil War, and World War I.

What Drives the Long-Run Gold Price

There is a tight inverse relationship between gold and the U.S. dollar. Figure 11.6 shows the gold price and the trade-weighted dollar back to 1969. It is evident that the two great bull markets in the gold price—in the 1970s and the 2000s—have been associated with steep declines in the dollar. The period of tightest correlation was 1969 to 1980. The bear market rally in the dollar from mid-1973 to late-1976 was associated with a correction in the gold price. The dollar rallied from 1980 to 1985 and gold fell sharply. The dollar fell from 1985 through 1987 and gold rallied. The same inverse relationship mainly held from 1988 to early-2001, when the dollar was strong and gold weak. However, the relationship broke down temporarily and then resumed with a vengeance through 2009, including the countertrend rally in the dollar and sell-off in gold during the panic in 2008 and early-2009.

The future of the dollar is clearly critical for the future of the gold price. As discussed in the preceding chapter, the long-run outlook for

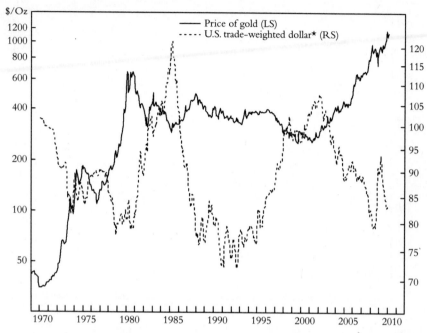

Figure 11.6 Gold and the U.S. Dollar, 1969–2009
*JPMorgan Chase & Company.
Source: Chart courtesy of BCA Research Inc.

the dollar is bearish because there are too many of them and the supply will only increase. The U.S. dollar is the principal reserve currency and almost $4 trillion worth is held by central banks. A reserve currency should have some scarcity value, not be a glut on the market as a result of massive monetary stimulus, near-zero interest rates, out-of-control budget deficits, sharply rising government debt, and persistent balance of payments deficits.

The United States increased its net short-term liabilities to foreigners at a very high rate for decades by running deficits with other countries. Clearly, the precarious position of the U.S. dollar as a result of the massive U.S. liabilities to foreign central banks is a major factor in the appeal of gold.

Even though the United States is not on the gold standard, it is useful to see what the theoretical price would have to be to raise the value of the U.S. gold stock high enough to pay off all of its

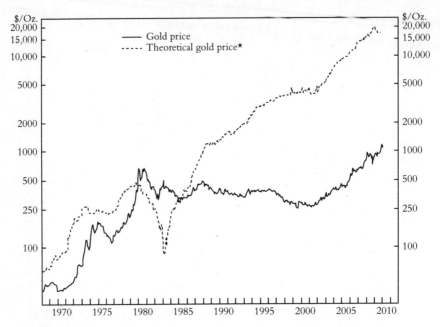

Figure 11.7 Price of Gold Required to Cover Net Liquid Liabilities
*The price of gold at which U.S. gold stock equals net liquid liabilities.
Source: Chart courtesy of BCA Research Inc.

short-term liabilities. We show the series back to 1969 in Figure 11.7
along with the actual gold price. There was a fairly close relationship
between the two until about 1985, but since then, the theoretical
gold price has exploded upward, recently reaching a level of $20,000 per
ounce. It seems totally unrealistic to think of the gold price moving
to these levels, but it does put into perspective the massive imbalance
in the global monetary system and the potential for gold to move
up should the United States fail to get its twin deficits—fiscal and
international—under control. In that case, monetary chaos would
eventually be guaranteed.

There are other ways to gain perspective on the gold price.
One is the bilateral relationships between the price of gold and oil,
and gold and other commodities. This is shown in Figure 11.8. All
three were undervalued in the late 1960s. When general inflation
took off and gold was allowed to float freely, all three rose sharply.
We have based the ratio of gold/Commodity Research Bureau

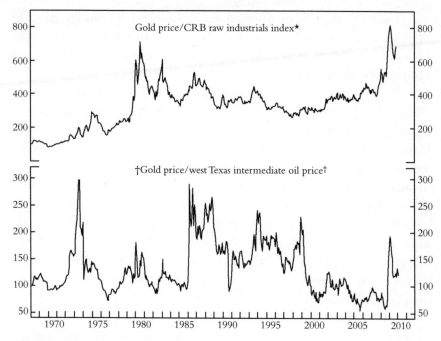

Figure 11.8 Gold, Commodities, and Oil
*Commodity Research Bureau; ratio rebased to 1914 = 100.
†Ratio rebased to 1968 = 100.
Source: Chart courtesy of BCA Research Inc.

Index at 100 in 1914 (to take into account the inflation from 1914 to 1968), and we based the gold/oil ratio at 100 in 1968 because both were officially controlled. It is interesting to note that, in spite of the great volatility over the past 40 years, the gold/oil ratio is not far off its starting point, with gold slightly ahead. However, gold has outpaced commodity prices by a factor of five since 1968. The conclusion from these data is that gold may not have a lot of upside in the near term unless oil and other commodities move up quite sharply from late 2009 levels.

Gold as an Investment

Let's put aside for the moment the motivation for holding gold as a safe haven, protector of wealth, and hedge against catastrophe. There is no question that gold has always lived up to its reputation for those in perilous situations. But for most of us, this is not particularly relevant now or in the foreseeable future. The focus should be on whether gold can consistently add value to a diversified portfolio.

There are several things we need to look at, just as we do for other assets. First, it is important to know how gold has performed since it was set free in August 1971, vis-à-vis total returns achieved by U.S. stocks and U.S. 10-year Treasuries over the same period. These trends are shown in Figure 11.9a. The record shows that gold and 10-year Treasuries have done about the same but U.S. stocks have done better. However, the starting point is critical. In 1969, gold was hugely under-valued and bonds and stocks were at the cusp of a major secular bear market. When the comparisons are made from 1980 to 2009, as shown in Figure 11.9b, both U.S. bonds and stocks outperformed gold by a very wide margin even after the inclusion of the recent rise in gold and the poor performance of stocks since 2000.

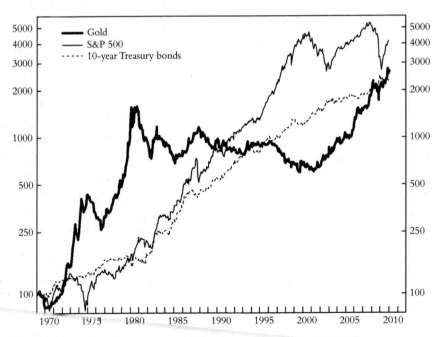

Figure 11.9a   Total Return: Gold, Stocks, and Bonds, 1969–2009
Note: All series rebased to January 1969 = 100.
Source: Chart courtesy of BCA Research Inc.

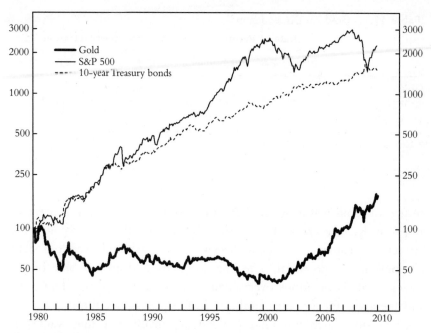

Figure 11.9b Total Return: Gold, Stocks, and Bonds, 1980–2009
Note: All series rebased to January 1980 = 100.
Source: Chart courtesy of BCA Research Inc.

One way of reducing the starting point problem is to calculate total returns based on trend lines (slopes) that give a geometrical compound return, which is much more meaningful. The return on gold was about 4.5 percent per annum in the 1970–2009 period and about 1 percent since 1980. Stocks and bonds have averaged 12.5 percent and a bit over 9 percent respectively, regardless of the starting point. Volatility is measured by the standard deviation around the trend line and has been less for gold than for stocks and bonds. However, the better record on this score pales in comparison to the relative long-run rates of return on the three assets. These are summarized in Table 11.1 for the periods 1970 to 2009 and 1980 to 2009.

It is evident from the data in Table 11.1 that gold has not been such a wonderful investment on a long-term buy-and-hold basis. However, gold has experienced two enormous bull markets—1970 to early 1980 and 2001 to 2009, which may not be finished yet. The total

Table 11.1　Gold, Stocks, and Bonds

	Rate of Return*		Standard Deviation	
	1970–2009	1980–2009	1970–2009	1980–2009
Gold	4.5	1.0	0.3	5.6
S&P 500	12.5	12.5	9.0	18.5
10-Year Treasuries	9.1	9.4	3.9	7.1

*Compound annual returns based on the trend.

return on gold was a pretty dramatic 2,400 percent and 446 percent, respectively, in each of those moves. These are the sort of gains that attract speculators like bees to honey. No one should ever lose sight of gold's mania potential. The inflation scare and gold bubble of the 1970s created enormous overvaluation at the top in 1980. The most suitable assets for a mania, outlined in Chapter 6, are those that cannot be easily valued. Gold has no yield, and investors, if they want, can justify any price in the short term. However, manias are bubbles and they always burst. They are exciting on the way up but do not create profits that most people keep.

Proponents of gold have argued that it is a useful asset in portfolios because of its negative correlation with stocks and bonds. This was true in the 1970s when gold went up while stocks and bonds fell sharply. However, since then, the evidence is much less clear. In fact, from 2002 to 2008, all three assets were closely correlated. In 2009, gold has again been positively correlated with stocks and bonds (particularly corporate bonds). Overall, even including the experience of the 1970s, gold has not provided much long-run diversification benefit since 1969. Gold and S&P total returns have had a correlation of .52. Gold has had a .65 correlation vis-à-vis Treasury bonds over the same period.

Therefore, from a diversification perspective, it is hard to make a strong case for gold in a balanced portfolio. However, that is a separate issue from the insurance motivation to provide a hedge or protection against geopolitical and/or financial catastrophes. Those are rare events and do not lend themselves to correlation statistics.

Some Investment Tools for Gold

Those who want to invest in gold need to have some objective tools to rely on for purposes of adjusting exposure. Figure 11.10 shows the gold price since 1969 along with its trend line. The two dashed lines on either side of the trend line show one and two standard deviations. Gold was undervalued prior to the beginning of the first mania by two standard deviations and undervalued by one standard deviation prior to the second. At the top in 1980, gold was more than two and a half standard deviations on the expensive side. In late 2009, gold appeared to be moderately overvalued based on this measure and, therefore, had moved into risky territory, although nothing like the frothy peak in 1980.

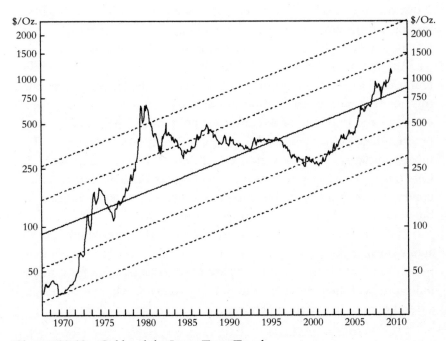

Figure 11.10   Gold and the Long-Term Trend
Note: Dashed lines represent one and two standard deviations about the mean.
Source: Chart courtesy of BCA Research Inc.

Valuation measures, as we have emphasized, are not very helpful in identifying turning points in a timely way. Trend-following tools, such as moving averages discussed in earlier chapters in Part II, can be helpful. While we would never use these in isolation, they can sharpen timing when investors perceive that the fundamentals are pointing to an approaching change in trend. Figure 11.11 shows the gold price, together with three-month and nine-month moving averages, around three key turning points as well as the period since 2007 shown in the top panel. Followers of those trend-reversal indicators could have used them to support timely entry into the two big bull markets, post-1970 and post-2001 and a timely exit from the post-1980 bear market. The current bull market shows no sign at this point in time that a trend reversal is imminent.

These momentum indicators are particularly helpful when used in conjunction with the long-run trend indicating whether gold is cheap or expensive relative to its trend line, as expressed in Figure 11.10. However, investors should never underestimate the difficulty of interpreting trend-following devices. They often give whipsaw signals, which is why they must be used in conjunction with the fundamentals.

Another factor investors should always keep an eye on is bullish enthusiasm or bearish pessimism. At the start of the chapter we pointed out how the recent price action in gold combined with massive media coverage and dramatic proliferation of gold ETFs (the retail investor's product) have clearly indicated that a second gold mania has started. Two other indicators of psychological extremes are shown in Figure 11.12. One is net speculative positions as a percentage of open interest on futures contracts. The other is bullish market sentiment. Both series indicate that bullishness on gold was at an extreme in late 2009.

The problem with sentiment indicators is that they don't tell you about turning points, only risk from the perspective that "everyone is bullish" and vice versa. That is why we need to supplement fundamental indicators with measures, like the moving averages, which should signal a trend reversal in a fairly timely way.

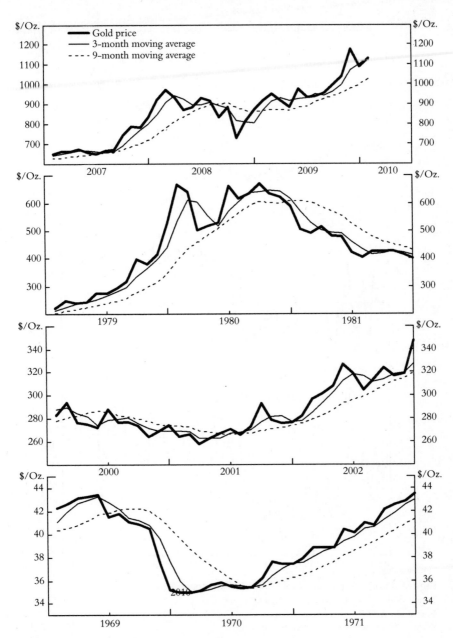

Figure 11.11 Gold and Moving Averages
Source: Chart courtesy of BCA Research Inc.

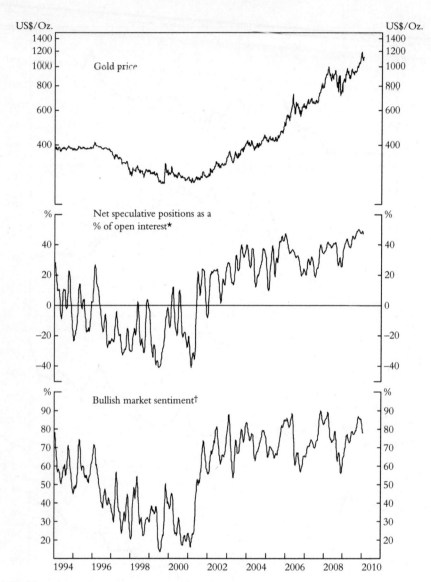

Figure 11.12   Gold and Gold Market Sentiment
*Source of data: Commodity Futures Trading Commission.
†Source of data: Marketvane.net.
Source: Chart courtesy of BCA Research Inc.

Conclusion

This chapter has emphasized that Gold Mania II is under way. Investment demand is essentially speculation, whether overt or explicit. Hedge funds and wealthy individuals are loading up because it has been one of the best games in town. However, momentum going into 2010 was slackening. There are thousands of small investors as well who are caught up in the hysteria, even buying small bars of gold in department stores. They may believe that they are investing, but the reality is that they are speculating—buying solely on the hopes that another buyer will come along and pay a higher price. In part, this demand is a function of paltry returns on cash and liquid deposits at banks. The very low opportunity cost of holding gold is likely to continue. Gold demand is also based on a disgust with the stock market as a result of prices still being significantly below the level of 10 years ago. In addition, the many articles in the media focusing on the potential for a dollar collapse and sharp rise in inflation have provided additional impetus to gold demand. The price is tracking quite closely that of the first gold mania from 1969 to 1982. The current run could well have a lot further to go. Based on its long-term trend line, gold is overvalued but not by as much as in 1980. That is true to varying degrees according to other measures discussed in this chapter. But a true mania takes prices far beyond rational valuation. Gold is the perfect target as it has no income stream to value and it does not take a huge amount of money to move the price sharply. Central banks have started buying again. Momentum is rising strongly.

The bottom line is that the gold price could go a lot higher if mass hysteria—already high—accelerates. Some have already made fortunes on the rise so far, and others will get very rich if it does turn out to be a true mania. But investors must remember the lesson from Chapter 6. A mania creates a bubble, and bubbles burst with little or no warning.

(continued)

Gold from a rational long-term investment perspective does not have a compelling case at these levels. However, gold is as much an emotional issue as it is rational, if not more so. The Great Reflation is the greatest monetary and fiscal experiment in peacetime history. Millions of people fear that the Great Reflation will have a bad ending for paper money and paper investments, and they want to have some protection. The Swiss (and many others) have famously recommended that families interested in long-term wealth preservation should hold an insurance position in gold of 5 to 10 percent of their assets. Given the future uncertainty and potential threats of wealth destruction, we would also recommend that long-term investors keep such an insurance position and hope they don't need it.

Speculators and short-term investors in gold may make money in the near term if fears of U.S. monetary debauchery escalate. But it is not cheap. It is a crowded trade (i.e., millions are on the same bullish side) and dependent on the "greater fool" theory to keep prices rising. That theory says that if you are using momentum as your main tool, you have to be betting that there is another buyer ready to take your position when you want to sell.

Chapter 12

Commodities

Nearly every time I strayed from the herd, I've made a lot of money. Wandering away from the action is the way to find the new action.

—Jim Rogers[1]

After the crash, it didn't take long for commodities to get back into play again. The gains from the lows have been quite spectacular. By late 2009, gold, silver, copper, and oil were up by between 60 percent and 150 percent, and the broader indexes were up by between 40 percent and 45 percent. Once again the media are beating the drum and many investors are contemplating what role, if any, commodities should play in their portfolio decisions. Jim Rogers is unquestionably an investment genius and a commodities guru. His recommendation, to avoid the popular investment themes of the day and look for the undiscovered, is universally sage advice.

Do commodities as an investment class, given all the recent attention, hype, and speculation, still meet the requirement of being away from the herd? Undoubtedly, they did in 2001. The main commodity indexes then were much lower than they were in 1980, as can be seen in Figure 12.1. Rallies over the following 20 years were brief and mild and the underlying trend was down. After 2001, it was a different story, and a forceful case for commodities could be made based on 20 years of underinvestment by producers and poor returns for investors. All the major commodity indexes exploded upward after 2001, gaining around 250 percent by the peak in mid-2008. Fortunes were made and Jim Rogers's fame spread from professional circles to Main Street America.

Mania, as we discussed in Chapter 6, is an appropriate term to describe the commodity frenzy before the bubble burst in the second half of 2008. The decline took the broad commodity indexes down about 35 percent, and some, like oil, natural gas, and copper, fell by between 70 percent and 85 percent. Commodity prices generally lag the business cycle upturn, as it takes time to work off excess inventories. However, in this cycle, commodities bottomed in March 2009 coincidentally with the stock market, a highly unusual phenomenon, and rallied sharply through the rest of 2009. It seemed apparent that the bullish investment thesis for commodities before the crisis was left intact.

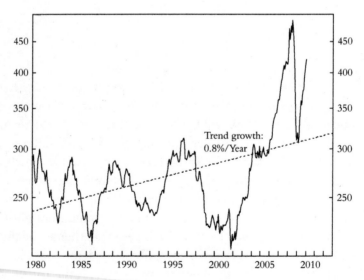

Figure 12.1 CRB All Commodities Index, 1980–2009
Source for data: Commodity Research Bureau.
Note: Dashed line represents trend from 1980 to 2009.
Source: Chart courtesy of BCA Research Inc.

Hedge funds and pension funds, which are the institutional component of the herd, have continued to pour money into commodities with the rationalization that they are an attractive asset class that is uncorrelated with traditional stock and bond investment classes.

Exchange-traded funds (ETFs), which cater to the retail investor, have exploded in volume. They are products that are affordable to virtually anyone and their popularity is worth noting because the retail investor is the other part of the herd. The explosion in ETFs and commodity futures as well has also caught the attention of the authorities, who are worried about upward pressure on the price of energy and other sensitive commodities. This is another indication that the renewed bull market in commodities is well observed, mainstream, and a potential mania candidate. The other side of the story is that when an asset class has become highly popular to nonprofessionals, the makings of a major setback are usually being put into place. A little background should be helpful to investors trying to decide whether to play the commodity game.

Some Background

Commodities are products that generally get consumed as inputs into physical products. Think copper, crude oil, natural gas, coffee beans, sugar, pork bellies, cotton, and potash. When they are consumed, they disappear. This is even true to some extent with gold and other precious metals, much of which goes into jewelry and the arts. However, precious metals don't really disappear, and, if the price is high enough, can be melted down and returned to the market. It can also be true with base metals. It wasn't so long ago, for example, that copper coins were melted down in a previous bull market because the copper content was worth more than their face value.

Commodities must be produced in ever-larger quantities to service a growing world population that aspires to a higher living standard. To increase supply, you need time, money, and expertise. These properties make commodities a real, as opposed to a financial, asset. It is not easy to increase the supply of many commodities, and rising costs eventually must be reflected in rising prices. Governments can print money but they can't print oil, copper, or soybeans, and this appeals to a lot of investors. Most of the well-known, heavily used commodities have liquid markets, either for cash payments or as listed contracts that trade in markets called futures. The latter require very small down payments, relative to the size of the total contract. Often it can be as little as 5 percent. The down payment is called margin. Trading in futures has existed for centuries because it has great advantages over the cash market. You don't have to store the wheat or copper in your backyard. You never have to take delivery; when, say, your September contract is about to come due, you sell it and buy a further-out contract. You can maintain your position by continuing to roll one contract into another indefinitely, as long as your margin holds out (i.e., the price of the commodity doesn't drop to the point where your margin is below the required minimum). Another advantage of futures markets is not so well known. Studies have shown that the commodity futures markets outperform the cash or spot market considerably.[2] The futures markets also allow actual producers to hedge against a decline in price. For example, farmers can reduce the risk of a big price drop when their crops are ready for market by selling them in the futures market at the price prevailing at the time of sale, rather than the price prevailing at the time they actually deliver their crops to the market.

Commodities traders have been around for centuries. Some are specialists, while some are speculators who believe they can beat the professionals, or just enjoy the gambling. With the proliferation in recent decades of futures markets in dozens of different commodities, the investment appeal has broadened dramatically. Supply always rises to meet demand, and this has been evident in the creation of new commodity products. Investors can now buy a variety of commodity index contracts, commodity funds, and commodity ETFs, which provide diversification. ETFs are investment products with very low fees that trade like stocks on the stock exchange. With the surge in new products, commodities markets have become democratized. It is very easy to put your money to work, either in individual commodities or in a basket of commodities, and, for a few thousand dollars or less, anyone can play.

Since commodities are considered a real asset as opposed to a paper asset, many people believe that they offer protection from inflation. The evidence, discussed next, is not so clear-cut. However, with the wall of money unleashed by the Great Reflation, investors may want to take a serious look at owning some as part of a broader diversification strategy for their portfolios. Before jumping in, they need to look closely at the investment case.

The Investment Case

Commodities as an investment class have received a lot of attention over the past eight years, perhaps way too much. They have been hyped in the media by investment advisers, commodity services, and popular books. Many well-known and successful pension funds and endowments, encouraged by investment consultants, have helped to popularize the notion of investing in commodities as a separate, alternative asset class.

There is a simple reason why commodities have become so popular. Figure 12.2 shows how well they did from the top of the tech bubble in early 2000 until the great crash in 2008–2009, outperforming the stock market by a very wide margin, although they have only just matched

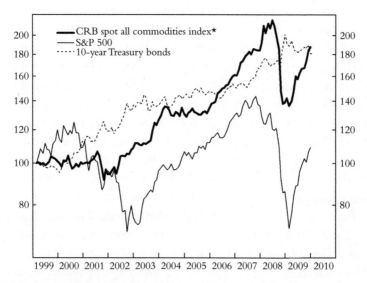

Figure 12.2 Total Return: Commodities, Stocks, and Bonds
*Source for data: Commodity Research Bureau.
Note: All series rebased to January 1999 = 100.
Source: Chart courtesy of BCA Research Inc.

the total return on bonds. Profits in commodities can be spectacular over short periods because prices are volatile and people frequently employ a lot of leverage. Even taking into account the 35 percent fall in commodity prices after the 2008 peak, the main indexes are still up 80 percent from 1999 compared with zero total return on the S&P. Therefore, in spite of their big setback during the crisis, the reputation of commodities as a stellar mainstream portfolio performer is still intact. Bullish sentiment has already heated up again with the early signs of U.S. economic recovery in 2009. More important, the huge Chinese infrastructure spending has stimulated that country's appetite for commodities once again. Moreover, China has trillions of dollars in currency reserves and Chinese enterprises have been buying resource companies and tying up future production with special financial deals, adding extra spice to the commodity story. However, there are always two sides to every investment thesis.

First, let's look at the potential positives. Commodities are a diverse asset class in their own right, negatively correlated according to a number of studies with stocks, bonds, and other financial instruments.[3] Commodity indexes are usually positively correlated over the short to intermediate term with generalized price inflation. That was particularly true in the 1970s. However, it was not so in the blow-off that occurred from 2002 to 2008. If the impact of sharply rising energy and food prices were removed from the general price index, the latter did not show any significant gains at all; that is, commodities and general inflation were not correlated in that six-year period. In addition, during the 2002–2008 period, commodities, stocks, and bonds all moved together. This period is long enough to cast serious doubt on whether the previous negative correlations will hold in the future, and hence investors need to take the diversification story with a grain of salt. The one exception is the U.S. dollar. It does seem that all periods of dollar weakness coincide with rising commodity prices. This was true of the 1970s, 2002–2008, and after March 2009. Moreover, commodities fell and the dollar rose in the nine months ending March 2009.

The widespread expectation is that the unprecedented reflationary stimulus will continue to cause depreciation of the U.S. dollar against all major floating currencies. Additionally, as we discussed in previous chapters, the U.S. reflation will stimulate strong monetary expansion and spending in countries like China that have pegged their currencies to the dollar. As a result, commodities, in general, will get a positive push from both these sources.

The second reason commodities should be of interest to investors is that they have been a good play on the spectacular recent growth in China, India, and other rapidly developing countries. This is a structural story, separate from the cyclical recovery now underway in developing countries. Their per capita consumption of most commodities is very low compared to the West and has a long way to go to catch up. For example, China's per capita consumption of energy is one-sixth and one-quarter that of the U.S. and Korea, respectively. By investing in commodities or commodity-producing companies or countries, investors can participate in their growth but avoid the complexities of investing directly in their stock markets.

The third reason for considering commodities is that there are dozens of individual commodities to choose from. There are foods, textiles, metals, energy, and so on, each of which responds to its own supply and demand pressures, as well as general macro forces. There is always a bull or bear market somewhere, even though the commodity indexes themselves may be flat for an extended period, and the diligent, energetic sleuth can find opportunities if prepared to invest the time and energy.

The Long-Term Trend

Cycles are always seductive because there appears to be a deterministic element that can be used as a substitute for time-consuming careful analysis. Investors should guard against this temptation; they need to always take a hard look at the facts. Most important, it is necessary to keep in mind that prices are determined by demand in the short run and supply in the long run. The evidence is overwhelmingly clear that over very long periods of time supply has always risen sufficiently to sustain a very powerful long-term inflation-adjusted decline in commodity prices as a whole. The reason is that the world has abundant natural resources, and where these have tended to run out, technology has always come to the rescue, driven by profit incentives to create either more supply or close substitutes. Demand in the long run has also done its bit in adjusting to high relative prices by shifting to alternatives.

This long-term story of declining real prices of commodities through history has been well documented in an excellent research piece by Martin Barnes,[4] a longtime managing editor at the *Bank Credit Analyst*. Over the past 210 years, as shown in Figure 12.3, industrial commodities adjusted for general inflation have fallen about 70 percent. Three bellwether commodities – wheat, cotton and copper – have fallen between 75 percent and 85 percent over this period.

These declines are a sobering reminder to investors that the bull case always faces a huge headwind. Moreover, the declines occurred over a period in which world population grew from one billion to six and a half billion and per capita real incomes grew much faster. Clearly, demand has grown sharply for 200 years; inflation-adjusted prices fell because supply is extraordinarily elastic over long periods.

As a result of these secular trends, commodities have proven to be a disastrous long-term investment. Figure 12.4 shows industrial commodities relative to total return on equities, bonds, and cash. Since 1900, relative to equities, industrial commodities have fallen 99 percent. Relative to bond returns the decline has been 90 percent, and relative to cash it has been almost 95 percent. This is a fundamental lesson that commodity investors should never forget—huge demand increases do not lead to rising prices in the long run. And relative to financial assets, long-term investors are throwing money away by investing in commodities on a buy-and-hold basis. Commodities may be a hedge against inflation in the short term, but the evidence shows they are not over long periods.

The 18-Year Cycle

There is a popular case for commodities vis-à-vis equities based on cyclical trends. Proponents claim that we are only halfway through an 18-year rising cycle, a view that could be consistent with the bull case based on the potentially inflationary consequences of the Great Reflation. This view has been used to support strong recommendations that investors hold significant positions in commodities. For that reason, it is worth examining in some detail.

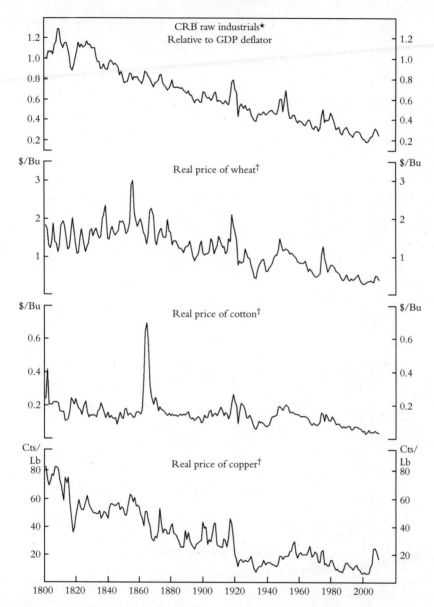

Figure 12.3 Real Commodity Prices: Long-Term Bear Market, 1800–2009
*Source of data: Commodity Research Bureau.
†Adjusted by the GDP deflator.
Source: Chart courtesy of BCA Research Inc., *Bank Credit Analyst*, July 1996.

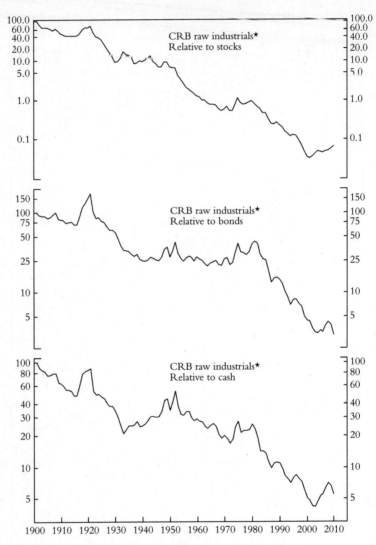

Figure 12.4 Commodities: Relative Returns, 1900–2009
*Commodity Research Bureau.
Note: All series rebased to 1900 = 100.
Source: Chart courtesy of BCA Research Inc.

The cycle authors, Barry Bannister and Paul Forward,[5] looked at data back to 1870 to show that stocks relative to commodities moved in a cyclical pattern averaging about 18 years. We reproduce the chart as Figure 12.5. The basic conclusion from their study that is relevant for the present is that the bull market relative to equities that started in 2000 will extend out toward 2018.

A close look at the data indicates the following: From 1870 to about 1910, there was a 40-year relative bear market for commodities (i.e., stocks outperformed). From 1910 onward, Figure 12.5 shows that there were three other periods of underperformance, one lasting 10 years, the other two lasting 20 years. The average underperformance for the four periods was almost 23 years. Figure 12.5 also shows four periods when commodities outperformed stocks, the first two associated with World War I and World War II, the third in the 1970s, and the fourth since 2000. The range is eight to 12 years, and the average is 10 years.

By separating bull and bear markets, a quite different interpretation from the one generally put forward by commodity bulls is warranted. First, it is evident that two of the four periods of commodity outperformance were related to war. Therefore, barring another major war in the near future, the bull thesis based on historical data and the cyclical pattern must

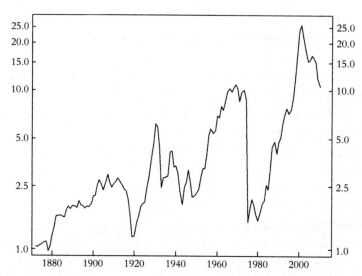

Figure 12.5 Stock Prices Relative to Commodity Prices, 1870–2009
Note: Rebased to 1870 = 1.
Source: Chart courtesy of BCA Research Inc.
Source for data: Warren and Pearson data from 1870 to 1890; WPI BLS from 1891 to 1913; PPI All Commodities Index from 1914 to 1973; CRB Spot All Commodities Index from 1974 to date, Commodity Research Bureau.

be suspect. Moreover, even apart from wars, it makes no sense to average the bull and bear cycles together to get the magic 18-year cycle because the former are only half as long as the latter. Rather, a more useful interpretation of what is pretty shaky cyclical evidence is that commodity bull markets last about 10 to 11 years. The current relative bull market started in 2000, almost two years before the actual rise in commodity prices as stocks fell faster than commodities after the tech crash. Therefore, for what it's worth, by the end of 2009, commodities based on a deterministic interpretation of the data may have covered about 80 to 90 percent of the up cycle, not the 50 percent suggested by the 18-year Bannister-Forward cycle. Therefore, it is not improbable that the recovery in commodity prices since March 2009 may turn out to be a bear market rally and fade much earlier than the hardcore bulls believe. This would still leave room for another cyclical bull market in commodities several years from now, based on sustainable economic recovery and another long wave expansion. In the meantime, most commodities are in surplus and the world remains very deflationary.

Commodity Investing in the Shorter Term

The short-term case for investing in commodities as an asset class rests on five major factors; low U.S. interest rates and enormous liquidity, a falling dollar, massive demand from China and other fast-developing countries, the potential for a general asset mania, and underinvestment in most commodities in the previous 30 years.

Let's look at the first four bullish factors. Later we look at the fifth—the underinvestment thesis. First, U.S. short-term interest rates have been near zero for over a year and will continue to be low for some time. Therefore, the cost of holding commodities is almost nonexistent. The world is awash in liquidity. Second, the dollar is weak and the long-term trend will remain down. Third, demand from China and other rapidly developing countries has recovered markedly and industrial economies have turned up in the second half of 2009. Fourth, the Great Reflation against the backdrop of weak general inflation and low capacity utilization and massive liquidity in developing economies means that there is great potential for a resumption of the financial mania prevailing before the crash. The avalanche of new money has to go somewhere, and if it is not going into rapid economic growth, it will go into investable assets, as the theory goes. Figure 12.6 compares the current commodity cycle, which started in late 2001, with the mania cycle that began in 1971. Like the gold comparison shown in the previous chapter (Figure 11.3), the two commodity cycles are tracking closely. Although commodities in late 2009 are somewhat lower than they were at the same point in the previous cycle, it is clear that the potential for another leg up in the commodity mania exists.

Undoubtedly, there is considerable support for this view, and plenty of emotion in the commodity arena is evident, which could easily drive prices higher in the near term. Some exposure to commodities or commodity-producing corporations in today's uncertain world is not a bad idea. However, there are also grounds for caution.

First, this is not a new story. As Jim Rogers himself pointed out, he likes to be away from the herd. Figure 12.7 highlights two measures of sentiment. The first shows net speculative positions as a percentage of open interest on commodity futures, the second the percentage of bullish commodity market traders. Both measures show that the degree

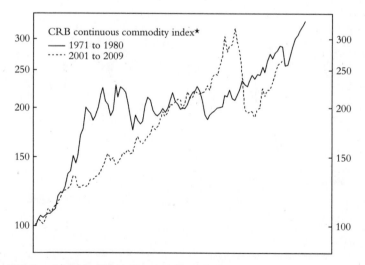

Figure 12.6 A Tale of Two Commodity Manias
*Source of data: Commodity Research Bureau.
Note: Both series rebased to 100 at start of bull market.
Source: Chart courtesy of BCA Research Inc.

Figure 12.7   Commodities and Two Measures of Sentiment

*Source of data: Commodity Research Bureau.
†Source of data: Commodity Futures Trading Commission; futures contracts include 17 commodities.
‡Source of data: Marketvane.net; includes 10 commodities.
Source. Chart courtesy of BCA Research Inc.

of bullishness has risen sharply. It is normal for it to rise with commodity prices but extreme readings are a danger sign. The readings in late 2009 were still below the peaks of 2008, but the rising trend is clear evidence that the bull market has been discovered.

Moving averages are another tool investors can use to decide how aggressively they want to be positioned in commodities. We discussed this tool in previous chapters. Figure 12.8 shows the CRB Index and the three and nine-month moving averages. Investors could have entered the post 1971, 2002, and 2009 bull markets and exited the post 1980 and 2001-2002 and the 2008 bear markets in a timely way by following the moving averages relative to the Index and looking for crossover signals and trend reversals in the moving averages. However, we repeat our earlier warning. Trend reversal indicators can give whipsaw signals and must be used with fundamental indicators.

One of the most important of the fundamentals that investors should follow is supply and demand. Investors tend to look mainly at the latter because it is more visible. However, supply is also critical. The fact is that high prices for many commodities have prevailed for almost a decade, enough time for new investment to start increasing supply, particularly as interest rates are low. Even after the decline in 2008–2009, prices are still 50 to 60 percent above the levels of 1980 to 2000, and average costs of production reflecting global deflation have been falling. Already capital markets are making funds available to create new supply and finance corporate acquisitions. Rising stock prices of commodity producers lower their cost of capital and speed up investment in new projects.

There is another supply factor that will be important in coming years. A high proportion of commodities are produced by developing countries and many are strapped for money. As a result, they are speeding up development and softening terms for foreign investors. Mongolia, for example, recently signed a huge, long-delayed mining development project, Oyu Tolgoi, that will become one of the world's largest copper producers. This may be the tip of the iceberg as other developing countries rush to speed up resource projects.

The world economy is still far below the 2007 level, and the prospect of slow recovery means that most commodities will remain in surplus

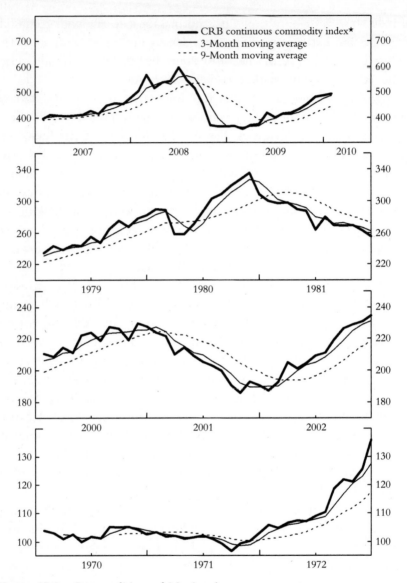

Figure 12.8   Commodities and Moving Averages
*Source of data: Commodity Research Bureau.
Source: Chart courtesy of BCA Research Inc.

for years. Thus, there are plenty of supplies of almost everything to satisfy demand from China and other developing countries for the foreseeable future—a demand that is likely to be less robust than before the crash once artificial infrastructure stimulus abates.

Higher prices and luck have also had time to stimulate technology to create new supply and close substitutes. For example, shale gas technology has vastly expanded natural gas supplies and knocked the price down over 50 percent from the peak a few years ago. New technologies in wind, solar, batteries, and conservation will, in time, reduce demand for oil in developed economies and slow increases in developing countries. This is classic adjustment to high relative prices that have been the hallmark of commodity economics for thousands of years.

There is another factor warranting some caution. Investors should be well aware, from the experience of 2008 and earlier, that a major rise in the price of key commodities such as food and energy can derail economies, particularly those that are large net importers. For example, every big rise in the price of oil since the 1970s has led to a U.S. recession. In 2008, the spike to $150 oil and the run-up in food prices pummeled U.S. consumers, draining incomes at a time when they were already struggling with too much debt and falling house prices. Therefore, investors should never ignore the broad economic impact of sharp commodity price increases. Owners of commodities profit, but not for long, as a large relative price increase always damages other investments by knocking out the underpinnings from the economy and debt structure. Fragility in both will likely prevail for at least a few years. The world simply cannot take another big shock like 2008 in commodity prices. If that were to happen, all investors should run for cover, including those invested in commodities.

Conclusion

Conservative investors should tread carefully when it comes to investing in commodities as an asset class. Most of the bullish arguments don't hold much water from a long-term perspective, including the hedge against inflation and the negative correlation with stocks and bonds. The demise of the private debt supercycle and the long wave decline in the United States and much of the developed world provide a story of deleveraging and deflation. There will be no general inflation for the next

(continued)

few years at least, and one thing is clear—commodities are no hedge against deflation.

The best case for commodities is in the short run and is based on fears of U.S. monetary excesses and a U.S. dollar collapse as a consequence of the Great Reflation. This fear has generated enormous financial demand for commodities as opposed to consumption demand, and in the short run it could undoubtedly drive prices higher and even create another leg to the mania that could ultimately rival that of the 1970s. However, it would be a bull run based on speculation and the greater fool theory (an endless procession of speculators prepared to pay higher and higher prices) without much real foundation.

It is crucial to keep in mind that a major commodity price rise on the back of a fragile world economy and financial system is a recipe for disaster—another economic downturn, financial crisis, and bear market in commodities. So our advice would be to own some commodities if you must but not too much, be conservative with leverage, and be ready to exit if the market gets really frothy as indicated by the sentiment indicators in Figure 12.7. Remember, financial/investment demand is fundamentally different from consumption demand. In the latter case, supply mostly disappears. In the former, it can come back on the market with a vengeance if sentiment reverses.

Chapter 13

Real Estate

I just love real estate; it's tangible, it's solid, it's beautiful. It's artistic from my standpoint and I just love real estate.

—Donald Trump

The U.S. real estate market was the epicenter of the economic and banking earthquake that shook the world in 2008 and 2009 because that is where the most egregious lending and borrowing practices occurred. The epic story of the real estate mania and bust is a very large part of the private sector debt supercycle described in Part I of the book.

Real estate is by far the biggest asset owned by households. In fact, at the top of the real estate market in 2006, households held $22 trillion of real estate versus $9.5 trillion in equities. The problem, as always, was way too much debt. Because rising nominal house prices for so many years came to look like the closest thing to a bulletproof investment, people started to borrow a larger and larger proportion of house values. House prices, in turn, were inflating after 1996 at the fastest rate in over 100 years, if we exclude the brief catch-up period from very depressed levels right after World War II. Lenders became eager coconspirators in this unprecedented house price mania.

Commercial real estate also began to inflate sharply after 2000. That bubble burst with the housing collapse, but it has been following a somewhat different cyclical pattern. Commercial property has long time lags because the process of downward rental adjustment and refinancing of debt, usually undertaken with a five to 10-year maturity, gets spread over a number of years. Hence, the commercial property sector could remain in a downward spiral for some years.

In this chapter, we look at both residential and commercial real estate.[1] It is a market that is highly specialized and dependent on regional characteristics. It is heterogeneous within regional areas and quality varies tremendously. We are not going into details of real estate investing but rather take a top-down look and make a few general observations that we hope will be helpful to the nonspecialist.

Real Estate: Some Background

A diversified portfolio of income-producing commercial properties has produced a real (inflation-adjusted) return of about 5 percent per year over the long run. It is an income play; there has been no significant real appreciation of prices over time, and the return to owners essentially comes from rental income. It is a good inflation hedge and a good portfolio diversifier.

Residential property is quite different. The long-term rate of real price appreciation has been less than half of 1 percent per annum. Real house price data back to 1890 is shown in Figure 13.1 along with the trend of population in the United States. By the end of the 1930s, real house prices were 30 to 40 percent below the 1890s level in spite of a doubling of the population. It wasn't until 1950 that inflation-adjusted prices got back to the 1890s level, and they remained there until the mid-1990s when the mania began. After 1950, the population doubled again and, in particular, household formation, a big driver of housing demand, was extremely high from 1946 to the 1970s, but that was not sufficient to move real house prices upward until the mid-1990s.

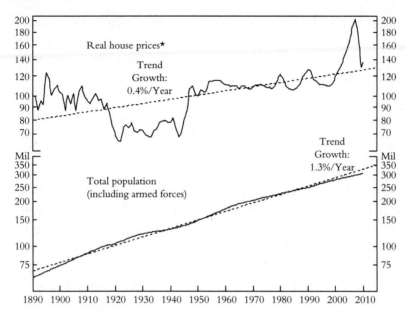

Figure 13.1   Real House Prices and Population Growth since 1890
*Source for data: Robert Shiller.
Note: Dashed lines represent long-term trend.
Source: Chart courtesy of BCA Research Inc.

The long-term data are important to note because they conflict with the widespread notion that houses appreciate steadily and rapidly over time. They do not; when real prices rise above the 0.4 percent trend line shown in Figure 13.1, they always come back to it and usually fall below. In other words, owners of homes, in general and over long periods of time, don't make much money on their homes after adjusting for inflation. What they do get instead is a flow of real, not monetary, benefits that go with living in their own house. That is their return. They also get a proven inflation hedge over the very long run because house prices do appreciate slightly faster than the general price index.

Naturally, there are cycles, as in all markets, and those who buy after a big surge in prices do badly. Those cherry-picking after a big decline, as for example in 2009, can do extraordinarily well if they are patient. Real estate is inherently illiquid and tends to be financed with a lot of debt—over 100 percent was common in the buildup to the housing bubble. Generally, loan-to-value ratios of 70 to 75 percent are the extent of leverage in commercial property, but prices have typically been much more volatile than in the residential sector.

Residential Real Estate

The roughly 32 percent decline nationally in housing prices between 2006 and 2009 was the greatest real estate crash in the past 90 years. The perversion of lending standards relating mainly, but not exclusively, to the subprime lending and securitization orgy has often been blamed, but this is only one part of the story. The seeds of this crisis go back much further—to the supercycle of private debt discussed in Chapter 2.

From 1996 to the peak in June 2006, U.S. nominal house prices increased nationally by 139 percent, an annual compound rate of 9.1 percent.[2] Some markets, like Las Vegas, Miami, and Phoenix, did much better than average. While 9.1 percent may sound rather modest compared with the 18 percent return on equities from 1982 to 2000, it is an extraordinary rise and pretty well matches the return on U.S. stocks from 1996 to 2006. Figure 13.1 shows clearly the extent of the bubble over the 10 years to its top. Prices, according to the Real Home Price Index, rose almost 70 percent above the long-term trend line. And, it must be remembered, home buyers almost always use a lot of leverage. Accounting for that, returns on real estate, even after allowing for mortgage interest, were fabulous. With 30 percent down, the average homeowner's investment would have returned approximately 345 percent over the 10-year period, a 16 percent compound annual return. With more leverage, the profits were even juicier; a 10 percent down payment would have generated a return of close to 940 percent, or about 26 percent compounded annually. A homeowner who could barely scrape together a down payment ended up beating 99 percent of Wall Street's best money managers during this magical era for real estate.

The total value of the stock of U.S. housing increased by about $14 trillion between 1996 and 2006. Where did all the money come from to drive values so high? In the early stages, the market was supported to some extent by profits created by the technology mania.

But the real money came from mortgage lenders, particularly the banks and government enterprises like FNMA and GNMA, and through securitization, a variety of other lenders. By 2000, real estate was seen as an investment capable of producing safe, reliable returns, whereas stocks were seen as risky gambles, having declined 50 to 90 percent during the tech bust.

House buyers were more afraid of being left out of the housing market than they were of making an investment that was leveraged 10 or even 20 to one. In the late stages, banks were bribing people to take the risk, as they required no down payments and granted mortgages for all, and sometimes for more than the value of the house. Real estate speculation became the one casino where you could play with other people's money and keep the winnings for yourself. Anyone with a part-time job or even no job could become a mini Donald Trump. A proliferation of TV shows captured the mood nicely, such as *Property Virgins, Flip That House,* and countless renovation and design reality shows that classified 3,000 square feet as cozy.

As long as a greater fool could be found to keep bidding up prices and credit was plentiful, affordability seemed to be irrelevant. Prices lost touch with people's ability to service debt, and new buyers simply hoped to keep up with interest payments. A perversion of this Ponzi finance frenzy was the flood of home equity extraction. A highly leveraged and increasingly speculative investment could become a piggy bank—a source of income to buy a new car, renovate a bathroom, or put an addition on an already overpriced suburban home. Better yet, why not double up and buy a second house or a couple of condos and rent them out?

The amount of credit wrung from home equity extraction was huge, as owners kept increasing leverage as fast as their house prices were rising. This also depressed the country's aggregate savings and investment, which had disastrous economic effects for the country as a whole. This was discussed in Part I of the book.

In the end there are never enough fools to keep a mania going indefinitely. A crash is inevitable, its magnitude proportional to the size of the bubble. The one-third fall in house prices nationally after the peak wiped out the equity of millions of homeowners, creating unprecedented foreclosures and repossessions.

The Future of House Prices

The housing market has been rigged since the Great Depression. Mass unemployment then led to a very real threat of a workers' insurrection. The perceived failure of free markets and the lack of social safety nets created a dangerous environment for the U.S. political structure. The Roosevelt administration implemented the New Deal, which created a wide range of government agencies and initiatives. Among these, the Federal Housing Administration (FHA) was established to encourage home ownership by backing mortgage lenders with federal insurance and encouraging lending up to 80 percent of the purchase price for up to 20 years. This was a revolutionary change as ready access to credit triggered the beginning of the first property-owning democracy.

Home ownership rates climbed sharply, which is hugely supportive of a stable democracy. However, a government-rigged market always creates moral hazard. Almost everyone came to believe that prices were on a one-way street north.

The crash has now led to even greater and more explicit government intervention in the housing market, with a number of new programs, including tax subsidies, mortgage subsidies, and outright government lending or guarantees for virtually all new mortgages. This has definitely helped to break the downward spiral of house prices, foreclosures, and forced sales. Key questions are whether and when a new bull market might start, supported by huge government intervention. Or, conversely, are those supports just a temporary Band-Aid with more price declines ahead when the government backs away from the subsidies?

The unprecedented collapse in house prices from the peak raises two questions. First, have prices made a full downward adjustment in the competitive, mainly central U.S. markets that do not have supply constraints? The answer is probably yes. On the demand-determined, less competitive, and mainly coastal markets, the full adjustment of prices will be known only after income and employment have stabilized. This may take more time but seemed to be occurring by late 2009. In general, prices nationally have dropped back to the level of the cost of building a new dwelling, which includes land acquisition, building costs, and profit for the builder. In addition, inventories have shrunk very significantly.

The second question is a perennial one after a burst bubble. Will prices, having gone far above the trend line, stop on the way back down at the trend line where they were in late 2009, or fall below? A trend line is determined by the area above it, which is created during the bull market, being offset by a roughly equal area below the trend line. Figure 13.1 shows this to have been true following all bull markets since 1890 and even the minor ones in the late 1970s and 1980s.

The adjustment after the bull market of the mid-1950s was a bit different. Prices never fell sharply but they did remain in a relative decline for almost 20 years, falling from a point above the trend line in the late 1950s to below the trend line. Prices did not move back above the trend line until 1978, and that was temporary. The relative weakness is remarkable as that period was one of high household formation when housing was in great demand.

To gauge where house prices may be heading, we have to take into account both postwar historical experience and the lingering effects of the postcrash environment. Postwar experience would suggest that the most optimistic outcome for the housing market in the period ahead is for inflation-adjusted prices to approach the trend line shown in Figure 13.1 as they have done, and then slide gently below it for a period of years, possibly like the period after the early 1970s. However, it must be emphasized that these are inflation-adjusted prices. If inflation were to ramp up in the years ahead, then nominal dollar prices could actually rise but real (inflated-adjusted) prices fall if the rate of general price inflation is above the appreciation rate of house prices. Owners of houses would then fall behind inflation. They would have to find better inflation hedges if they hoped to keep their overall financial positions from depreciating in real terms. If the general price level were to fall, as in Japan for much of the past 20 years, the trend in house prices would almost certainly resume its decline from current levels.

The postcrash environment does not provide much support for an optimistic scenario. First, the stimulus program has created artificial supports for housing and the apparent stabilization may prove temporary. First-time buyer subsidies, mortgage subsidies, depressed general interest rates, and a temporary moratorium on foreclosures may mean that another decline in prices is in store in 2010 and beyond.

Approximately 20 to 25 percent of all mortgages are under water (i.e., the value of the house is below the outstanding mortgage).

Second, world deflation of general prices is likely to continue for some years. This will negatively affect price expectations, household formation, and risk attitudes of buyers and lenders. The legacy of excess debt of most households will remain an albatross and cause sustained deleveraging. The heavily indebted average household had lost between 25 and 30 percent of their net worth as a result of the crash in both housing and the stock market at the low point in March 2009. It has recovered some of the loss since. The subprime mortgage market, which played a big role in the bubble, is finished until a new generation of idiots and crooks comes along. Conventional mortgage lenders have barely resumed lending and only on a more traditional basis, requiring 20 to 25 percent down payments. With the average house costing between $172,000 (existing home) and $217,000 (new home), a cash down payment of between $35,000 and $45,000 is required. However, the median net worth of renters under 35 years of age— the group most likely to be first-time buyers—is just $7,500. Therefore, entry-level demand for housing will remain extremely weak as first-time buyers will have to start saving and hope for inheritances and gifts from their families. Without first-time buyers, housing markets struggle. Thus government mortgage lenders will have to continue financing almost all first-time house purchases, a questionable situation in the face of out-of-control fiscal deficits.

The combination of the looming pension nightmare for retirees, the demographics of both aging and declining fertility rates[3] (i.e., shrinking birthrates) guarantees two things. First, there will be huge numbers of people forced to liquidate their homes to pay for their old age, and, second, there won't be enough new entrants to the housing market to buy them. This will add substantially, and for years to come, to the supply of homes on the market. Finally, the inevitability of sharply higher taxes to pay for the spiraling fiscal deficits of federal, state, and local governments will also negatively affect the demand for housing by sapping discretionary income.

All is not black for the housing market, though. There are some positive factors, as indicated in Figure 13.2, which should not be ignored. Affordability has greatly improved, driven by low mortgage rates and

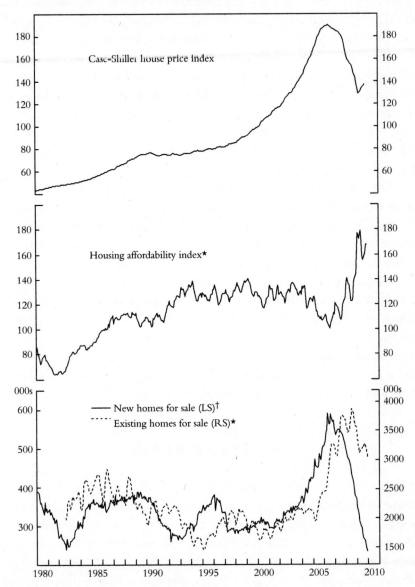

Figure 13.2 House Prices, Affordability, and Inventories

*Source for data: National Association of Realtors.

†Source for data: Department of Commerce.

Source: Chart courtesy of BCA Research Inc.

the 32 percent fall in nominal prices. In addition, inventories of unsold homes have fallen sharply. The socialization of mortgage lending and the pro–home ownership government policy could also be helpful, although dangerous if it encourages people to extend themselves beyond their means. The resets on previously made subprime mortgages are mostly behind us and foreclosures in this area should wind down in the next year or two. However, even if we assume that a more solid housing base is achieved by 2011, these positives are unlikely to do more than just soften the negatives.

Our conclusion is that owning a home, in general, will be a poor investment in the future. Houses will continue to provide great benefits to owners who can comfortably afford them. Houses, on a nationwide basis, are much more affordable and they do not carry the financial risk that existed before the bubble burst. But in a world of deflation, prices, at best, will be lucky to hold their own. Should general inflation return in a few years on account of the Great Reflation, house price appreciation is likely to lag. There have been two lengthy periods when real house prices fell, eventually going below the long-term trend. The first was after the 1890s. Prices did not get back to those levels until the late 1950s. The other period was after the 1950s peak and the low was not reached until the mid- to late-1990s.

Commercial Real Estate

It is not surprising that a massive bubble in the commercial property sector paralleled the bubble in residential real estate. Generally, people assess trends in commercial property by looking at what is happening in the business districts of approximately 30 major metropolitan centers. This is shown in Figure 13.3. Prices rose about 50 to 60 percent from 2002 to the peak in early 2008, approximately half of which reflected multiple expansion (i.e., a higher price for the same income stream); the other half, a sharp escalation in rents. The risk in commercial property is the same as residential—a combination of leverage plus the well-established tendency for inflated prices to fall back to at least their underlying trend line. Rents are cyclical, debt has to be serviced, and it dries up in periods of stress. Forced selling in an illiquid market always

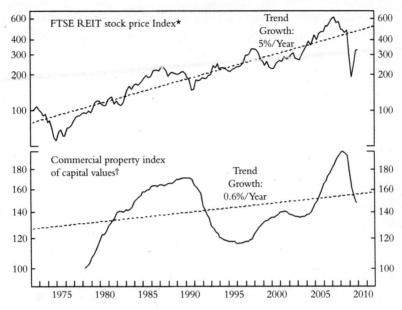

Figure 13.3   Commercial Real Estate: Stock Prices and Property Values
*Source for data: Financial Times Stock Exchange (NAREIT).
†Source for data: National Council of Real Estate Investment Fiduciaries (NCREIF).
Source: Chart courtesy of BCA Research Inc.

translates into steep price declines or, at a minimum, prolonged periods of flat prices in nominal terms and falling real prices when inflation is subtracted.

The precrash bubble was, like most bubbles, fed by easy credit, reduced lending standards, and investor conviction that it was a one-way ride. The slide in commercial property prices after the crash was slower in the beginning than in house prices and started quite a bit later. But this does not mean that the final adjustment will be less. It simply reflects the normal lags. First, properties are usually financed with five-to 10-year terms. As long as the debt is serviced, lenders do not panic. Because rents lag the business cycle, reflecting the long-term nature of most leases, cash flow on buildings holds up initially. But over time, particularly with a recession, vacancies build and leases expire. They are renegotiated down, as debt comes due; prices slide and lenders worry.

By late 2009, prices in this commercial real estate bear market were down about 30 percent or so on average. However, leverage—the loan-to-value ratio—is typically 75 percent and often higher. Large leverage means equity wipeout as prices fall. A 30 percent decline in the face of 25 percent original equity means the mortgage is 5 percent under water. As the loan comes due, no lender in its right mind will renew without a huge injection of new equity. Banks still have in excess of a trillion dollars of write-offs ahead and will remain very risk-averse. Buildings will continue to get thrown on the market, forcing prices down further, which, in turn, feeds the spiral.

It frequently takes years for the full adjustment to occur, and the Great Reflation is unlikely to change this for a very good reason. The bull market of 2002 to 2008 was different from others because commercial rents were inflated by a 25-year bubble in debt, asset prices, and employment in the industries benefiting from the bubble. Inflated sectors such as banking, mortgage lending, and real estate brokerage—anything to do with finance, investing, and real estate—are discussed in Chapter 3. They are big users of office space and there will be a structural contraction in employment in those areas for years. The demographics of aging and low fertility rates will further shrink demand, as we discussed earlier. Thus, very high vacancy rates in office buildings and pressure on rents are likely to be sustained for some time, even as the economy begins to improve.

Conclusion
The real estate hangover is not likely to go away very quickly. Values have improved sharply, and residential prices, on average, are back close to their long-term trend line after adjusting for price inflation. However, we live in a world of deflation, and house prices generally spend some time below the trend line after a surge in prices.

Homebuyers, by all means, should search out good values if they are well capitalized and looking for a place to live as opposed to a speculative investment. Bargains can frequently be found, as there remain plenty of forced sellers. But, on average, inflation-adjusted house price indexes, like the Case-Shiller, are likely to remain flat, at best, for years in areas that are competitive.

Commercial property has not completed its full downward adjustment. Forced sellers will continue to create great opportunities for the well-financed, the patient, and the knowledgeable. Capitalization rates (income yields) have improved substantially, providing some protection. But, like the residential area, don't expect capital appreciation for years as measured by the basic indexes.

Part III

THE FUTURE: IS A RETURN TO LASTING STABILITY POSSIBLE?

Chapter 14

Declining America: Will It Recover?

There is a lot of ruin in every nation.

—ADAM SMITH

I n Part III, we look at some of the broader issues arising from Parts I and II. The Great Reflation, as we discussed earlier, is an effort to pump air back into the 25-year credit and asset bubble that deflated so suddenly and dramatically in 2008 and early 2009. However, it would be naive in the extreme to think that this effort will make the economy and financial system whole again, and that somehow it will restore stability and prosperity without having any seriously negative consequences.

On one level, the financial crisis of 2008 was a manifestation of the failure of the American economic and political systems. The realization that certain key components of the American economic model do not self-regulate is no longer open for debate. On a political level, key individuals were aware of the dangers inherent in the high-risk practices of banks but did not act. The fundamental problem is that these failures go far beyond negligence to the system itself. The ultra-free market, credit-infused model that seemed to be so successful in generating extraordinary growth in the United States is broken and it will not be so easy to fix.

The fundamental reality for investors is that they must deal with a highly uncertain future. Part II discussed asset allocation issues to help investors make practical portfolio adjustments in the face of this great uncertainty.

Part III also looks at some deeper issues lurking beneath the obvious economic and financial distress the United States is now trying to deal with. Clearly, America is in a state of relative economic and political decline, a trend that has been evident for several decades. Some aspects of the decline were masked by the euphoria that resulted from the debt and asset bubble. But now that it is history, the United States must face a darker reality than just trying to clean up after the crisis.

To be sure, much of the developed world is facing many of the same issues; but the fact is that the United States is still the world leader and hegemon in the economic, financial, and geopolitical spheres. Decline of the dominant power has always created huge problems and major dislocations throughout history. When there is a changing of the guard, as there was in the 1920s and 1930s, decision making gets complex, difficult, and frequently ineffectual, and risks inevitably increase.

The Decline of the American Empire

Talk of decline in America has been a popular sport for decades, and the proponents of such views have been pilloried mercilessly. However, the fact remains that, by many measures, the United States is grappling with a number of disturbing long-term problems without much success. In Part I, we talked about the transformation of a 25-year private debt supercycle into a new public sector debt supercycle that will compromise U.S. fiscal flexibility for decades. We also discussed the fallout from deleveraging of the private sector at a time when the long wave economic downturn has resumed.

The latter two are separate but complementary forces. They are powerful, pervasive, long-term, and slow-moving. They will affect all aspects of our lives and well-being and are difficult for the average person to understand. When both the private debt cycle and the long wave are in a positive, rising phase, life is very good. The converse is true when both are in the down phase, as is currently the case. Disequilibrium is prevalent, and painful adjustments have to be made.

It is important to understand that each of the two long-term cycles—the debt and the long wave—are different in their timing phases and different in character. One is purely financial, whereas the other is economic. However, they interact in important ways that create feedback mechanisms. In Chapter 3, we pointed out how, for example, inflation-ary policies were put in place to counter the early negative effects of the long wave downturn, which we believe began around 1972 or 1973. The persistence of inflationary monetary policies, massive fiscal def-icits, and runaway private credit creation had unintended consequences. They created a series of asset bubbles that temporarily interrupted the long wave downturn by overstimulating important parts of the economy. The implosion of the latest asset bubble in 2008 and 2009 caused the deepest economic recession of the postwar period and very nearly triggered a debt deflation at least as severe as the one in the 1930s. The danger was magnified by the fact that the incipient debt deflation after the crash occurred while the long wave was still in its declining phase, a double negative. That is also what happened after the crash in 1929.

In stark contrast to the experience of the 1930s, the authorities this time pulled out all the stops to reflate their way out of the crash and debt crisis. Depression was short-circuited but the reflation and bailouts have created a totally artificial economy, leaving great uncertainty as to what will happen after the government supports are removed.

America's decline also shows up in demographics,[1] another slow-moving, long-term force. The two major factors are the aging of the population and the decline in the fertility rate discussed in the previous chapter. This combination will cause a sharp increase in the old age dependency ratio, the number of old people having to be supported by the working-age population. In the United States, it will amount to a near doubling from about 19 percent to about 35 percent by 2050. Though a less negative prospect than for Europe and Japan, it still represents a seismic shift and raises questions about how the United States will achieve the growth and tax revenue needed to control public deficits while the labor force is shrinking rapidly relative to the retired population.

The other demographic trend that bodes ominously for the United States will be its rapidly shrinking population relative to the rest of the world. The planet is expected to add three billion more people by 2050, almost all of whom will be located in the Middle East, North Africa, and sub-Saharan Africa. They will be young, aggressive, and, in good part, out of work, posing additional security threats for the West and the United States, in particular.

Security costs a lot of money, as the U.S. experience of the past several years in Iraq, Afghanistan, and with homeland security, has demonstrated. The United States is already far overextended financially. This is also true from a military perspective. The United States is having a difficult time recruiting for the army. The suicide rate in the military has doubled since 2004, indicating a deep-seated malaise. On the battle-field, results in Iraq and Afghanistan do not provide much comfort. The nation's inability to deal with Iran, North Korea, and even Somali pirates is further grounds for concern. Writing more than 20 years ago, Paul Kennedy[2] drew attention to the United States' overreach of geopolitical power and how it was paralleling the experience of other great powers that went into serious relative decline. He, like many, pointed out that power can be maintained only by a prudent balance between the creation of wealth and the fiscal capacity to maintain military expenditure at the necessary levels. The United States simply isn't cutting it. The country has become increasingly impotent in meeting its geopolitical commitments. This will be further compro-mised by the enormous fiscal costs of the financial crisis and the resulting sharp decline in fiscal capacity. The connection between shifting resources away from growth and toward military and other non-growth expenditures has always hastened the decline of great powers.

While the long-term trends are clearly disturbing, it is not self-evident that the United States is doomed to terminal decay. The coun-try has demonstrated an inherent ability to regenerate and adapt when faced with difficult situations in the past. However, it does need the wisdom to recognize its problems and the ability to deal with them. This will require exceptional political skills, leadership, and enlightened policies.

Is the United States up to the challenge? Historically, the country acts in a unified and decisive way only after a huge crisis. The experience of 2008–2009 does not seem to qualify because the pain for most people was transient. The reflation has started up the music and people are dancing once again.

Carlo Cipolla[3] has also provided some important insights into the subject of empires in decline. Like Kennedy, he also draws attention to finances running out of control, and the public sector debt burdens squeezing the private sector with inflation and taxation. Change hurts vested interests, and Cipolla draws attention to the evidence that all empires eventually develop resistance to the sort of change that is needed for reform, particularly to generate growth, production, and an increased tax base, and to reverse structural weakness in the economy. For example, we must all wonder what the consequences are of U.S. manufacturing falling to just 12 percent of the economy from 23 percent in the 1960s and 1970s. If the current trend continues, at some point no one in the United States will make anything anymore.

Cipolla points out that empires in decline exhibit arrogance, conceit, and complacency; the focus of people shifts to rights from duties, and the public spirit falters. There are, at such times, many people who make the right diagnosis and forecast the continuation of decline, yet are widely ignored.

Robert Nisbet[4] has useful thoughts on the social and political dimensions of what he calls the "twilight ages." He observes that in such situations of decline, there is a feedback mechanism between declining institutions and eroding values on the one hand, and growing concentration of political power on the other. In the case of the United States, he points to the decline of traditional authority—family, religion, political parties, local communities, voluntary associations, and even class structure. The result is alienation and a rootless mass of people while the bureaucratic state becomes increasingly powerful, and beholden not to moral principles and doing the right thing, but rather to the latest polls and pressure from well-financed lobbyists.[5]

Corruption in such an environment flourishes as we learned so well after the recent crisis and the previous one as well. Social ills—drugs, crime, poverty, obesity, poor health, infant mortality, a huge prison population—become entrenched and are shocking to witness in such a wealthy country. Political paralysis in the United States has become a fact of life, and the warnings of Kennedy, Cipolla, and Nisbet resonate with all thoughtful people. As a result, while we must remain hopeful that the country will pull out of its long slide, we must also be realistic and look for evidence and milestones that policies and outcomes are actually changing for the better. We will return to this theme in the next chapter. For now, it is important to emphasize that the issue of long-term decline of empire does impact and complicate the more immediate challenges of managing through the postcrash environment, the resumption of Kondratieff's long wave economic decline, and the need to get public sector debt under control.

The Long Wave Revisited

As indicated in Chapter 3, there is every prospect that the U.S. economy may well be in the late stages of the long wave downturn, the so-called winter period that precedes the next long wave upturn. We emphasized then that these long cycles are useful as a framework, as a way to think about markets and the process of capitalist evolution. It is not a deterministic model or theory and should not be used to support either apocalyptic or rosy forecasts. It is only one among many influences on our lives. It is a realistic, historical description of technical change and innovation, albeit with painful adjustments along the way. But it does have an upside.

The basic message from past experience is one of eventual economic and financial renewal and progress. This should give us considerable hope, in a currently bleak environment, that eventually the United States will be able to cope much better with all of the negative forces relating to empire decline. What goes down comes back up. The period of renewal and resurgence, however, is a difficult sea change for many who are too old to adapt to new ways of doing things, new technologies, and new institutional arrangements. New skills and retraining are crucial. But history has shown that over very long periods, things do get much better for most people, even though empires come and go. Moreover, as an empire slips past its zenith, the decline is frequently, though not always, long and slow. It is usually a decline relative to other countries, not an absolute. Therefore, we should not be too quick to judge where the United States will be in five, 10, or 20 years.

The long wave analysis does, of course, draw everyone into the issue of timing the overall length of the cycle and, in particular, the different phases. However, even though we reject the idea of determinism and regular periodicity, and much prefer to think in terms of a framework for analysis, we are necessarily forced into consideration of when the current downturn might end. Our view, and it is based on intuition as much as anything else, is that five to 10 years is likely to see us through—subject, of course, to the avoidance of catastrophic policy mistakes, the subject of the next chapter.

It is likely that the crash of 2008–2009 and its aftermath have jump-started the corrective adjustment to the credit excesses and associated speculation of the past 25 years, as well as the need to eliminate excess capacity. Repair and healing will certainly take a lot of time. There will be an extended period of creative destruction, which is an essential part of the bottoming process of the long wave in economic life. It forces consolidation of maturing industries and releases resources —financial, physical, and human—to be used in the next upswing. During this period, it is all too easy to dwell on the obvious negatives of high structural unemployment, economic dislocation, declining industries, bankruptcies, and financial loss and extrapolate them indefinitely into the future. The reason is their high visibility. The more profound interpretation is the opposite—the time for recovery is actually getting closer. However, because movements in the long cycle are slow and their impact complex and less visible, they are not easily understood by the vast majority of people.

It is important to focus on the things that will bring about renewal and the next upswing. First, the long wave downturn has run far beyond its normal life expectancy, suggesting intuitively that an end cannot be far away. Second, the deleveraging of the private sector is under way. While that is a short-term negative, it is an essential part of the reliquefaction of the economy prior to the next long wave upswing. Third, powerful new technologies have been created in recent years and are being put in place. The stage has been set, as in all previous bottomings of the long wave, for innovative new industries to appear and disseminate technologies across a much wider spectrum of the economy.

The key for the United States will be to have a leadership role in the new technologies and innovations, and, on this score, there are grounds for optimism. It is a clear leader in microprocessing, computer technology information processing, supply chain management, and the implementation of technology more generally in all areas of life. It is also among the world leaders in energy technology. Breakthroughs there would have a dramatic impact on U.S. living standards and reduce dependence on supplies from unstable foreign countries, sharply improve the balance of payments, and reduce or eliminate dependence on foreign capital.

There are a variety of other potential game-changers out there, as is always the case near the bottom of the long wave decline. It is never possible to see very clearly how the world will transform or to gauge the timing with any accuracy. This can never be known, but we can watch for signposts along the way that will indicate progress through the bottoming process and whether prospects for growth and stability are improving or deteriorating. The key will be getting from here to there without renewed financial instability and more crises of the sort outlined in Part I.

Will America recover? The answer certainly is yes. The uncertainty is over how well, how quickly, and how durable the recovery might be. In short, will recovery be just another countertrend rally or a genuine, lasting renewal? Unfortunately, we cannot be sure yet that the right policies will be put in place to ensure the happier outcome; it is possible but far from guaranteed. Investors should be hopeful but realistic and vigilant.

One of the signposts for the start of a Kondratieff upswing in the economy would be an increase in production and capacity utilization in the capital goods industry. That is an important sign of deep-seated recovery, because excess capacity is concentrated there during the long wave downtrend. However, it is important to monitor capital goods production that serves industries that are in a secular uptrend. In recent years, the capital goods industry has been devastated by a continuation of falling profit margins from the long wave decline and foreign competition, and the collapse of savings and investment generally in the United States. This must reverse if a sustainable recovery is going to happen.

Nominal interest rates on Treasury securities are also an important indicator, although interpretation of the trend will be complicated by the enormous demands from the Treasury to finance deficits. Extended deleveraging and a reduction in the real rate of interest on corporate debt is also meaningful in timing the next long wave upswing. Around the trough and early stage of the upswing in the 1890s and early 1900s, it was around 3.25 to 3.5 percent. Inflation started to rise slowly in the early 1900s, thus reducing interest rates in inflation-adjusted terms to around 2 percent. In the mid to late 1940s, around the end of the last long wave decline, real corporate bond yields were close to zero. In contrast, by late 2009, real interest rates on medium-grade corporate bonds were around 5 to 6 percent, much higher than was the case around the troughs of the previous two long waves. They must drop back to foster sustained recovery, and that will be another signpost for investors to watch for.

Conclusion

A consequence of three distinct, but not independent, long-term negative trends has created a grim situation in the United States. One trend derives from the bursting of the debt and asset bubble of the past 25 years. A second is the resumption of the long wave economic downturn, the winter phase in the Kondratieff/Schumpeter analysis. The third is the apparent relative decline of the U.S. empire and the discrediting of significant parts of the U.S. economic and political models. The interaction of these three long-term trends has obviously created a huge challenge for U.S. policy makers. It has also created a huge challenge for investors as well, as they have to grapple with the resulting risks and uncertainty.

Unfortunately, the long run eventually catches up with everyone and becomes the here and now, as the United States has discovered. The economic and fiscal costs of the financial crisis are massive. They will continue to drain financial resources that could otherwise be used to relieve or reverse the forces of decline in the United States. The historical evidence is clear; rising fiscal

(continued)

burdens hasten the demise of empires. America's overextended commitments will become increasingly difficult to meet at a time of geopolitical pressure from many hostile countries and groups. Demographic trends will compound these risks; the U.S. population is aging rapidly, so the relative proportion of workers will shrink while the tax burden on them will rise sharply. The long wave decline still has some years to run before the next major upswing gets under way. The authorities are struggling to reflate the economy, but deleveraging of the private sector in the next few years will create a significant headwind.

Adam Smith wisely observed 250 years ago that "There is a lot of ruin in every nation." By that he meant that every nation has its problems and we must be careful not to get too pessimistic about the United States. Plenty of other major countries, notably in Western and Eastern Europe, Japan, and Russia, have even more severe problems than the United States. India and China, in spite of their high growth rates, also have major problems. However, with the United States, it is an entirely different story. When the hegemonic power weakens, bad things tend to happen. As the saying goes, "When the cat's away, the mice will play."

The United States certainly has what it takes to pull out of this situation. Whether it does will depend on politics, policies, wise leadership, and the recapture of the public spirit that made the United States a great power in the first place. It must shake free from the inherent tendency of declining empires to get locked into a political stalemate of vested interests, which hinders change and reform of sclerotic institutions. The next chapter takes a look at politics and some policy options at this juncture.

Chapter 15

Politics and Policies in the Long Wave Trough

I've always believed that America's government was a unique political system—one designed by geniuses so that it could be run by idiots. I was wrong. No system can be smart enough to survive this level of incompetence and recklessness by the people charged to run it.
—THOMAS L. FRIEDMAN[1]

In the preceding chapter we pointed out that there is a confluence of several negative forces at work in the United States—a sort of perfect storm—combining the after-effects of the banking crisis, deleveraging of the private sector, resumption of the long wave economic decline, and evidence of a significant waning of U.S. superpower status, reinforced by rapidly deteriorating fiscal viability.

We also warned of the dangers of excessive pessimism. People have a tendency to extrapolate the recent past indefinitely into the future. It is entirely appropriate to be realistic about the obvious challenges facing the United States, but we have to keep in mind that the outlook for the world has been bearish for the past 50,000 years! Somehow things do get better over time, and that has a lot to do with the long wave, which is essentially one of progress, decline, and progress again, through invention, innovation, and the birth of new industries and institutions that raise living standards and the quality of life.

Whether we are optimistic or pessimistic has a lot to do with time horizons. The basic message from the long wave is bullish, but not yet. Another golden period for the economy could lie ahead, starting in a few years, if the government does not mess it up with counterproductive policies. The stock market has had two major crashes in the last 10 years. Real estate and corporate bonds have also been a disaster for investors. But that was yesterday; markets look ahead. There are plenty of grounds to expect considerable volatility and instability, and we could be some years away before the next secular bull market really gets going. But there is an excellent chance that March 2009 saw the end of the long bear market in stocks that started in early 2000. This may also be true of most categories of risky assets. However, there is no shortage of potential problems, and the financial system will remain fragile, even on the most optimistic assumptions, for at least another two years. That is why we must pay particularly close attention to politics and policies. With wisdom and leadership, we could skate through the next few years relatively unscathed. Wrong policies and poor leadership could easily destroy the shaky grounds for optimism.

From Conservatism to Parochialism

The long wave's power and slow, inexorable movement create feedback into social and political institutions. The MIT System Dynamics Group[2] has researched these issues back to 1850. They studied Democratic and Republican party platforms, State of the Union addresses, and a variety of speeches in European countries. Their work details shifting political and social values that fit a repetitive pattern over the course of the long wave. This is summarized in Figure 15.1.

During the onset of the decline phase, a pronounced shift to conservative values occurs. In the late 1970s, this became evident in the

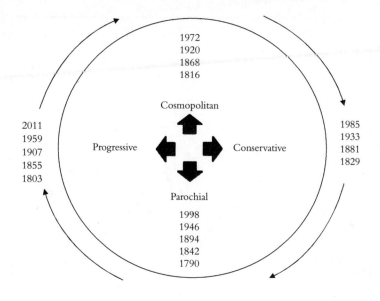

1972
1920
1868
1816

Cosmopolitan

2011   Progressive   Conservative   1985
1959   1933
1907   1881
1855   1829
1803

Parochial

1998
1946
1894
1842
1790

Political value shifts
during the long wave

Economy	Politics
Expansion	Progressive
Peak	Cosmopolitan
Decline	Conservative
Trough	Parochial

Figure 15.1   Long Wave in Political Values
Source: Chart courtesy of BCA Research Inc. Data taken from a talk given by John Sterman at a
BCA. Conference and published by the *Bank Credit Analyst* in October 1992.

United States and United Kingdom with Ronald Reagan and Margaret
Thatcher. Other countries have experienced similar shifts. In the latter
stage of the long wave decline, politics turn from conservative to parochial,
an MIT euphemism for nasty, divisive, inward-looking, and protec-
tionist attitudes. There is an increasing tendency for people to look
out only for themselves or their group at the expense of the collective
welfare.

This is the really dangerous phase of the long wave when structural
unemployment spikes. Figure 15.2 shows that by late 2009, it had
risen to over 35 percent of total unemployed workers from 10 percent in

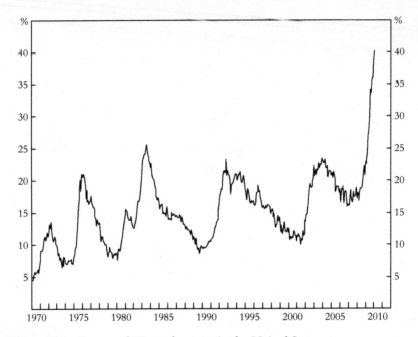

Figure 15.2   Structural Unemployment in the United States
Note: Persons unemployed for over six months as a percentage of total unemployment.
Source: Chart courtesy of BCA Research Inc.

early 2000 and 5 percent in 1970. This is the biggest deterioration
since the 1930s. Huge income inequality, a widely documented phenomenon in recent years and also in the late 1920s, creates mass resentment when major industries go into terminal decline and bankruptcies
spiral. Politicians are then tempted to exploit public resentment to
buy votes. The finger of blame is pointed at others as people look for
scapegoats. During the previous down wave in the 1930s, the world
experienced extreme polarization in politics between the left and right.
Free market capitalism was almost buried. Nazis and Japanese milita-
rists gained power, and fascism took over in many other countries in
Europe; divisiveness in France, the United Kingdom, and the United
States created political paralysis in the face of the obviously growing
economic and geopolitical threats.

The 1870s, 1880s, and part of the 1890s made up another long wave
decline marked by very difficult economic and political conditions.

There were three stock market panics and depressions in less than 20 years and very high structural unemployment. Real wage growth was less than 1 percent a year, less than half of the growth rate during typical upswings. During the latter part of this decline, many intellectuals embraced Marxism and communism, which then began to gain traction in much of Europe even before World War I. Trade unionism took off and governments began implementing far-reaching social policies as a defensive measure. In the United States there was also great political divisiveness. Socialists, radicals, and anarchists began agitating, and bitter strikes occurred for the first time in many cities, factories, and railroads.

There does seem to be a lot of validity in the concept that at the beginning of downturns people become conservative to try to keep a tight grip on their wealth, which they sense is being threatened. At the bottom of the long wave decline, when wealth has become impaired or lost, they become angry, lose faith in the capitalist system, and are tempted by bold economic and political experiments. The worse conditions become, the more desperate people search for radical solutions.

After the current long wave decline had run for a few years, conservative popularity peaked with the end of the Reagan-Thatcher era in the late 1980s. The parochial period followed with a lag. The ending of the Clinton/Blair period ushered in the usual pattern of nasty and divisive politics, which gained momentum under Gordon Brown in the United Kingdom and George W. Bush in the United States. The surprising narrowness of President Barack Obama's victory and the rise of the Sarah Palin phenomenon (which celebrates ignorance and stupidity) in the face of the disastrously failed presidency of George W. Bush speak volumes about the ongoing polarization and loss of faith in U.S. social and political values and the relative ease of exploiting the ill informed. Although we have focused mainly on the United States and United Kingdom, similar political developments have been evident in many other countries. History has shown that this is to be expected. During the bottoming period, the political life expectancy of politicians is short; reelection is difficult, and policies blow with the shifting political winds as the public searches for quick solutions to the economic turmoil.

Future U.S. Policy: Constructive or Destructive?

There is a clear message that history delivers during the parochial (bottoming) stage of the long wave downturn—leaders must manage the process with wisdom and the public must exercise patience. There are no quick fixes. The huge risk is that governments and political parties will do the wrong thing in response to social polarization. The rise of nationalism, fascism, and socialism in the 1930s is a sobering reminder. President Roosevelt, in response to public clamor, imposed as part of the New Deal the National Industrial Recovery Act (NIRA),[3] which some scholars[4] now believe seriously delayed the recovery and sustained unemployment in the 25 percent range until World War II spending started to bring it down. There were, to be sure, a variety of other foolish policies imposed in the 1930s that contributed to the magnitude and duration of the Depression, including the imposition of the Smoot-Hawley[5] tariff regime and the adherence to the rigid gold standard until early 1933.

The Japanese provide another stark reminder of the consequences of policy failures during a long wave downturn. Stock prices are still 75 percent lower than 20 years ago, the economy has stagnated, and gross government debt has ballooned to 220 percent of gross domestic product (GDP) according to the IMF. Japan's policies impeded adjustment in the banking and corporate sector and failed to address pro-growth strategies.

Restructuring

The key for the government is to focus on high-impact policies—those that will speed up the transition to the next long wave upswing. The authorities must avoid rocking the economic and financial boat, which will not be very seaworthy for a few more years. At the same time, do-nothing policies can be disastrous. For example, those enamored with the libertarian right argue that the government should just let failing institutions and companies go under—a completely hands off policy. There are some good arguments for such policies under normal circumstances. Government bailouts create moral hazard which encourages excess risk-taking in the future. Bailouts also slow the needed adjustment and create artificial competition for viable enterprises. However, in extreme cases of systemic debt deflation and incipient financial and economic collapse, standing aside and letting the fire burn itself out can be catastrophic, as we know from experiences like those in the 1930s and in the nineteenth century. Depressions were longer and deeper than they needed to be because of the self-feeding nature of debt deflation, in which falling prices continue to increase the burden of debt, triggering more debt liquidation, which depresses prices further in a self-reinforcing cycle.

Fortunately, the government has avoided this approach, pursuing the wiser course of recapitalizing banks, restructuring some large manufacturing companies, and allowing the fiscal deficit to rise in order to offset the collapse in private spending. No doubt there will be plenty of wasted money and pork-barrel purchasing of votes as political quid pro quo, but in general, liquidation and restructuring should occur in a much more orderly and far less damaging way. Managing the process is critical but adjustment must occur and be thorough. Bad debts and unviable businesses must eventually be liquidated, something the Japanese strenuously resisted.

The example of the Resolution Trust Corporation experience in the early 1990s, which worked to liquidate bankrupt savings and loan companies in an orderly way, served the United States well. Japan, at the other extreme, tried to hide its debt problems for years after its bubble burst at the end of 1989.

Monetary

The next long wave upswing will not happen until much of the excess debt incurred since 1982 is purged. However, deleveraging is difficult in a weak economic environment. The government has tried to ease the pain with bailouts, monetary ease, ultra-low interest rates, and fiscal stimulus. The Federal Reserve has played, and could continue to play, a crucial role in financial repair by keeping short-term interest rates very low, underwriting (together with government) the solvency of the banking system, and injecting large amounts of liquidity. These policies can help to improve prices in the housing, stock, and credit markets, which, in turn, will greatly speed up balance sheet repair and improve private sector liquidity.

Low interest rates ease the burden of debt servicing, and allow financial restructuring to proceed more quickly. That, together with a secure banking system, reduces the perception of risk. Low interest rates on government debt reduce the cost of financing deficits and make the rise in government debt-to-GDP ratio more tolerable.

Low real interest rates on private debt are even more important because, ultimately, it will be corporate capital spending and prudent household borrowing and spending that will lift the economy out of the doldrums. Figure 15.3 shows that interest rates on private debt have fallen sharply vis-à-vis Treasury bond rates since the panic in early 2009. However, by the end of 2009, the 10-year BBB corporate bond yield was about 5.5 percent, far too high. History has shown that long wave upswings have great difficulty getting started until real interest rates on private credit have fallen to low levels. This is particularly important for upstart companies in new technological fields. Low real interest rates tend to raise stock prices and the appetite for risk, which also favors newly emerging companies and industries.

A little help from rising asset prices will go a long way toward financial healing so long as it does not trigger another mania. General price inflation will remain nonexistent through the rest of the troughing process but expectations of inflation will not necessarily remain subdued. The Federal Reserve must ignore such fears in the short run and avoid raising interest rates prematurely. Otherwise, it will risk another bear market in stocks, recession, and extension of the long wave decline. Further balance sheet deterioration would result. The Federal Reserve did such a thing in 1936–1937, causing a steep stock market decline and another recession. The Japanese central bank was also guilty of premature tightening in the midst of their post-1989 deflation, with similar results.

Should asset price inflation in the United States become a bubble while the economy remains fragile, there are policies available other than a general rise in interest rates. The authorities, for example, could increase margin requirements on commodities and equities, require larger down payments on homes, and intrude in other ways to control credit-financed purchases of assets that are deemed to be inflating dangerously.

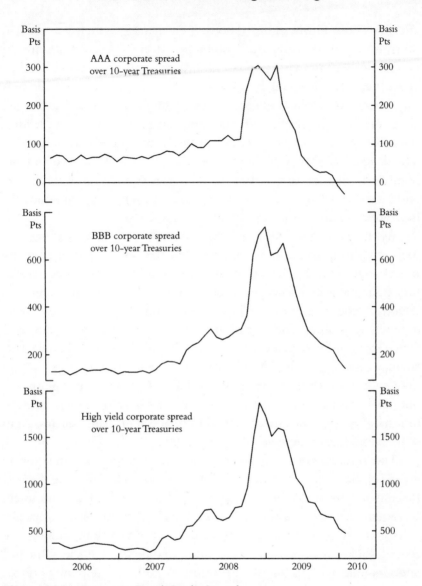

Figure 15.3 Corporate Bond Credit Spreads
Source for data: Merrill Lynch.
Source: Chart courtesy of BCA Research Inc.

Regulation

There is no dispute over the huge role played by financial institutions in the crisis, and the public outrage is palpable. As a result, new and meaningful regulations in the financial arena appeared to be a certainty after the crash. Financial institutions, their managers, their perverse pay incentives, and the egregious lending practices in recent years are the perfect scapegoats, and populist politicians can look good to their constituents by pillorying bank executives at public hearings. Certainly no objective observer would argue against tougher, more effective regulations on financial institutions' practices, particularly to do with lending standards, balance sheet risk, and properly structured pay incentives. The dangers, as always, lie in the potential to create badly thought-out regulations that fail to improve the workings of the system while creating distortions and excessive costs that push entrepreneurs into the back alleys where they can once again evade controls.

As the year 2009 advanced, the effort to reregulate was increasingly caught up in political squabbles and the outcome is not certain. It is crucial to break the grip of self-interested lobby groups on regulatory policy and its execution. Proper authority and accountability are essential; otherwise reform will fail. Raging turf battles across the many different regulatory bodies and among lawmakers do not bode well for effective reform. Regulation is far too political and influenced by corrupt lobbying in the United States. If that does not change, we can fully expect a return to the abuses of the past. Regulatory failure will not derail the next upswing, but it would certainly encourage a return to instability once the current mood of financial prudence abates. Signs of this were becoming evident by late 2009.

The most important regulatory area of dispute is whether supervision of financial institutions should be removed from the Federal Reserve and given to a new, powerful regulatory body. There are useful precedents for such a structure. In Canada, which did not experience a systemic banking crisis and required no bank bailout money, the central bank has responsibility for monetary policy and the Office of Superintendent of Financial Institutions (OSFI) has responsibility for the soundness of financial institutions. It is a federal body, professionally staffed and apolitical, equipped with both authority and accountability. OSFI has the power to close down financial institutions and no one messes around with it.

A powerful, apolitical federal institution to regulate the U.S. banks and other financial institutions would go a long way toward ensuring future stability and dramatically reducing the risk of financial institutions speculating on the back of weak balance sheets. However, in the end, it is not so much the rules as the competence and integrity of the regulators that will ensure a sound financial system. The key is to remove politics, theology, and lobbyists from regulation and end overlapping jurisdictions, fuzzy authority, and lack of accountability; and staff it with nonpartisan people having wisdom and integrity. We can hope, but the track record is not comforting.

The Fiscal Deficit

Chapter 4 outlined the potentially catastrophic explosion in fiscal deficits and the rising government debt-to-GDP ratio that lie ahead. Both government and private calculations consistently show that the government debt-to-GDP ratio is heading towards 100 percent in a few years and much higher in the long run. Japan has given us a test tube experiment of what happens when policies to deal with a deflating economy and fiscal deficits are mishandled. Japan has had sustained massive deficits and a spiraling debt-to-GDP ratio of 220 percent, unprecedented in peacetime in Western-oriented countries. In spite of, or perhaps because of this, there has been little or no growth. The deficits have surely helped to avoid a depression and have supported reliquefaction of the economy, but they have not allowed Japan to avoid stagnation.[6] The economy's growth from 1989 to 2009 has averaged just 1 percent.

The U.S. fiscal deficits will continue to be absolutely necessary in the short term to pull the economy out of the current slump and, in particular, to support the deleveraging of the private sector. The deficits reflect a collapse in tax revenues, massive bailouts, and an increase in automatic stabilizer payments such as unemployment insurance. They are antideflationary. The deficits will not, per se, cause inflation or higher interest rates until well after deflationary pressures disappear.

The United States can live with a much higher government debt-to-GDP ratio in the near term. It did so after World War II when debt reached close to 120 percent of GDP. The United Kingdom has had even higher debt-to-GDP ratios. They reached 250 percent after the Napoleonic Wars and World War II and 175 percent after World War I. Calamity did not happen after these war-related debt episodes because growth resumed once peace was established and the public maintained confidence in the integrity of the monetary standard. The key to confidence is to establish a credible structural plan that is linked to growth; that is, the government takes a growing share of a growing pie. The problem is going to be getting growth in the next five to 10 years alongside deleveraging and an extension of the long wave decline.

The United States must institute the same sort of policies that were associated with previous escapes from high government debt ratios once stability is established. Credit rating agencies are already considering downgrades to sovereign debt issued by countries like the United States and the United Kingdom because they do not yet see a credible plan of deficit reduction. Such policies must be overwhelmingly focused on growth, which will in itself generate much higher tax revenue. It is always easier to take from a growing pie. Increases in tax rates may well be necessary, but they should be of a nature that minimizes the impact on growth and avoids perverse incentives. Populist governments in political trouble cannot be expected to take this approach.

Managing the reduction in the U.S. government debt ratio will not be easy. There is a danger that the government might impose excessive tax increases, impose them on the wrong targets, and get the timing wrong, as Japan did in its struggle to balance stimulus with excessive deficits. There is also a danger that the government may ignore deficit reduction until it is too late out of fear of political backlash. It may push for more social expenditure increases—for example, on health insurance—to buy votes. This would add to the deficit and make eventual tax increases that much more burdensome. Another potential danger caused by precarious government finances would be that the United States reverts to isolationism and cuts military expenditures. This has occurred in similar situations in the past. If so, it would do irreparable damage to confidence in the United States as an effective geopolitical police officer and partner. It would encourage U.S. enemies and would-be regional hegemons to become much more aggressive and would risk more substantial wars.

Social Policies

The late stages of the long wave decline create a huge army of disadvantaged and resentful people—workers, managers, homeowners, investors, and the unemployed. The demands for more and improved social policies spiral upward, while the ability of the government to meet those demands declines. Subpar economic activity, incomes, and profits translate into inadequate tax revenues while bailout and social safety net funding soars. Recently, the International Monetary Fund (IMF) published a study showing that the permanent loss in output (which reduces tax revenue) from serious crises is about 10 percent after seven years.

Managing disappointed public expectations is extremely difficult and requires great political leadership. The United States has been sorely lacking comprehensive medical insurance for approximately one-sixth of the population, roughly 45 million people. President Obama was elected in good part on fixing this. New legislation is moving through Congress and the cost, if enacted into legislation, could be in the trillions of dollars at a time of rapidly rising government debt ratios—hardly what the country needs from an economic and financial perspective.

International Monetary Reform

At this point, it is time to circle back to our views outlined at the beginning of the book. Chapter 1 stated that the key to achieving long-term financial stability and ending the Age of Inflation is to properly fix the international monetary system. This will require the imposition of international and domestic monetary discipline and limiting growth in credit to growth in the economy (i.e., no more debt supercycles). Discipline has been sorely lacking for most of the time since 1914. Exceptions occurred briefly in the 1930s (at the wrong time) and in the early post–World War II years.

The transition through to the end of the long wave decline will continue to have very high structural unemployment and slow, halting growth. There will be no lobby for monetary discipline, whether in the United States or elsewhere. Even China, which calls repeatedly for monetary discipline in the United States, behaves quite differently when its own unemployment is an issue. A case in point is recent Chinese monetary stimulus. A major part of their overall reflation plan focused on increasing bank loans to almost anyone. By late 2009, they were rising at an annual rate of 35 percent.

We are living in a world of parochial politics and there are no financial superpowers with the clout that the United Kingdom and United States wielded in 1944 when they pushed through the Bretton Woods agreement (BW I). The Chinese and other surplus nations will continue to make plenty of noise over potential U.S. monetary debauchery, but in the final analysis, they will hold their noses and buy U.S. dollars—at least for the time being. No major exporter wants its currency to fall against the U.S. dollar in a time of economic distress and potential deflation. The world of Bretton Woods II (BW II)[7] is alive and well and will continue. It is based on a floating dollar for the developed world and currency pegs against the dollar for most of the rest of the world.

However, this period of uneasy international monetary stability— a "balance of financial terror," in the words of Larry Summers—will not last for long, perhaps three to four years. A new system must be put in place during this breathing spell. It will be a Herculean task because the international financial world is totally divided on the big issues and there is no leadership available with the experience, financial power, and credibility to make it happen. The United States is in significant, relative decline on a number of fronts, and the United Kingdom has been for many decades. Moreover, the European Union and Japan have serious problems of their own and do not demonstrate effective leadership.

The United States is still the reserve currency country of the world, and as a result of massive current account deficits for years has run up a huge tab with foreigners, totaling $4 trillion to central banks alone. China, Japan, Germany, Russia, and the Organization of Petroleum Exporting Countries (OPEC) are the main surplus countries with positive current account balances averaging about $1.2 trillion over the past two years. Together they hold about $2 trillion, roughly half the dollar holdings of all central banks. Even they will not be able to force change on the United States. The best they can do is complain and use their dollars to diversify into assets that will protect them from dollar depreciation and the long-term threat of price inflation. However, the United States would be extremely unwise to remain complacent about its precarious financial position. Failure to deal with it will guarantee a major dollar crisis at some point in the future.

There has been no end of proposals for international monetary reform since the cracks began to appear in BW I in the early 1960s. Robert Triffin and Jacques Rueff[8] famously debated the issues then, and that discussion remains highly relevant today. Both agreed on the cause of the problem: Dollars held as reserves by foreign central banks create an inflationary bias—both money and credit—in the international monetary system, and lead to persistent current account deficits in the reserve currency country. This ultimately undermines confidence in both the reserve currency and the country behind it, and eventually leads to deflation because of excessive debt and overbuilding of capacity in the inflated areas. Fragility and the risk of crises grow over time. Rueff wanted a return to the gold standard at a revalued gold price high enough for the United States to pay off its liabilities. Chapter 11 pointed out that this would now require a gold price of $20,000 per ounce, an indication of just how big the U.S. foreign debt has become. Triffin wanted a world central bank, similar to Keynes's proposal in 1944. There have been many other proposals since then. It is not our purpose to review them. They have ranged from the intellectually clever but naive to the crazy fringe.

The point is that there are no serious, practical proposals on the table that deal with the four fundamental problems. First, what do you do with the massive dollar balances held by central banks that overhang the market and threaten a dollar collapse? Second, how do you reimpose monetary discipline into the system when the biggest player has fought for 50 years to avoid external discipline? Third, if the system were reformed, how do you stop foreign central banks from reaccumulating dollars or other national currencies again? Fourth, even if central banks were able to deal with the first three problems, how would they deal with future asset inflations? These occurred repeatedly in the nineteenth century, even when the gold standard was flourishing and purchasing power of money was stable. While the problem is partly amenable to domestic resolution with more direct regulation of credit, the globalization of finance has made it a global problem and it must be dealt with as such.

Our conviction is that there will be no effective reform of the international monetary system any time soon. BW II will, de facto, continue because it suits the major protagonists. The United States wants the freedom to inflate, and China and many other countries want the freedom to keep their currencies from rising to sustain competitive advantage for export-led growth. Other countries are experiencing painful currency revaluations, which essentially means they are importing U.S. deflation. The system will, therefore, continue to be prone to great instability after the crisis-driven enthusiasm for cooperation declines. Toughened lending standards around the world will help to police credit creation for a while, but it will not last. Creative minds and new institutions will find a way to get around any new regulations, and competitive pressures will force others to follow, as they always do, in the fight for market share and profits.

As we have emphasized, the international monetary system will remain in a delicate, fragile balance in the short run. How long that is no one can say. But the signs of breakdown are everywhere, and failure to fix it soon carries serious risks. One of these is another asset inflation, clear signs of which were evident in late 2009. If it were to gather a lot of momentum, central banks would be forced into tightening that could be inappropriate for a deflationary economic world. Another risk is protectionism in the United States. If surplus countries don't pursue policies that would allow the U.S. current account deficit to contract, and if U.S. structural unemployment (Figure 15.2) doesn't fall, Congress will be highly motivated to exploit the situation for populist election purposes. And the President's diminishing political fortunes could easily bring him into that camp.

Another obvious risk is that the quiet, back-door exit from the dollar turns into a mass stampede, creating a dollar crisis, U.S. government debt funding problems, and a major spike in interest rates. This, in turn, would threaten a new banking crisis at a time when the U.S. fiscal position has little or no capacity for more bailouts. It is not difficult to imagine other risks. The point is, the international monetary system desperately needs credible and quick reform. This is essential if the United States wants to remove a major risk while the economy is undergoing the painful adjustment to lower private debt and the long wave decline has not yet terminated.

Conclusion

The United States faces peacetime policy challenges that are unprecedented in severity since the 1930s. There is the potential to meet these challenges, and the political leadership could steer the economy safely through the years of difficult adjustment lying ahead before the next big renewal in the economy gets under way.

However, this chapter and the previous one make it clear that investors must be realistic. There is plenty that could go wrong, and policy makers' recent track record is not very encouraging. The conservative stance for investors is to be skeptical and take a "show me" attitude. That means looking for positive milestones over the next one to three years, watching what policy makers actually do while ignoring the political rhetoric.

Summary
and Conclusions

When the music stops, in terms of liquidity, things will be compli-
cated. But as long as the music is playing, you've got to get up and
dance. We're still dancing.
— CHARLES PRINCE, FORMER CEO OF CITIGROUP,
JULY 9, 2007

The Great Reflation has pumped some air back into the balloon. The world economy started recovering in the second half of 2009. Financial markets had accurately forecast that when they bottomed earlier in March. As the year came to a close, the music was indeed playing again, and a lot of people were back out on the dance floor. But to many, there was a huge disconnect, a pervasive aura of unreality, as we had just survived a near-death experience in the economy and financial system. Banks and hedge funds were making a lot of money again, their bonuses were under attack by governments, and their headhunters were back hunting. Worries of a new asset inflation were expressed frequently in the media and research reports. Was the crisis just a bad dream or a one-off accident? Will life return to what people had come to believe was normal? In short, should all investors be back out on the dance floor?

One of the main purposes of this book is to explain and help investors understand why the crisis was not a rare event. Rather, it was a logical outcome of the asset and credit bubble of the past 25 years, which gave us an artificial prosperity. That is over now. The private sector debt supercycle has morphed into a public sector debt supercycle. Near-zero interest rates will make it cheap to finance the government's deficit, but only for a while. Interest rates at some point will have to normalize and will go much higher if fears of inflation heat up. The Great Reflation took the downside out of the crisis in the short run. It aborted what easily could have been another Great Depression. But there is no way it will make the economy and financial system whole again and lead to sustainable growth and prosperity.

The so-called Great Moderation, the cliché used during the Greenspan years to describe what most observers thought was a permanent, happy state of affairs, is dead and buried. It turned out that the Great Moderation was an illusion, based on too much debt, reckless overspending, falling price inflation, unsustainable asset inflation, and surplus savings in developing countries. It required a foreign willingness to recycle dollars back to the United States so Americans could continue overspending and undersaving. It was artificial, unsustainable Alice-in-Wonderland economics. The massive stimulus and bailouts from the Great Reflation may have started up the economy and got the markets going again, but once more, it is artificial. No one has any idea what economic and financial conditions will be like when the stimulus is removed, when government debt ratios go to much higher levels, and when the rating agencies downgrade sovereign debt of some major countries.

Investing in the Aftermath of the Great Reflation

Investors unfortunately must deal, not with the should-be world, but with the real world and its greatly elevated risk and uncertainty. Parts I and II of the book detailed a list of serious problems facing the United States. These include an unwinding of a 25-year private sector debt bubble; an explosion in public sector debt that will hit 100 percent of gross domestic product (GDP) in a few years; U.S. $4 trillion indebtedness to foreign central banks; a sinking U.S. dollar and serious doubts about whether the decline can be halted; near-zero interest rates required to get the economy going but also triggering another round of speculation in financial assets; a resumption of the long wave downturn; and a seriously flawed international monetary system.

The flaw in the international monetary system is probably the most fundamental of these problems and was the basic cause of the banking and economic collapse in 2008–2009. The United States has been living in an Age of Inflation for many decades. Inflation is ultimately deflationary because it leads to too much debt, overpriced financial assets, and excessive investment in housing, office buildings, and industrial capacity. In today's globalized world, much of the overinvestment in real estate and industrial capacity occurred mainly outside the United States and hence is less visible to most Americans.

Inflation leads to distortions in relative prices and gives the wrong signals to people making investment decisions. It leads to instability, volatility, and financial crises. It undermines confidence in currencies, which leads to speculative manias in gold and other commodities.

The Bretton Woods II system of partly floating, partly pegged currencies is the only game in town. It is essentially unstable, keeping the dollar from collapsing by a "balance of financial terror." Countries with floating currencies import U.S. deflation. Countries with currencies pegged to the downward-floating dollar have de facto adopted Federal Reserve monetary policy, and they experience asset bubbles in stocks, real estate, and capital spending in their countries.

In a world of deflation, no one wants their currency to rise and no one wants to risk the chaos that would surely occur with a dollar collapse. As a result, the United States will remain complacent and exploit the lack of leadership elsewhere to reform the world's monetary system. The Fed will keep pumping money into the system for as long as it can. But this ensures that the system cannot last. How long? That is anyone's guess, but it may be longer than most people think.

The United States clearly has other fundamental problems that compound the financial ones. These relate to the aging of the population, geopolitical overcommitment, divisive politics, and a decline of the public spirit. Chapters 14 and 15 discussed how all these problems, while developing on separate tracks, are converging to create a toxic brew. Policy makers will have to deal with them soon or more severe crises may occur.

There are potential grounds for optimism on the policy front, but the government's recent track record in doing the right thing is poor. It is important for investors to be realistic; the conservative posture is to remain skeptical and take a "show me" attitude, watching what politicians do and paying little heed to the rhetoric.

The world will remain a very deflationary place for some time. Unfortunately, the financial system suffers from constipation; the Federal Reserve bought $1.3 trillion of assets of dubious quality in 2009 to get the credit-generating mechanism moving again, but by late in the year it was not functioning well. Commercial banks have continued to hoard reserves, money growth has been weak and bank loans contracting. However, excess liquidity created by the Fed must find a home. With a backdrop of deflation and weak underlying economic growth, it has washed into gold and commodity markets, developing country stock markets, and to some extent stock markets in developed countries.

The Great Reflation is an experiment, something we must all keep in mind. Like all true experiments, the outcome is not known in advance. Precise forecasts of where the dollar or U.S. stocks, for example, might be in a year or two are not worth much and no one should pretend to know. Unfortunately, investors, whether they like it or not, have to play the game. The dilemma is painful. Keeping money in safe, liquid, short-term assets provides returns of between zero and one-quarter of 1 percent, hardly better than keeping dollar bills under the mattress. To get better returns, investors have to take on levels of risk far beyond their comfort zone.

Many people ask whether the Great Reflation will work. In one sense it already has; the crisis of 2008–2009 could have caused a depression but it didn't. But the Great Reflation, as we have emphasized, certainly doesn't solve any of the real problems we have discussed throughout the book. It did put some air back in the balloon but that was just Act I. Investors should be preparing for Act II. That will be all about correcting the structural problems, distortions, and disequilibriums that came with 25 years of money and credit excesses and the series of asset bubbles.

The function of prices is to balance supply and demand and correct disequilibrium in the economy and financial system. Governments can delay the adjustment but only for a while. The key prices to watch are currencies and interest rates. For example, when there are too many dollars on the market, the dollar will fall to correct the imbalance. When the demand for credit is too big relative to the supply, interest rates will rise. If the quality of corporate debt deteriorates, interest rate spreads vis-à-vis the risk-free rate will rise, reducing supply and increasing demand. Prices have a job to do, and investors should always remember that. They should monitor them to track how and when the adjustments to disequilibriums are occurring. Investors using a road map with milestones will be much further ahead than those relying, in a highly uncertain world, on the apparent certainty of point estimates of price and time.

The Markets

Investors, as we have emphasized, must function in the real world of high risk and uncertainty. Part II discussed the main asset markets that investors can use to allocate their investable capital. The purpose was to provide a framework for understanding the markets and tools to help make decisions more confidently. Investors have to place their money where they think they can get the best returns for the risk they are prepared to take on. They must also diversify thoughtfully across enough asset classes to further reduce the risks of hitting an unforeseen pothole, or worse.

The stock market is one place investors should bet on because there is a very high probability that the secular bear market that began in early 2000 bottomed in March 2009. Two crashes in less than 10 years have created value and opportunities. Stocks may not have entered a new secular bull market yet, but careful investment could generate decent returns.

Stocks have done well in other long wave troughing periods following major financial crises. The recurring ingredients are a cheap starting point, low and stable price inflation, low interest rates, anticipation of a new long wave upswing, and a narrowing of credit spreads based on accurate perceptions of declining systemic risk. By late 2009, these conditions were falling into place, but the fact remains that a lot of uncertainty will linger for years. Investors will have to decide their comfort level of exposure. Our advice is to have less exposure than normal and to focus on high-quality companies. Those investors who have experienced a big hit to their net worth from the crash and who are not in a position to absorb another should obviously be even more conservative. The fact is that the investment world is still a very risky place, and a buy-and-hold equity strategy will likely do as badly in the near future as in the past 10 years. A sound strategy for the average investor is to try to reaccumulate capital slowly and patiently until higher levels of risk can be tolerated and to use the strategies outlined in Chapters 7 and 8 to increase and decrease exposure.

Investors should, naturally, seek out promising areas of potential growth. Equities in well-managed commodity-producing countries should be attractive. A partial list would include Canada, Australia, New Zealand, Norway, Colombia, and Brazil. They will be beneficiaries of world recovery from the banking crisis and the transition toward the next long wave upswing. It is also a good way to benefit from growth in rapidly developing countries such as China without actually investing in those markets. However, we also believe those markets will do well as a result of their own internal growth, and historically, they have been huge beneficiaries of low U.S. interest rates. Some, like China, have undervalued currencies and will experience currency appreciation against the dollar over time. The emerging markets are not for the fainthearted, though. They are subject to frequent asset bubbles as speculative money floods in, and the reverse when money floods out again. Most of them dropped much more than the United States did during the crash. However, compared to stock market levels of five years ago, countries like China, India, Russia, and Brazil are all far ahead of the S&P 500. In short, you will get more growth in emerging markets but also more volatility.

Investors should also seriously consider well-managed small companies (as measured by their value). Important qualities are good valuation relative to their assets and income prospects, along with sound balance sheets. Over the long run, small value companies have outperformed all other classes of stocks by a wide margin. A good entry point is essential, and the crash of 2008–2009 provided one. However, they can be volatile and very illiquid in the short run and thus are not for everyone.

Energy, particularly oil, should remain an attractive area as the evolving supply/demand picture will continue to push relative prices higher over time. Crude oil supplies will begin to flatten out in a few years and then start to fall, while demand from developing countries will continue to grow as they seek to catch up to levels of developed country prosperity. Rising prices will be required to allocate diminishing world supplies among oil-thirsty countries. Innovation designed to exploit rising relative prices will continue to create huge new investment opportunities in alternative energy.

The sharp panic drop in Treasury yields (rise in prices) during the financial crisis probably marked the end of the long secular bull market that started in 1982. Hence, returns to investors will be meager; however, yields won't likely rise much for a few years. The world will remain relatively depressed, flirting with deflation from time to time. The private sector debt reduction is far from over, and this will blunt the negative effects of large government deficits. They will remain relatively benign until there is a lot more vigor in the economy. Corporate bonds are a better place for investors to get extra returns as perceptions of credit risk will continue to decline with deleveraging, narrowing the spread between corporate and Treasury bonds.

Low interest rates, rapid monetary expansion, and sustained large fiscal deficits are a recipe for a weaker dollar. However, investors should keep in mind that a world worrying about deflation and high unemployment is a world where every country wants a cheaper currency to maximize export growth and protect domestic industries. The dollar will continue to erode, but not collapse, once again frustrating the apocalyptic forecasts. However, there will remain an uneasy truce in the foreign exchange markets and investors should continue to bet on a falling dollar over time. They should protect themselves accordingly, either with investments that will benefit from a lower dollar, such as equities of companies that have the bulk of their assets and earnings in strong currency countries, or directly with currency hedges.

Gold has begun what looks like a mania. So far its price has been tracking closely the pattern followed in the 1968–1980 gold mania. Since the low point in 2001, the gold price has quadrupled, a far sharper rise than other major asset prices except crude oil. It has been responding to a weak dollar, extreme U.S. monetary ease, and fears of future price inflation. This could continue if the emerging bubble gets more fuel, but it is a risky play. Value is relatively poor compared with other asset classes that have lagged behind. Gold is important as an insurance policy, and the often recommended 5 to 10 percent of assets in gold is a good long-term investment policy. However, for those buying now, it is very expensive insurance.

Commodity price indexes are also tracking the path they took in the previous mania in the 1970s. They also could go higher in the near term as the new liquidity finds a home. One can never be too sure how strong investment demand might be. Many investors still favor commodities as an asset class for several reasons. They can, at times, provide diversification, are a play on developing country growth, are a real (i.e., physical) asset, and are attractive to those fearing renewed inflation. However, investors need to be cautious because commodity prices, in general, face a significant headwind for the next few years while the world economy is struggling to recover.

Most commodities are in surplus and will be for years. New supply will come onstream from mothballed production. Moreover, many developing countries are suffering from declines in income and are speeding up processing for new foreign investment. Portfolio demand for commodities against this backdrop could be inadequate to offset the negative effect of new supplies. Investment demand, should it falter, could turn into supply as speculators disgorge their holdings. Industry demand, however, generally leads to consumption of commodities. Thus a sustainable bull market will have to wait until final demand is on a decisive uptrend.

Real estate is heterogeneous and regionalized and hence it is usually not very helpful to make general predictions. An exception was in the years leading up to 2007–2008. Every indicator pointed to a massive speculative bubble in both residential and commercial real estate. The former was pretty much deflated by the end of 2009. Well-financed homebuyers, taking a long-term view and focusing on value and strategic locations, should not suffer price erosion in the future and may well see some appreciation. But there will be no early return to the bubble period. Commercial real estate will likely remain in trouble for some years. Forced selling will create opportunities for the well-financed professionals, but amateurs should look for safer, more liquid opportunities.

Wealth Preservation

Unfortunately, there are no magic bullets that will solve the great dilemma now facing all investors: how to get a decent return while keeping risk at tolerable levels. Investors should be extremely wary of simplistic advice and promises of high and quick rewards. The Great Reflation has virtually eliminated returns on liquid, safe, short-term deposits or money market funds, while guaranteeing a world of high future risk and volatility.

The quarter century from 1982 to 2008 was the asset and credit bubble period. That was the time to make a lot of money. But it was artificial and the increase in wealth and living standards temporary. Now it is payback time. Near-zero interest rates and the substitution of public for private debt excesses will not make the problems go away and restore what people used to think of as normal.

Investors will have to be much more proactive in allocating their funds across different asset classes, including rebuilding liquidity when the time is appropriate. A key theme running through Part II of the book is to avoid running with the herd. Take money off the table on major rallies and put it to work after major declines. Be disciplined about value and avoid chasing runaway prices. The period ahead could see frequent asset bubbles as the avalanche of money created by the Federal Reserve and other central banks seeks a home. But the overriding conclusion from the analysis in this book is that wealth preservation and maintenance of a margin of safety will be the critical strategy for most people. The long run in the investment world does not exist anymore.

The music has started playing again and people are out on the dance floor. But remember, there are a lot of things that can go very wrong on very short notice. Keep your eye on currencies and interest rates as key benchmarks, keep lots of liquidity, and cut risk early when the indicators start flashing. This is musical chairs, and when the music stops, there won't be a chair for everyone.

Notes

Preface

1. Richard Dana Skinner, *Seven Kinds of Inflation* (New York: Whittlesey House/ McGraw-Hill, 1937).

2. A. Hamilton Bolton, *Money and Investment Profits* (Homewood, Ill.: Dow Jones-Irwin, 1967).

Chapter 1: The Age of Inflation

1. Richard Dana Skinner, *Seven Kinds of Inflation* (New York: Whittlesey House/McGraw-Hill, 1937).

2. William McChesney Martin, Federal Reserve chairman from 1951 to 1970, popularized this colorful expression indicating that the central bank's job was to stop the party before it got too rowdy.

3. Jacques Rueff, *The Age of Inflation* (Chicago: Henry Regnery Company, Gateway Edition, 1963).

4. See Niall Ferguson, *The Ascent of Money* (New York: Penguin Press, 2008).

5. Johann Wolfgang von Goethe, *Faust*, trans. Philip Wayne (Baltimore: Penguin Books, 1959), as cited in Rueff, *Age of Inflation*.

6. See Michael D. Bordo, *Concise Encyclopedia of Economics;* Brian Kettell, *Gold* (Cambridge, MA: Ballinger Publishing Company, 1982); Barry Eichengren,

Golden Fetters: The Gold Standard and the Great Depression, 1919–1939 (New York: Oxford University Press, 1992).

7. Barry Eichengren and Michael D. Bordo, *The Rise and Fall of a Barbarous Relic: The Role of Gold in the International Monetary System* (Cambridge, MA: National Bureau of Economic Research Working Papers 6436, January 1998).

8. Barry Eichengren, *Globalizing Capital: A History of the International Monetary System* (Princeton, NJ: Princeton University Press, 2008), 27.

9. Rueff, *Age of Inflation;* Robert Triffen, *Gold and the Dollar Crisis* (New Haven, CT: Yale University Press, 1961); Richard Duncan, *The Dollar Crisis: Causes, Consequences, Cures* (Hoboken, NJ: John Wiley & Sons, 2003).

10. Duncan, *Dollar Crisis,* Chapter 8, "Deflation."

Chapter 2: The Debt Supercycle, Illiquidity, and the Crash of 2008–2009

1. Irving Fisher, "The Debt-Deflation Theory of Great Depressions," *Econometrica* 1, (1933): 337–357.

2. Supreme Court Justice Potter Stewart (January 23, 1915–December 7, 1985) was an associate justice of the United States Supreme Court. On the Court, he made major contributions to criminal justice reform, civil rights, access to the courts, and Fourth Amendment jurisprudence, among other areas.

3. John Maynard Keynes, *The General Theory of Employment, Interest and Money* (London: Macmillan Cambridge University Press, England, for the Royal Economic Society, 1936).

4. Walter Bagehot, *Lombard Street: A Description of the Money Market* (London: Henry S. King, 1873).

5. The special drawing right (SDR) is an interest-bearing international reserve asset created by the International Monetary Fund (IMF) in 1969 to supplement other reserve assets of member countries. The SDR is based on a basket of international currencies comprising the U.S. dollar, Japanese yen, euro, and pound sterling. It is not a currency, nor a claim on the IMF, but is potentially a claim on freely usable currencies of IMF members. The value of the SDR is not directly determined by supply and demand in the market, but is set daily by the IMF on the basis of market exchange rates between the currencies included in the SDR basket.

6. Hyman Minsky, "The Financial Instability Hypothesis," Levy Economics Institute Working Paper Archive 74, May 1992.

Chapter 3: The Long Wave in the Economy

1. Lao tzu, *Tao Te Ching,* 1. Written around the sixth century B.C., the *Tao Te Ching* is central in Chinese religion for religious Taoism and Chinese Buddhism.

2. Nikolai Kondratieff, *The Major Economic Cycles* (Moscow, 1925); *Long Wave Cycle*, trans. Guy Daniels (New York: Richardson & Snyder, 1984).

3. Joseph Schumpeter, *Business Cycles: The Theory of Economic Development* (Moravia, Czech Republic, 1911); Thomas McCraw, *Prophet of Innovation: Joseph Schumpeter and Creative Destruction* (Cambridge, MA: Belknap Press, 2007).

4. Walter Rostow, *The Stages of Economic Growth* (Cambridge, England: Cambridge University Press, 1960); Jay Forrester, *Industrial Dynamics* (Bala Cynwyd, PA: Pegasus Communications, 1960); John Sterman, *Business Dynamics* (New York: Irwin/McGraw-Hill, 2000); Ernest Mandel, *Long Waves of Capitalist Development* (Cambridge, England: Cambridge University Press, 1980); James B. Shuman and David Rosenau, *The Kondrateiff Wave: The Future of America until 1984 and Beyond* (New York: Dell Publishing); Martin Barnes, *Bank Credit Analyst,* June 1995, July 1997, and various BCA issues in the 1980s.

5. See William A. Sheridan, *The Fortune Sellers* (New York: John Wiley & Sons, 1997).

6. George Soros, *The Alchemy of Finance* (New York: John Wiley & Sons, 1994).

7. Prominent supply-side economists of the period were Walter Eltis (Oxford University), Robert Mundell (Columbia University), and Arthur Laffer (a member of President Reagan's Economic Policy Advisory Board, 1981–1989).

Chapter 4: Government Deficits and the Great Reflation

1. Adam Smith, *An Inquiry into the Nature and Causes of the Wealth of Nations* (London: Strahan and Cadell, 1776).

2. Richard C. Koo, *The Holy Grail of Macro Economics: Lessons from Japan's Great Recession* (Hoboken, NJ: John Wiley & Sons, 2008).

3. Irving Fisher, "The Debt-Deflation Theory of Great Depressions," *Econometrica* 1, (1933): 337–357.

4. Scylla and Charybdis are two sea monsters of Greek mythology that were situated on opposite sides of the Strait of Messina between Sicily and Calabria in Italy. They were located close enough to each other that they posed an inescapable threat to passing sailors; avoiding Charybdis meant passing too closely to Scylla and vice versa.

5. Carmen Reinhart and Kenneth Rogoff, "The Aftermath of Financial Crises," paper presented to the American Economic Association meeting, January 3, 2009.

6. The Center on Budget and Policy Priorities (CBPP) is a nonpartisan research policy institute working on federal and state fiscal public programs.

7. A national sales tax, called value-added tax (VAT) in Europe and goods and services tax (GST) in Canada, is an obvious possibility as the United States is about the only developed country that doesn't have one.

8. Koo, *Holy Grail*.

Chapter 5: Money and the Great Reflation

1. Milton Friedman and Anna Schwartz, *A Monetary History of the United States 1867–1960*, (Princeton, NJ: Princeton University Press, 1963).

2. Andrew Dickson White, *Fiat Money Inflation in France*, Cestunlivre LLC Publication, 1923.

3. The Bullion Committee Report of 1810 is a historic document of great importance. It began the debate over what money is, how should it be controlled, its relationship to inflation, and currency depreciation. The Committee recommended that the United Kingdom return to the gold standard to stop the over issue of paper money and return the pound to its prewar parity and maintain its stability.

4. Milton Friedman, *A Program for Monetary Stability* (New York: Fordham University Press, 1960); *The Optimum Quantity of Money* (Chicago: Aldine Publishing, 1969).

5. See N. Gregory Mankiw, *Macroeconomics* (New York: Worth Publishers, 1992), 426–427.

6. Jacques Rueff, *The Age of Inflation* (Chicago: Henry Regnery Company, Gateway edition, 1963); Robert Triffen, *Gold and the Dollar Crisis* (New Haven, CT: Yale University Press, 1961); Richard Duncan, *The Dollar Crisis: Causes, Consequences, Cures* (Hoboken, NJ: John Wiley & Sons, 2003).

Chapter 6: Financial Manias and Bubbles

1. Charles Kindleberger, *Manias, Panics, and Crashes: A History of Financial Crises*, rev. ed. (New York: Basic Books, 1989).

2. Gustav Le Bon, *The Crowd: A Study of the Popular Mind* (New York: Macmillan, 1896); Charles Mackay, *Extraordinary Popular Delusions and the Madness of Crowds* (London: R. Bentley, 1841); Hyman Minsky, *Stabilizing an Unstable Economy* (New York: McGraw-Hill Professional, 2008); Edward Chancellor, *Devil Take the Hindmost* (New York: Plume Books, 2000).

3. Minsky, *Stabilizing*

4. Richard Duncan, *The Dollar Crisis: Causes, Consequences, Cures* (Hoboken, NJ: John Wiley & Sons, 2003), particularly Chapters 4 and 7.

5. Carmen Reinhart and Kenneth Rogoff, "The Aftermath of Financial Crises," paper presented to the American Economic Association meeting, January 3, 2009.

Chapter 7: Asset Allocation: Investing in a Turbulent World

1. Carl von Clausewitz was a Prussian officer, famous for his strategic insights in *Principles of War II*, 1812, and *On War*, 1832.

2. Bookstores are full of informative material on personal finance, and these can explain the many options available to investment beginners.

3. See, for example, Charles Ellis, *Winning the Loser's Game* (New York: McGraw-Hill, 2002).

4. Elroy Dimson, Paul Marsh, and Mike Staunton, *Triumph of the Optimists: 101 Years of Global Investment Returns* (Princeton, NJ: Princeton University Press, 2002).

5. Jeremy Siegel, *Stocks for the Long Run* (New York: McGraw-Hill, 1998).

6. Ibbotson & Associates, *Stocks, Bonds, Bills and Inflation*, Harvard Year Books.

7. Siegel, *Stocks for the Long Run*.

8. Efficient markets in this context means that markets at any point in time incorporate all available information and investors cannot outperform the market consistently, after adjusting for risk. The theory says that they would do just as well choosing stocks by throwing darts at the stock sheets. Almost all academics are firm believers in the theory, and Warren Buffett teases them mercilessly on account of his great track record.

9. David Dreman, *Contrarian Investment Strategies in the Next Generation* (New York: Simon & Schuster, 1998).

10. David F. Swensen, *Unconventional Success: A Fundamental Approach to Personal investment* (New York: Free Press, 2005).

11. Steven Leuthold, *The Myths of Inflation and Investing* (Chicago: Crain Books, 1980).

Chapter 8: The Stock Market

1. John F. Mauldin, ed., *Just One Thing* (Hoboken, NJ: John Wiley & Sons, 2006).

2. Philip A. Fisher, *Common Stocks and Uncommon Profits and Other Writings* (New York: Harper & Brothers, 1958); Benjamin Graham, *The Intelligent Investor: A Book of Practical Counsel* (New York: Harper & Brothers, 1949; 4th revision, with Jason Zweig, New York: HarperBusiness Essentials, 2003); Robert G. Hagstrom, *The Warren Buffett Way*, 2nd ed. (New York: John

Wiley & Sons, 1997); Peter Lynch, *One Up on Wall Street: How to Use What You Already Know to Make Money in the Market* (Philadelphia: Running Press, 2001); Jeremy Siegel, *Stocks for the Long Run: The Definitive Guide to Financial Market Returns & Long Term Investment Strategies* (New York: McGraw-Hill, 1994).

3. John Maynard Keynes, *The General Theory of Employment, Interest and Money* (London: Macmillan Cambridge University Press, England, for the Royal Economic Society, 1936).

4. A. Hamilton Bolton, *Money and Investment Profits* (Dow Jones–Irwin, 1967). The Bank Credit Analyst (BCA) has been the foremost research group in using this approach to anticipate changes in markets. A. Hamilton Bolton, the founder, maintained that markets respond to changes in liquidity, not the level of liquidity. Even more important is the rate of change—acceleration of new liquidity into the market or the rate of deterioration of liquidity is what really matters. The BCA approach is to build indicators that reflect liquidity changes and turn them into tools that are useful, in a timely way, to anticipate changes in the markets.

5. T. Congdon, "Money and Asset Prices," *Monthly Economic Review,* Lombard Street Research, 2004; T. Congdon, "15 Years of Monetary Trends," *Monthly Economic Review,* Lombard Street Research, 2004; T. Congdon, "Money and Asset Prices in Boom and Bust," *Hobart Paper,* 152, London: IEA, 2005; M. Friedman and A. Schwartz, *Monetary Trends in the United States and the United Kingdom: Their Relation to Income, Prices, and Interest Rates, 1867–1975* (Chicago: University of Chicago Press, 1982); David Laidler, *The Demand for Money—Theories and Evidence* (Scranton, PA: International Textbook Company, 1969); G. T. Pepper, *Money, Credit and Inflation,* Research Monograph 44, IEA, 1990; G. T. Pepper, *Money, Credit and Asset Prices* (London: Macmillan, 1994); Beryl W. Sprinkel, *Money and Stock Prices* (Homewood, IL: Richard D. Irwin Inc., 1964).

6. James Montier, *Behavioural Finance* (Hoboken, NJ: John Wiley & Sons, 2002).

7. David Dreman, *Contrarian Investment Strategies in the Next Generation* (New York: Simon & Schuster, 1998).

8. Ned Davis, *The Triumph of Contrarian Investing: Crowds, Manias, and Beating the Market by Going Against the Grain* (New York: McGraw-Hill, 2003).

9. Robert D. Edwards and John Magee, *Technical Analysis of Stock Trends* (Springfied, MA: J. Magee Publisher, 1948); Martin J. Pring, *Technical Analysis Explained* (New York: McGraw-Hill, 2002); Tony Plummer, *Forecasting Financial Markets: The Truth Behind Technical Analysis* (London: Kogan Page, 1989); Tony Plummer, *Forecasting Financial Markets: Technical Analysis of the Dynamics of Price* (New York: John Wiley & Sons, 1991).

10. Gerald M. Loeb, *The Battle for Investment Survival* (New York: John Wiley & Sons, 1996).

Chapter 9: Interest Rates and the Bond Market

1. See Franz Pick, "Pick's Currency Report." Franz Pick was for many decades one of the world's leading experts on inflation, devaluations, and monetary debauchery. He was born in Bohemia, came of age during the European hyperinflations and currency destructions of the early 1920s, and was a paymaster in the Czech underground during World War II. He was an outspoken critic of U.S. government policies during the rampant inflation and devaluations of the U.S. dollar in the 1970s, when he coined the term *mini-dollar*.

2. For the newcomer to bonds, this inverse relationship can seem obscure. The way to think about it is as follows: A bond, for example, with an interest rate of 5 percent to an investor can provide a higher return to the next investor only if the bond can be bought at a lower price.

3. Henry Kaufman, *Interest Rates, the Markets and the New Financial World* (New York: Times Books, 1986); Bill Gross, *Investment Secrets* (Hoboken, NJ: John Wiley & Sons, 2004); Sidney Homer and Richard Sylla, *A History of Interest Rates* (Piscataway, NJ: Rutgers University Press, 1991); Richard Ferri, *All About Asset Allocation* (New York: McGraw-Hill, 2006), Chapter 8; James Van Horne, *Financial Market Rates and Flows* (Englewood Cliffs, NJ: Prentice-Hall, 1984).

4. Van Horne, *Financial Market Rates and Flows,* particularly Chapter 3.

5. John Sterman, *Business Dynamics* (New York: Irwin/McGraw-Hill, 2000).

Chapter 10: The U.S. Dollar

1. William Rees-Mogg, *The Reigning Error: The Crisis of World Inflation* (Kensington, UK: Hamish Hamilton Ltd., 1974).

2. Michael P. Dooley, David Folkerts-Landau, and Peter Garber, *An Essay on the Revived Bretton Woods System* (Cambridge, MA: National Bureau of Economic Research, 2003).

Chapter 11: Gold

1. William Rees-Mogg, *The Reigning Error: The Crisis of World Inflation* (Kensington, UK: Hamish Hamilton Ltd., 1974).

2. Ibid.

3. Roy W. Jastram, *The Golden Constant: The English and American Experience 1560–2007* (Cheltenham, UK: Edward Elgar, 2009); Brian Kettell, *Gold* (Cambridge, MA: Ballinger Publishing Company, 1982).

Chapter 12: Commodities

1. Jim Rogers, *Hot Commodities: How Anyone Can Invest Profitably in the World's Best Market* (New York: Random House, 2007).
2. Ibid.
3. Gary Gorton and Geert Rouwenhorst, "Facts and Fantasies about Commodities Futures," Yale School of Management, Yale ICF Working Paper 04-20, July 14, 2004.
4. Martin Barnes, "The Long-Run Bear Market in Commodity Prices: Will It Ever End?" BCA, July 1996.
5. Barry Bannister and Paul Forward, "The Inflation Cycle of 2002 to 2015," Equity Research Industrial Portfolio Strategy, Legg Mason, April 2002; Barry Bannister, "War, Legacy Debt, and Social Costs as Catalysts for a U.S. Inflation Cycle," Legg Mason, May 2003.

Chapter 13: Real Estate

1. There are a number of excellent sources I have drawn on for this chapter, particularly the work of Joe Gyourko, Martin Bucksbaum Professor of Real Estate and Finance at the Wharton School, University of Pennsylvania. Useful references are as follows:

   • E. Glaeser, J. Gyourko, and A. Saiz, "Housing Supply and Housing Bubbles," *Journal of Urban Economics* 64, (2008): 198–217.
   • Joseph Gyourko, "Real Estate Returns in Public and Private Markets," *Wharton Real Estate Review,* Spring 2004.
   • Joseph Gyourko, "Understanding Commercial Real Estate: Just How Different from Housing Is It?" National Bureau of Economic Research Working Paper w14708, February 2009. Available at SSRN: http://ssrn .com/abstract=1344690.
   • John R. Talbott, *Contagion* (Hoboken, NJ: John Wiley & Sons, 2009).
   • Whitney Tilson and Glenn Tongue, *More Mortgage Meltdown* (Hoboken, NJ: John Wiley & Sons, 2009).
2. This is an estimated gross return, which represents the compound annual return of national house prices between 1996 and June 2006 based on Case-Shiller house price data.
3. George Magnus, *The Age of Aging: How Demographics Are Changing the Global Economy and Our World* (Hoboken, NJ: John Wiley & Sons, 2009).

Chapter 14: Declining America: Will It Recover?

1. George Magnus, *The Age of Aging: How Demographics Are Changing the Global Economy and Our World* (Hoboken, NJ: John Wiley & Sons, 2009).

2. Paul Kennedy, *The Rise and Fall of the Great Powers: Economic Change and Military Conflict from 1500 to 2000* (New York: Random House, 1987).

3. Carlo Cipolla, *The Economic Decline of Empires* (London: Methuen & Co. Ltd., 1970).

4. Robert Nisbet, *The Twilight of Authority* (New York: Oxford University Press, 1975).

5. John R. Talbott, *Contagion* (Hoboken, NJ: John Wiley & Sons, 2009).

Chapter 15: Politics and Policies in the Long Wave Trough

1. Thomas L. Friedman, "Rescue the Rescue," *New York Times*, September 30, 2008.

2. John D. Sterman, speech delivered at a Bank Credit Analyst conference, October 1992. See also John Sterman, "An Integrated Theory of the Economic Long Wave," *Futures* 17 (1985): 104–131.

3. The National Industrial Recovery Act (NIRA) of 1933 authorized the president to regulate industry, permit cartels and monopolies, and protect collective bargaining rights for unions. It was implemented by the National Recovery Administration (NRA) and the Public Works Administration (PWA).

4. Harold L. Cole and Lee E. Ohanian, "New Deal Policies and the Persistence of the Great Depression: A General Equilibrium Analysis," Federal Reserve Bank of Minneapolis, Research Department Staff Report, February 2003.

5. Jude Wanniski, *The Way the World Works* (New York: Basic Books, 1978).

6. Richard C. Koo, *The Holy Grail of Macro Economics: Lessons from Japan's Great Recession* (Hoboken, NJ: John Wiley & Sons, 2008).

7. Michael P. Dooley, David Folkerts-Landau, and Peter Garber, *An Essay on the Revived Bretton Woods System* (Cambridge, MA: National Bureau of Economic Research, 2003).

8. Jacques Rueff, *The Monetary Sin of the West* (New York: Macmillan, 1972).

About the Author

Tony Boeckh's economic and financial writings have been widely followed by individual and institutional investors in every major country in the world for over 40 years. He has been referred to as the "expert the experts rely on" by Louis Rukeyser of *Wall Street Week*. His analyses and forecasts have been most closely associated with the Bank Credit Analyst (BCA), which he developed into its modern form; he was the Chairman, CEO, and Editor-in-Chief of BCA Research Inc. from 1968 to 2002. Under his leadership, BCA grew from a small firm to become one of the world's leading independent investment research companies. He has a PhD in finance and economics from the Wharton School, University of Pennsylvania.

He first gained experience in economic and financial research at Canada's central bank in the early 1960s. He taught economics and finance at McGill University in Montreal for a number of years. He coauthored *The Stock Market and Inflation*, published by Dow Jones-Irwin in 1982.

He was involved in the investment management business as chairman of Greydanus, Boeckh and Associates, a fixed income investment firm, from 1985 to 1999.

Tony has been a longtime supporter of free market economic principles. He is a founding trustee of the Vancouver-based Fraser Institute, an economic think tank dedicated to free market principles.

Currently, he and Ian Boeckh manage Boeckh Investments Inc., a family office and private investment firm specializing in small public companies. The firm periodically organizes investment conferences for family offices. Tony has lectured at economic, financial, and investment seminars and conferences around the world, and has been sought after by the media and others for his insights and analysis. He is also very active in charitable work in the area of mental health and has established, with his family, the Graham Boeckh Foundation toward that end.

Tony has been a longtime student of investment cycles, financial manias, and crises. The financial crisis of 2008–2009 prompted him to set out his thoughts in *The Great Reflation: How Investors Can Profit from the New World of Money*. He also coauthors *The Boeckh Investment Letter* with Robert Boeckh, which is available on the Web at www.boeckhinvestmentletter.com. The publication follows the principles outlined in *The Great Reflation* and is focused on helping investors make portfolio decisions.

Index